GARLAND PUBLICATIONS IN AMERICAN AND ENGLISH LITERATURE

Editor
Stephen Orgel
Stanford University

GARLAND PUBLISHING, INC.

Elektra in Exile

Women Writers and Political Fiction

Victoria Middleton

GARLAND PUBLISHING, INC.
NEW YORK & LONDON 1988

Copyright © 1988
Victoria Middleton
All Rights Reserved

Library of Congress Cataloging-in-Publication Data

Middleton, Victoria.
Elektra in exile : women writers and political fiction / Victoria Middleton.
p. cm. — (Garland publications in American and English literature)
Originally presented as the author's thesis (Ph.D.)—University of California, Berkeley, 1979.
Bibliography: p.
8SN 0-8240-6398-8
1. Political fiction, English—Women authors—History and criticism. 2. Women and literature—Great Britain. 3. Shelley, Mary Wollstonecraft, 1797-1851. Last man. 4. Eliot, George, 1819-1880. Felix Holt, the radical. 5. Woolf, Virginia, 1882-1941. Years. 6. Lessing, Doris May, 1919- Four-gated city.
I. Title. II. Series.
PR830.P6M53 1988
823'.009'9287—dc 19   88-16264

Printed on acid-free, 250-year-life paper
Manufactured in the United States of America

DEDICATION

To my parents.

TABLE OF CONTENTS

Chapter		Page
1.	ELECTRA IN EXILE	1
2.	EXILE, ISOLATION, ACCOMMODATION IN THE LAST MAN: THE STRATEGIES OF A SURVIVOR	27
3.	GEORGE ELIOT'S POLITICAL FICTION: THE LEGACY OF THE FATHER	77
4.	DOUBT AND "DELIBERATE FAILURE" IN THE YEARS	126
5.	DORIS LESSING'S CHILD OF VIOLENCE	174
SELECTED BIBLIOGRAPHY		233

Chapter 1

ELECTRA IN EXILE

"A man has been termed a microcosm; and every family might also be called a state."[1] Mary Wollstonecraft's Enlightenment generalization has a special import that its abstractness conceals. Her use of the masculine noun as a universal reference reflects her assumptions about political power and those of her culture as a whole. Power over one's self or over a society is ascribed to men. Women were "other," outside the norm, when the subject was politics. As Wollstonecraft says in <u>A Vindication of the Rights of Women</u>, they were at once "despots" and "slaves" because of their exclusion (until the early decades of the twentieth century) from legitimate, recognized participation in politics.[2] Describing political power in fiction was as problematic for women as wielding it. The limited nature of women's political experience (like that of other disenfranchised groups), has been a source of strengths as well as weaknesses in their political novels.[3] The woman writer's disenfranchisement has had particular emotional and literary consequences. These consequences and the form they take in life and art are the subject of this study, an analysis of the political vision in the work of Mary Shelley, George Eliot, Virginia Woolf, and Doris Lessing.

As Mary Wollstonecraft's homology implies, for English women in the nineteenth and early twentieth centuries, the family <u>was</u> the state, the primary social unit to which they belonged in any political sense.

For a woman, any contest for power between the individual will and the collective could, in general, only be enacted in the home. A woman who desired to write on the subject of politics--the varieties, uses and value of power over oneself and others--inevitably drew upon the primal power relationships of family life.[4]

The child's experience constitutes a universal basis for a writer's delineation of authority and obedience in a political novel, and women have been privileged as well as oppressed by their necessarily close observation of family life. Women are not, of course, the only observers of the home scene. In the novels of Dickens and Charlotte Brontë, of Orwell and Doris Lessing, family life becomes a symbol, as it is the source, of the repression exacted by society. Often the child's dependency is transmuted into the adult's felt powerlessness in society at large.[5] From the tyrannical schoolmasters of Hard Times and Jane Eyre, it is not far to the faceless bureaucrats of Nineteen Eighty-Four and The Memoirs of a Survivor, for all are in a sense parental surrogates. Often, in a political novel, the individual's power over himself and others takes its energy and form from the distribution of power in the family.

Yet the mythos of childhood contains more than one plot, and these variants depend to some extent on differences of sex. Both Oedipus and Electra sought power and authority from their parents, but Electra could only obtain it through indirect means and masculine agency. In Freud's interpretation of their stories, the Electra complex is weaker than the Oedipal; the girl-child's ambivalence toward authority is stronger than her brother's. The boy wants to usurp the father's authoritarian role while the girl wants also to concilate and please. Otherwise she may find herself outside society altogether, like the fallen women in Victorian fiction, or even, like Antigone, buried alive. Electra's ambivalence toward power comes from the simultaneity of her desires: to win the father's approval <u>and</u> to abrogate his authority. Unlike Oedipus but like Lady Macbeth, the daughter who wants to assert her power in some work of her mind and hands has to unsex herself. A result of this inner conflict is an exile that is suffered inwardly: the self that is exiled from society's approval is exiled from its own wholeness. That is, the woman's ambivalence toward authority tends to turn against herself and produce self-division. She may simultaneously wish to assert herself and to desist, to obey, to conform to others' expectations.

Ambivalence toward one's own potency seems particularly strong in women writers who deal with political subjects. Novels such as Mary Shelley's <u>The Last Man</u>, George Eliot's <u>Felix Holt, the Radical</u>, Virginia Woolf's <u>The Years</u>, and Doris Lessing's <u>The Four-Gated City</u> crystallize tensions, conflicts felt by their writers toward the political autonomy of the self. Contradictions about power are visible in both the lives and the works of these women writers. Despite the independence, even audacity with which they lived, in writing about politics all four women were forced into compromises, if only unconsciously and implicitly. The political ambivalence of the Electra complex makes the woman writer ambitious for self-assertion at the same time that she criticizes its consequences for society as a whole. Such contradictions show up in the very form of the political novel, in which the narrative voice is in a sense a problematic version of the self. In each novel, the narrative perspective fuses the writer's ambivalence about self-assertion in private and public worlds.

Though The Last Man, Felix Holt, The Years and The Four-Gated City deal with elections, industrial debates, partisan policies and international conflicts, their topical subject matter is not my primary reason for calling these works political novels.[6] Rather, they are political because they dramatize a power struggle between human beings in which personal and public conflicts are interdependent.[7] Daniel Deronda is a political novel in this sense. Gwendolen Harleth's oppression by her husband (an oppression which George Eliot explicitly compares to colonial misrule) is set against Daniel Deronda's quest for a political mission. Both protagonists ultimately seek self-mastery in lieu of power over others, devoting themselves to larger social destinies. And Eliot's political conservatism is implicit in Gwendolen's submergence of her domestic will to power as much as in Daniel Deronda's selfless dedication to Zionism. The exercise of power is willfully reduced by Eliot to power over oneself, as even the foreground politics of the novel become metaphoric. In short, a political novel is the locus where two fictive worlds intersect: the public world of political conflict and the private world of character development.

The interlocking of private and public spheres in a novel mirrors the interrelatedness in society. Literature is Janus-faced, looking simultaneously toward its origin and its fulfillment, toward the culture out of which it is created and toward the reader's consciousness in which it lives. Reading a novel is a radically centripetal experience--we are drawn into the fictional world in a way that ultimately enhances our self-consciousness. But at the same time we feel a centrifugal force operating, referring us toward the novel's genesis in a historical epoch or entity. Whether history actively determines or is passively mirrored by a work of art, any literary analysis should take into account the complexity of connections between fictional and factual (social) reality implicit in the artifact. It is impossible, even if it were desirable, to pin down the causes of these connections. As Roland Barthes says in Writing Degree Zero, ". . . there is no need to invoke direct determinism to feel that History underlies the fortunes of modes of writing. . . ."[8] Instead, we can discuss the relation between novel and real world in terms of the individual artist who mediates between them. Georg Lukács puts it this way:

> It is the view of the world, the ideology or weltanschauung underlying a writer's work, that counts. And it is the writer's attempt to reproduce this view of the world which constitutes his "intention" and is the formative principle underlying the style of a given piece of writing. Looked at this way, style ceases to be a formalistic category. Rather, it is rooted in content: it is the specific form of a specific content.[9]

Fictional form emerges from "content," which includes the writer's consciousness of belonging to a class, race, or sex.

To discuss a writer's conception of the self in her society and her understanding of political relationships between discrete selves, we must remember the manifold and shifting nature of these entities. The self and its society must be described for each writer in her own terms; this description is the object of individual chapters in my study. Egotism, for example, means something different for Mary Shelley and George Eliot--whether conceived philosophically as solipsism or ethically as selfishness--than for Virginia Woolf and Doris Lessing, who live in an era dominated by ego-psychology. Before introducing the vocabularies of Shelley, Eliot, Woolf and Lessing, we need to review some of the ways self and society have been thought of outside literature, ways that have bearing upon literary conventions. These extra-literary categories should not be understood as more "real" than those found in a novel. By this I mean that sexual stereotypes and other social conventions are themselves "fictions," though their author may be anonymous and collective. Even the writer's life is, in a sense, a fiction: a text for interpretation.

The study of history, whether it is the history of an epoch or the history of an individual life, yields explanations that are no more definitive than the explication of a novel. Just as his choice of a genre determines some part of a creative writer's meaning, so it can be said that narrative forms and tropes shape the writing of history.[10] Our ways of thinking about historical facts--events? forces? laws?--influence what we will decide about their impact on an individual's life. To account completely for the pressure exerted by history on the imaginations and artifacts of women writers would be impossible. All that I would like to attempt here is a description of the triadic relation: history / life / text.

The history that bears upon women's political fiction is that of nineteenth- and twentieth-century English bourgeois life, particularly life in the family and its impact on the individual's relation to society.[11] Lawrence Stone has demonstrated how the decline of kinship, the rise of the modern state, and the Protestant hegemony all strengthened the power of the family, especially of the father, during the sixteenth and seventeenth centuries.[12] As real and symbolic power was concentrated in the father, the legal and emotional status of children and women decreased.[13] The father's authority in the home was corroborated by theories about the paternalistic basis of social organization. Patriarchal authority was a pervasive idea with roots that were anthropological, moral and ideological, as Gordon Schochet shows in <u>Patriarchalism in Political Thought</u>.[14] The Fathers in Heaven and on the throne were potent analogues and symbolic extensions of the governor at home. The paternalistic authority of the nuclear family over the individual's life declined in the eighteenth and nineteenth centuries.[15] But though the power of the real father was gradually transferred to the state, he retained an irrational yet imperious authority over his family.[16] For Shelley, Eliot, Woolf and Lessing, "society was a father," as Woolf wrote in <u>Three Guineas</u>.[17] The external political order drew its force from the still-potent authority of the biological father in their lives.

The father is of course an <u>inner</u> presence. Whether Freud's Original Sin of parricide is a primal impulse in the psyche or whether his theory criticizes his historical moment more than it describes innate structures of the mind is not a problem that can be resolved here. The point is rather that Freud's account of the relation between the family patriarch and the political authority of the state describes the experience of women who lived and wrote in the nineteenth and twentieth centuries in England. As he tells us in <u>Civilization and Its Discontents</u>, society requires the subordination of the individual's desire and potency to the interests of the community.[18] The repression of the id by the ego and superego is an essential fact of civilized life, punishment for the original Oedipal wish to kill the father and usurp his role. But the father is not defeated--he survives in the superego, the voice of authority that is perhaps hardest to silence.

Transgressing the law of the father--at home or in society--makes one feel guilty; it is the price of offending the authority figures without and within. If a woman is more desirous of placating the father than her brother would be, her guilt at rebelling against his law will be even greater than his, her self-assertion even harder to achieve.

Self-assertion--especially through aggression or appetite--was decried as hostile to culture in the works of many nineteenth-century English writers, including Arnold, Dickens, Thackeray, George Eliot and Meredith. It is as if the Victorian reaction against Romantic egotism and its political analogue, revolutionary fervor, represented a widespread guiltiness for killing the father--on the throne or in heaven. The patriarch's withdrawal from the human community created reactions ranging from Positivism (its Religion of Humanity an outlet for oceanic religious feeling) to the Victorian novel (with its intersubjectivity).[19] The Victorian needed to recover faith in some explanatory creed in a world where God, the religious patriarch, had "disappeared."[20] The result was often a life patterned on a rhythm of self-assertion and submission: ". . . personal dislocation, involving a threat to one's identity; a consequential, and somewhat desperate, search for that 'lost identity'; . . . a somewhat irrational counter-reaction which makes it absolutely essential . . . to be free of the burden of self . . . ."[21]

The anxieties of isolation became especially acute for the individual estranged from family, birthplace, or class.[22] Such estrangement, both literal and emotional, was caused or intensified by the requirements of the marketplace. Self-interest was the force behind capitalism and worldly success and was the source of self-destruction as well. The individual living in the heyday of capitalism had to contend with the pressures dividing him from other members of his family and his community, pressures that divided him internally as well. In the words of Mrs. Ellis, doyenne of Victorian domestic critics, it was an epoch when one could "almost fail to recognize the man, in the machine."[23] Religions of culture (like Arnold's) and Humanity (like Comte's) were not the only recommended antidotes to egotism. In a competitive world where one's autonomy was constantly threatened and constrained, men entrusted their emotional lives to the care of women. The emotional division of labor according to sex reached its apex in Victorian England, though it began in the eighteenth century and extended into the twentieth.

The head of the household was in danger of being mechanized in order to compete most profitably in the marketplace. But Mrs. Ellis's solution to this dehumanization, and the solution of nineteenth-century England as a whole, really exacerbated the division of the psyche created or promoted by bourgeois life. Women were called on to provide moral and affective guidance in the family, to guard their own "moral sensibility" from contamination by the world and to create an emotional and moral haven in the home.[24] This counsel was given even by the radical Mary Wollstonecraft in her Thoughts on the Education of Daughters (1787) and reinterpreted by countless social critics and artists throughout the century.[25] Coventry Patmore's Angel in the House was a feminine ideal endorsed by Tennyson, Ruskin, and Virginia Woolf's father Leslie Stephen, among others both early and late in the century. The Angel's ominous shadow hovered over the rationalistic household of William Godwin while Mary Shelley was growing up and was felt by

Virginia Woolf, as she testifies in "Professions for Women."[26]

The passivity and submissiveness of the woman in the family was partially a projection of the man's own desire for those qualities.[27] Resignation as an ideal for men and women, an ideal propounded by Tennyson, Arnold, Ruskin and George Eliot,[28] was however practiced more notably by women than by men. Women's moral power was really the superiority of the victim who has no practical power. It has been claimed that women have been particularly privileged observers of their society by virtue of being excluded from its sources of legal and political power.[29] Yet the privilege is offset by her Otherness; her power is mediated. The moral and psychological superiority of the outsider, exalted by Virginia Woolf in <u>Three Guineas</u>, is vitiated by the impotence and self-aggression ancillary to it.

The woman who writes about politics in her society may be politically sophisticated enough to see the evils of egotism and self-interest but at the same time she may be (if only unconsciously) desirous of self-assertion. Virginia Woolf's feeling that the vote was useful to impress people one despises sums up this ambivalence.[30] The woman writing a political novel can feel at the same time insecure about her familiarity with the economic and political machinery of society and repelled by political realities. Woolf confessed to experiencing such conflict about criticizing a social order that didn't value women's participation. George Eliot's problem was similar: to reject roles that were beyond a woman's reach. (Felix Holt is an unconvincing spokesman for this position, more because of its inherent contradictoriness than because of his implausibility as a working-class hero.) To demand a role in society means necessarily to endorse society's ways. To accept one's exclusion meant, for women in the nineteenth and much of the twentieth centuries, to forfeit recognition of one's self.

By the second half of the nineteenth century when women were calling for liberalization of their domestic roles and extension of their legal rights, their male sympathizers (like Meredith and Hardy) perhaps realized that protracted segregation of emotional and mental capacities impeded the wholeness of every personality. The liberation of women would not only make possible their self-assertion, it might permit men to express (rather than project onto women) what was "feminine" in themselves. Both sexes would benefit from a restoration of psychic harmony, an end to self-division.

Self-division, it is true, crosses sexual borders. The Doppelgänger motif informs Gothic novels as well as contemporary stories about schizophrenia; it is the property of Joseph Conrad as well as Mary Shelley. Current psychoanalytic and linguistic theories stress that the pronoun "I" is not single but has multiple cases: there are discontinuities "between the nominative and the accusative forms of the first person itself."[31] In the first-person pronoun, the absolute subject is divided from the ego, which becomes itself an object of consciousness.[32] Self-division--exile from wholeness of self --would seem intrinsic to the consciousness of any language user. But while the male writer may experience alienation because of psychological and political exigencies inherent in language itself, he is not burdened by the particular version of self-division imposed upon a woman. Women writers draw on a set of conventional assumptions that exacerbate self-exile in special ways. It is the schizophrenia of the pronoun "she," not the pronoun "I," that most tyrannizes them. This linguistic oppression, I would suggest, tells particularly on women writing novels about politics.

It has perhaps been easier for men to grant women the right to assert themselves than for women to do so. As Simone de Beauvoir wrote in The Second Sex, women are "Other" in their own eyes as well as men's.[33] The law of the father persists in more subtle and profound constraints than legislation against women studying, voting, divorcing and working as they please. Symbolically, the patriarchal law imbues the cultural inheritance of language, against and through which every writer struggles to express an original meaning. The individual's will combats cultural determinism--including political oppression--on the level of the sentence.[34]

No act of writing can be free of consciousness of sexual identity, whether that identity is considered to be psychologically or historically evolved. In the roles ascribed to their fictional protagonists, in their narrative personae, in the very language available to them, all writers--male or female -- inherit cultural conventions that implicitly attach values to sexual identity. When a woman novelist writes about "female" passivity, emotionality and dependency, she must regard herself as Other in a sense that no male novelist does. The fact that a superior objectivity is associated with maleness by George Eliot; that Doris Lessing calls the critical voice of the "self-hater" in Martha Quest's consciousness "he" rather than "she"; that Virginia Woolf defensively posits the use of a "feminine" sentence in A Room of One's Own--these facts and others indicate the difficulty for a writer of transcending the sexual conventions of her time.

Since writing is a compromise between the individual intention and the social code of language, frustration of the writer's purpose is inevitable. To have said what one wants is to get only part of what one desires--recognition by a reader/auditor; reduction of some need; gratification of some impulse. In women writing about politics, these desires converge. Women like Mary Shelley, George Eliot, Virginia Woolf and Doris Lessing do not write political novels because they cannot participate in the workings of government. Only for a Harriet Martineau was writing perhaps a secondary outlet for political participation. Woolf and Lessing were in fact active at times in politics; writing was their primary vocation out of choice, not necessity. But while their political novels do not take the place of political acts, the books seem uneasy compromises between private needs and publically acceptable articulations. Shelley, Eliot, Woolf and Lessing all have conflicting feelings about power--their own and society's--and these find complex expression in their fiction. As Lukács said, "the writer's ethic becomes an aesthetic problem of the work."[35]

In this study, I regard the author's life not as an explanatory cause but (in the words of Fredric Jameson) as "a text on the level with the other literary texts of the writer in question and susceptible of forming a larger corpus of study with them."[36] In analyzing political novels, I assume that the author's intentions can be deduced from a given novel and these deductions augmented by further study of the texts of an author's life--autobiographical essays and memoirs, journals, letters, and so on. One doesn't really need what Jameson calls "a semiotic account of the status of . . . 'autobiographical' passages, and of the specificity of those registers of a text in which authorial wish-fulfillment . . . is deliberately foregrounded" in order to talk tentatively about the author's presence in a work.[37] The idea of a "second self" is both more wieldy and more accessible. It is also traditional, having been coined by Edward Dowden in 1877 to discuss George Eliot's intentions as they were realized in one of her novels and simultaneously to disclaim certitude about the "real" George Eliot.[38] We can only postulate the relationship between historical personage and implied author in a novel. Bearing this in mind, I will foreshadow some connections between politics outside and within fiction that will be developed in subsequent chapters.

The four women whose work is the subject of this study had particularly strong attachments to their fathers. Mary Shelley lost her mother, Mary Wollstonecraft at birth and easily discounted William Godwin's shrewish second wife as an important emotional surrogate. George Eliot's mother was a weak presence for her, being (like Virginia Woolf's) preoccupied with caring for numerous children. Both Eliot and Woolf sought "mothering" in adult relationships with women (and to some extent with their husbands, who carefully guarded their careers) but were most strongly drawn to the roles of their fathers. Doris Lessing's regret for lost maternal love is stronger even than Woolf's. Yet in her case as in the other three, the father stood for a world of work (however inconclusive in Lessing's father's experience), of existential projects that made possible selfhood. Making something-- producing a novel, a philosophical treatise, a farm crop--meant making oneself. The author of such a work and such a self had authority, and his power was coveted by his daughter.

To some extent, Shelley, Eliot, Woolf and Lessing all think of writing as the legitimate exercise of power because it is an act by means of which they hope to transcend sexual identity. Mary Shelley speaks of the novelist's dual functions, dreaming and writing, as liberating her from limiting self-consciousness. George Eliot adopts a persona that is self-consciously "male" and a tone that emulates the "sexlessness" (her word) of the scientific method. Virginia Woolf insists that a great mind is androgynous, while Doris Lessing represents herself as an impersonal transmitter for a collective unconscious wavelength. All four want to believe that writing makes possible an imaginative escape from consciousness that is merely consciousness of one's _self_. All want to borrow what they think of as masculine rights and powers even as they deny sexual partisanship.

The lives of Shelley, Eliot, Woolf and Lessing oscillate between assertion and containment of power. The life histories of all four began at least by being more politically audacious than their political novels ever became. Mary Shelley ran away with a radical poet and had children out of wedlock; George Eliot lived unmarried with George Henry Lewes (as Kate Millett said, she "lived the revolution . . . but she did not write of it")[39]; Virginia Woolf left respectability behind for Bloomsbury; and Doris Lessing has allied herself with the most revolutionary political and intellectual movements of the post-war era, including Marxism and radical psychoanalytic theory.

The political careers of Shelley, Eliot, Woolf and Lessing follow a paradigm common to those of male writers as well, a Blakean regression from radicalism to conservatism. Shelley and Eliot conformed to the paradigm, first rebelling against, then assimilating into society. Both made amends for youthful disobedience of their real fathers and of society's law as well. Mary Shelley came to esteem the fabric of traditional society and expressed horror at social (as opposed to political) change. George Eliot counselled the conquest of private desire and the need to conform to public duty. She stressed self-perfection and tolerance of the social status quo. Virginia Woolf ascribed egotism and aggressiveness to men and tried to absolve herself of responsibility for reform of a world she found violent, irrational and ugly. Doris Lessing accepts historical determinism, admits that children of violence are not born aggressive but schooled to become that way, and yet despairs of changing society to eradicate violence. All four assume that, being outside the source of power, they can do no more than lament its exercise. But their work goes beyond the complaint of passive victims of a dysfunctioning social system.

The Last Man, Felix Holt, The Years and The Four-Gated City express latent resentment at the suppression of a woman's ambition, even her egotism. This ambition for power over oneself and others coexists (uneasily at times) with criticism of social structures that promote egotism and aggression. We can see resentment in the portrayal of the family in their fiction. Except for Doris Lessing, whose late work dwells on the deprivation of the infant, the novelists all depict childhood as a time of suppressed rebellion, not Dickensian pathos and need. Even Lessing (like Mary Shelley) stresses the adolescent's demand for independence from and recognition by her family and community. In To the Lighthouse and The Years, Virginia Woolf gives dramatic pictures of young anger. And George Eliot has Maggie Tulliver (in marked contrast to Dickens' Esther Summerson) drive nails into her doll's head to exorcise her passionate resentment of her family. Before Eliot preaches against egotism, she anatomizes it beautifully in the characters of Mrs. Transome and Gwendolen Harleth, suggesting that it holds some resisted attraction for her.

Why is this rebelliousness neither wholly suppressed nor harnessed? Perhaps the girl doesn't find herself drawn into society in roles that would compensate for and satisfy her ambitiousness. Perhaps she finds it difficult to identify with the male face of authority and to accept its surrogate, the superego, or whatever inner law stands for the outer law of society. The child rebels; the adult conforms. But the girl who rebels is deviating from sexual conventions, while the woman who conforms gets no greater reward from society for subordinating her own desires to its collective ones.

Reflecting their authors' ambivalence toward political power, many of the female protagonists and narrators in The Last Man, Felix Holt, The Years and The Four-Gated City end in exile. It is not necessarily social ostracism. In fact, Mary Shelley's characters leave solitude and comfort themselves with society (in its most superficial sense, paying calls and giving tea parties). In Perkin Warbeck, the widow of the rebel prince finds refuge in the court of her husband's political enemy. Still, Shelley's protagonists, like those of Eliot, Woolf and Lessing, experience exile from power. They are estranged from the sources of their personal power and autonomy, generally located in the family, and from society as a whole. The sense of emotional and political disenfranchisement is especially strong in these novels that examine the political relationships between self and society.

Mary Shelley's personal exile has several stages. Initially she was estranged from her family, having incurred the disapproval of the father she worshipped. But this chosen exile was succeeded by isolation all the more devastating for being imposed rather than willed. The loss of her children and husband (losses too sudden and enormous not to seem symbolically punitive) isolated her completely. Finally she came to feel separated even from her own emotional homeland: the anger, love and grief that inspired her to write and made possible her self-definition. In her novel The Last Man the consequence of this isolation is a political vision that upholds society's status quo at any cost. The novel is not so much conservative or anti-radical as it is anti-political.[40] No utopia, real or planned, can alter the fact that human relationships are both precious and ephemeral.

The narrative structure of The Last Man reflects Mary Shelley's ambivalence about self-assertion in private and in public. The narrator, Lionel Verney, changes in the course of the novel from a Romantic egotist to a Victorian scribe who writes to console himself for the loss of his community of loved ones. His story loses focus and form as he loses his private audience. The resulting garrulity is a sign of not self-indulgence but self-doubt and uncertainty about why he writes, as well as to whom. The movement toward third-person narration and realism in Mary Shelley's late novels begins in The Last Man and reflects her desire for political accommodation.

George Eliot feels as antipathetic toward social change as Mary Shelley, and her political quietism has a similar basis in repudiation of egotism. Eliot's real exile from her family, especially her adored brother and father, evoked extreme guilt in her. Their disapproval never ceased, and Eliot's faith in duty (without benefit of dogma) was a way of making amends for displeasing them. Dutifulness and authority became their own justification. And yet Eliot's novels all show the injustice and oppressiveness of the law of the father. Mr. Tulliver and the town of Middlemarch constrain the talent even as they subdue the will of Maggie and Dorothea. Eliot tells us of the need for this subjugation, but she shows the cost.

The potential conflict in her sympathy manifests itself in the narrative perspective of Felix Holt, where Eliot's appearance of objectivity conceals a partisanship. The "truth" she tells about radicalism is self-interested; her politics are based on a paradox. Eliot's desire to depict a version of social truth underlies her criticism of egotism, appetite and--desire.

The novels of Virginia Woolf describe nostalgically a lost harmony and wholeness that she attributes to childhood. The perfect happiness of a children's republic--when adults were excluded--is what Woolf lost with her mother's (and sister's and brother's) death. Adult society, and by extension history itself, was suspect because based on the repressive patriarchal family. Woolf's feminism was a brave but (even for her) unsatisfactory alternative to political activism in a world that she thought of as male-dominated. Women were "outside" power: free of blame for disasters like the world wars but equally powerless to prevent them.

In The Years, Virginia Woolf attempts to efface herself and let history tell itself; the result is a confusing, self-contradictory fiction. Its plot seems against, not for, the reader. The ambiguities implicit in the narrative structure of this family chronicle mirror

Woolf's hostility toward the family itself and its extension, the patriarchal state.

Early loss of a mother's love led Doris Lessing to pursue the vision of a maternal utopian homeland even more deliberately than Virginia Woolf. Granted more political rights from the first than were Shelley, Eliot and Woolf, Lessing turns even more quickly away from political solutions to social oppression, rejecting them as inadequate. Yet like Woolf, she shows the deforming or crippling effects of history on the individual while denying the individual's power to contest them. Her utopia would be realized not by political means but through genetic mutation.

Mary Shelley's tenuous control of her narrative finds an analogue in Lessing's The Four-Gated City. It concludes a lengthy autobiographical series called The Children of Violence in which the distinction between author and heroine threatens to dissolve in the novel's third-person narration. The narrative's looseness and sprawl reflect Martha's quest to lose herself in some larger collective entity. The effect is to dramatize Martha's neediness rather than her power to satisfy it. For Lessing, as for the others, suppressed desire to assert herself persists, if only beneath the surface of the fiction.

It should be clear that I am not arguing that aggressiveness, competition or selfishness are positive political attributes in women or men. In fact, Shelley, Eliot, Woolf and Lessing join male novelists in urging that compassion, altruism and sympathy have a part in political relationships between members of a society. My object is not to diminish this positive vision in their works but rather to show the problems that coexist with it: the de-formation in life and art that results when women writers confront political reality.

To say that women's political values find formal expression in a work of fiction is not to say that other values, aesthetic and moral, do not equally influence narrative form. Mary Shelley's "last man" fantasy not only draws upon the Gothic conventions of her era but uses a motif especially in vogue.[41] The realistic novel was for George Eliot the prevailing form as well as the appropriate vehicle to make her point about the need for the individual to assimilate into society. Woolf's anti-novel reflects not only her private war on the family (and its chronicles) but also the distrust of aestheticism prevalent in the 1930s. Finally, Doris Lessing's interest in science fiction is both traditional (in that utopias often have such a political message) and contemporaneous (in that it is a sign of our times).

Given that politics shapes narrative form, we must remember that narrative forms—intellectual patterns and trains of thought— shape politics. That is, the writer's idea of character influences her political vision. The nineteenth-century writers, Shelley and Eliot, stress the need for moral perfection, for character reform, in contrast to social or political change. The twentieth-century writers, Woolf and Lessing, hint that only a psychological revolution or mutation in the structures of the mind can overturn social and psychological laws that are inimical to the individual. The idea of the self changes, and its mutations alter literary visions of political possibilities.

Like the importance and meaning of individualism, the importance of society changes. The political conditions that militate against wholeness of self and harmony between separate selves have altered over two centuries. (George Eliot died little more than a year before Virginia Woolf was born, and the very different social and political conditions they lived through were mirrored in their novels.) But the need for love--for self-acceptance as well as approval from other people--does not change. Doris Lessing's utopian fantasies resemble Mary Shelley's in their impulse to escape from political oppression and private isolation, two kinds of exile that I have tried to show are interdependent. The political liabilities faced by women are the particular property of their disenfranchised state. The cost for the individual is made universally accessible in these novels. The political novels of Shelley, Eliot, Woolf and Lessing present an uneasy, temporizing truce between the demands of the self and the laws of society. Even internalized, as we shall see, the law of the father is only half-obeyed.

NOTES

[1] Mary Wollstonecraft, A Vindication of the Rights of Women, in A Wollstonecraft Anthology, ed. Janet M. Todd (Bloomington: Indiana University Press, 1977), p. 111. Wollstonecraft's point in A Vindication is not that women are powerless but that their power is irrational and despotic. My observation on this quotation is meant simply to draw attention to her word choice--to the implications of language use.

[2] Ibid., pp. 92, 107.

[3] In Patricia Meyer Spack's Imagining a Self: Autobiography and Novel in Eighteenth-Century England (Cambridge: Harvard Univ. Press, 1976), Spacks comments on the eighteenth-century woman writer's ability to turn handicaps into strengths: "Their strength derives from successful exploitation of the dichotomy between public passivity and private energy . . ." (p. 89).

[4] Chapter 3 of Spacks's Imagining a Self illuminates the eighteenth-century background of women's writings in many ways that bear upon my study; her discussion of women's relationships with men in their families is especially interesting.

[5] See Peter Coveney, The Image of Childhood; The Individual and Society: A Study of the Theme in English Literature (Harmondsworth, England: Penguin Books, 1967), p. 31 on the use of the child by nineteenth-century writers, including Dickens and Eliot.

[6] Most critics agree that the political novel is not a formal genre, that a novel is "political" by virtue of its subject matter, themes and intentions. See Morris Edmund Speare, The Political Novel: Its Development in England and in America (New York: Oxford Univ. Press, 1924), p. ix; Joseph Blotner, The Political Novel (1955); and Irving Howe, Politics and the Novel (New York: Horizon Books, 1957), p. 16.

[7] My stress on the relative power of individuals as the basis for political relationships in a novel owes something to Kate Millett's definition of politics in Sexual Politics (Garden City, N.Y.: Doubleday and Co., 1970), p. 23.

[8] Roland Barthes, Writing Degree Zero, trans. Annette Lavers and Colin Smith (New York: Hill and Wang, 1968), p. 2.

[9] Georg Lukács, Realism in Our Time: Literature and the Class Struggle, trans. John and Necke Mander (New York: Harper and Row, 1962), p. 19.

[10] Hayden White offers an exposition of possible narrative forms in which history is written in <u>Metahistory: The Historical Imagination in Nineteenth Century Europe</u> (Baltimore: The Johns Hopkins Univ. Press, 1973), p. 13.

[11] For a useful and lucid review of Marxist studies of the family see Chapters 3 and 4 in Martin Jay, <u>The Dialectical Imagination: A History of the Frankfurt School and the Institute of Social Research 1923-1950</u> (Boston: Little, Brown & Co., 1973). In addition to the Marxist/Freudian syntheses by Horkheimer, Marcuse, and others of the Frankfurt School, one may consider the work of R. D. Laing, which has bearing especially on the novels of Doris Lessing.

[12] Lawrence Stone, "The Rise of the Nuclear Family in Early Modern England: The Patriarchal Stage," in <u>The Family in History</u>, ed. Charles E. Rosenberg (Philadelphia: University of Pennsylvania Press, 1975), p. 13.

[13] Ibid., pp. 44, 50, 53.

[14] Gordon Schochet, <u>Patriarchalism in Political Thought</u> (Oxford: Basil Blackwell, 1975).

[15] Stone, p. 14.

[16] Jay, <u>The Dialectical Imagination</u>, p. 126.

[17] Virginia Woolf, <u>Three Guineas</u> (New York: Harcourt, Brace & World, 1963), p. 135.

[18] Sigmund Freud, <u>Civilization and Its Discontents</u>, trans. and ed. James Strachey (New York: W. W. Norton & Co., 1962).

[19] On Positivism see (among other studies) Robert D. Altick, <u>Victorian People and Ideas</u> (New York: W. W. Norton & Co., 1973), p. 235. On novelistic intersubjectivity see J. Hillis Miller, <u>The Form of Victorian Fiction</u>, p. 67.

[20] See J. Hillis Miller, <u>The Disappearance of God</u> (Cambridge: Harvard University Press, 1963).

[21] William Buckler, "A Dual Quest: The Victorian Search for Identity and Authority," <u>Arts and Sciences</u>, I, No. 1 (1963), 32.

[22] John Lucas, <u>The Literature of Change: Studies in the Nineteenth-Century Provincial Novel</u> (New York: Barnes and Noble, 1977), p. ix.

[23] Mrs. Ellis, <u>The Wives of England: Their Relative Duties, Domestic Influence, and Social Obligations</u> (London: Fisher, Son & Co., 1843), p. 56.

[24] Ibid.

[25] Mary Wollstonecraft, Thoughts on the Education of Daughters: With Reflections on Female Conduct, in the More Important Duties of Life (London: J. Johnson, 1787), pp. 56, 58.

There are numerous studies of the real and theoretical status of the woman in the nineteenth century. Among the earliest is Robert P. Utter and Gwendolyn B. Needham, Pamela's Daughters (1936). Non-literary analyses include:

Lee Holcombe, Victorian Ladies at Work: Middle-Class Working Women in England and Wales 1850-1914 (Hamden, CT: Archon Books, 1973).

Patricia Branca, Silent Sisterhood: Middle Class Women in the Victorian Home (Pittsburgh: Carnegie Mellon University Press, 1976).

In her "Introduction" to A Widening Sphere: Changing Roles of Victorian Women (Bloomington: Indiana University Press, 1977), Martha Vicinus warns against taking too seriously the Angel in the House as a norm for women's behavior in the nineteenth century (p. x). But she acknowledges that the "passivity, frigidity, and uselessness of the female model idealized during the Victorian era" (p. xi) was important as an idea. If nineteenth-century women were "not always the passive, submissive and pure creatures of popular idealizations, . . . neither were they ever completely free from this stereotype" (p. xix).

[26] Virginia Woolf, "Professions for Women," in The Death of the Moth and Other Essays (New York: Harcourt Brace Jovanovich, 1974), pp. 236-238.

[27] Eric Trudgill, Madonnas and Magdalens: The Origins and Development of Victorian Sexual Attitudes (New York: Holmes & Meier, 1976), pp. 74-75. See also Carol Christ, "Victorian Masculinity and the Angel in the House," in A Widening Sphere, ed. Martha Vicinus, p. 147.

[28] Donald D. Stone, "Victorian Feminism and the Nineteenth-Century Novel," Women's Studies, 1 (1972), 65-92.

[29] Vivian Gornick in "Woman as Outsider" in Woman in Sexist Society, eds. Gornick and Moran (New York: Basic Books, 1971) suggests that women are more careful observers because of their exclusion from an inner circle of decision making, while Lorna Sage maintains that social passivity transformed women into active victims in their fiction if not their real lives. See "Women and Literature--III: The Case of the Active Victim," Times Literary Supplement, 26 July 1974, pp. 803-804. Patrica Meyer Spacks, in Imagining a Self, says that an eighteenth-century woman writer made a "mythology of her victimization" (p. 73), turning weakness into strength, though never without cost to herself.

[30] The Diary of Virginia Woolf, Vol. I, ed. Anne Oliver Bell (New York: Harcourt Brace Jovanovich, 1977), Jan. 6, 1918, 104.

[31] Fredric Jameson, "Imaginary and Symbolic in Lacan: Marxism, Psychoanalytic Criticism, and the Problem of the Subject," Yale French Studies, No. 55/56 (1977), p. 340.

[32] Ibid., p. 343.

[33] Simone de Beauvoir, The Second Sex, trans. H. M. Parshley (New York: Vintage Books, 1974), pp. xix, xxxiv, 25, 79.

[34] See Roland Barthes, Writing Degree Zero, pp. 13, 16. Barthes distinguishes between language, style and writing ("écriture"). The first two are deterministic (historically and biologically), the last represents some freedom of choice in expression. See pp. xii and xiii in Susan Sontag's "Preface."

[35] Quoted in Lucien Goldmann, Towards a Sociology of the Novel, trans. Allen Sheriden (London: Tavistock Publications, 1975), p. 6.

[36] Fredric Jameson, "Imaginary and Symbolic in Lacan," p. 340.

[37] Ibid., p. 341.

[38] Edward Dowden, in A Century of George Eliot Criticism, ed. Gordon S. Haight (London: Methuen & Co. Ltd., 1965), p. 64. The term was revived by Kathleen Tillotson and popularized by Wayne Booth in The Rhetoric of Fiction (Chicago: The University of Chicago Press, 1961), p. 71.

[39] Kate Millett, Sexual Politics, p. 139.

[40] Lee Sterrenburg, "The Last Man: Anatomy of Failed Revolutions," Nineteenth-Century Fiction (1978), pp. 328, 331.

[41] Ibid., p. 327. See also J. de Palacio, "Mary Shelley and The Last Man," Revue de Littérature Comparée, 42 (1968), 37-49, for a discussion of the currency of the eschatological theme.

Chapter 2

EXILE, ISOLATION, ACCOMMODATION IN THE LAST MAN:
THE STRATEGIES OF A SURVIVOR

By birth and by marriage, Mary Shelley's intellectual connections are impeccable. The daughter of Mary Wollstonecraft and William Godwin, the wife of Shelley--unlike Virginia Woolf, Mary Shelley seems destined to be eclipsed by her illustrious connections. Her life as a woman and as a writer is often described as two epochs bifurcated by Shelley's death in 1822. Before the event, Mary seems to have been inspired by the heady atmosphere in which she found herself, swept along in the wake of genius--first Godwin's, then Shelley's. After, her life and her fiction lose lustre in the absence of Shelley's generative brilliance. Mary Shelley eludes us; we feel we lack "a solid sense of what she must have been like."[1] In part, this elusiveness stems from her own willingness to be known primarily as daughter and wife.

Patricia Meyer Spacks says of women novelists and autobiographers in the eighteenth century that "Women identifying themselves as daughters thus declared their dependency, their need, and their sense of where that need might be gratified, asserting their identifies to inhere in their roles rather than their deeds."[2] Mary Shelley was only too willing to please her relations, to comply with their expectations of her intellectually: "My husband . . . was from the first very anxious that I should prove myself worthy of my parentage and enroll myself on the page of fame," she confides in her 1831 introduction to Frankenstein.[3] After Shelley's death and Godwin's (1836), Mary took refuge in maternity, as her critics and defenders alike acknowledge. U. C. Knoepflmacher describes the exchange of roles in terms of her "becoming a militant mother rather than a daughter penitent for not being a son."[4] Daughter, wife, mother: Mary Shelley is all these. Yet she has another identity by which her contemporaries knew her in addition to a multitude of modern readers to whom the names Wollstonecraft, Godwin and Shelley are unfamiliar. She is "the Author of Frankenstein," as the title pages of her subsequent works proclaim. In this role, Mary Shelley found an existence independent of her relation to her family. It is as an author that she was able to possess a distinct sense of her self.

Creating a self in the act of writing fiction was the clearest, least ambiguous means of achieving an individual identity. Ironically, given Mary Shelley's background, being intellectually independent meant in a sense conforming to her parents' wishes. Both deplored domestic tyranny, whether in the guise of children's enslavement by adult force or women's moral submission to male possessiveness. Godwin advocated "independence" and "activity of mind" as "the greatest of all personal advantages,"[5] and wrote of parents:

> The right of the parent over his child lies either in his superior strength or his superior reason. If in his strength, we have only to apply this right universally in order to drive all morality out out of the world. If in his reason, in that reason let him confide.[6]

Mary Wollstonecraft argued that women's assumed, "artificial weakness produces a propensity to tyrannize, and gives birth to cunning, the natural opponent of strength. . . . ."[7] Mary Shelley endorses these views, for example, in Lodore, where she criticizes the hero's upbringing as the cause of his adult willfulness and advocates the education of daughters in self-reliance.

Nevertheless, though Mary Shelley echoes parental precepts in her fiction, her life and novels become increasingly conventional. Her late conservatism (her refusal to support liberal causes actively) connotes, ironically, an insidious rebellion against her political background.[8] Such rebellious "independence of mind," though not wholly unprecedented in her career, differs in kind and intensity from her early rebellion. Emotional conflict with her closest relations underlies much of Mary Shelley's early work. During the period of her greatest productivity, before Shelley's death, Mary's writing was an outlet for aggressive feelings against her father, her husband, even herself. Out of this quarrel with her world, domestic and social, she gave birth to a self. Rather, she almost succeeded in doing so. The process of self-creation was abortive.

Mary Shelley's emerging identity died with the deaths of her children and husband. Despite her temperamental and acquired propensity to seek rational explanations for events, she could not help reacting irrationally to the extraordinary tragedies that filled her early life. Indeed, the very sense of her own exceptionalness may have inclined her to heroicize her suffering. After all, many young mothers and wives of her day endured, even expected, frequent births and deaths. But for Mary Shelley, it must have seemed that her audacity in living unconventionally and willfully was punished by Providence, by "Necessity" if not by a deity.[9] The result of this cosmic admonition was that Mary Shelley retreated from actively defining her self and its relation to society.

The self in society is a primary theme of Mary Shelley's work. Her novels consistently present a Promethean conception of personality and an exaltation of the hero exiled from society through his superiority or willfulness. In Frankenstein (1818), Mathilda (1820), Valperga (1823) and The Last Man (1826), the Promethean figures--Victor Frankenstein, Mathilda's father, Castruccio, Raymond--are punished or at least criticized. Yet in these novels, independence of self is not wholly decried. There is a conflict between Prometheanism and a more modest, unheroic, yet still active selfhood, and in this conflict we perceive Mary Shelley's own struggle to assert her independence. That is, self-definition is achieved in the process of writing and is embodied in the novels' form.

Self-discovery in the early novels entails opposition to a male-dominated order which the protagonists find themselves outside of. The unheroic victims of Promethean heroes are not merely passive exemplars. The monster rages against his enforced isolation while Mathilda angrily, vengefully embraces hers. Underlying the plight of these rebellious victims is Mary Shelley's implicit quarrel with her father and husband. The monster avenges himself against his progenitor's neglect, theatening Victor Frankenstein, "'I shall be with you on your wedding night'" (Frankenstein, p. 161). Ostensibly, he complains at being denied his own bride; his jealousy of Frankenstein, however, really reflects Mary Shelley's Electral jealousy and rivalry. Mathilda is ecstatically happy with her father's love until its incestuous nature is made explicit to her. She equates her initiation into evil with rape ("I have compared myself to Proserpine"),[10] the ultimate violation of her self by a masculine power.

What Mathilda both dreads and desires is too horribly anti-social to be achieved in life. Her forbidden love is transmuted into a kind of necrophilia from the moment when she sees her drowned father's (phallic) corpse, "something stiff and straight . . . covered by a sheet" (p. 45). Mathilda comes to love the gentle poet Woodville, but his Shelleyan idealism is an inadequate surrogate for her father's demonic passion. She proposes a suicide-marriage:

> "Behold, my cheek is flushed with pleasure at the imagination of death; all that we love are dead. Come, give me your hand, one look of joyous sympathy and we will go together and seek them. . . . Oh! that I had words to express the luxury of death that I might win you. I tell you we are no longer mortals; we are about to become Gods. . . ." (p. 68)

Woodville encourages her to live, but Mathilda continues to woo death:

> In truth I am in love with death; no maiden ever took more pleasure in the contemplation of her bridal attire than I in fancying my limbs already enwrapt in their shroud: is it not my marriage dress? Alone it will unite me to my father when in an eternal mental union we shall never part. (pp. 77-78)

Mathilda's emotional history symbolically replicates Mary Shelley's--the daughter kills the mother when she is born; the father regards the daughter as his dead wife's image; after "wooing" his child he rejects and deserts her, leaving her only a memory and an insatiable longing for a reunion. Both Mathilda and Frankenstein's monster are unable to gratify their desires, and consequently both complain about the irrationality and injustice of their "fathers'" law. Ultimately, neither can adapt to any larger social will. The inadequacy of the patriarchal order exacts the individual's death, but each narrator records a powerful protest.

In the final novels--Perkin Warbeck (1830), Lodore (1835), and Falkner (1837)--aggressive self-assertion changes into accommodation. In real life, bowed by personal catastrophe, Mary Shelley retreated. In place of an individuated identity, she docilely accepted yet another social role: the widowed mother. The fiction of this period expresses this impulse in the form of victimized characters who most fear individuation and alienation. Orphans do not identify themselves as exiles, conscious (and perhaps secretly proud) of their alienation from society; they find or become parents, sometimes both. In Lodore, Ethel is above all a daughter who loses her father but finds her long-lost mother. In Falkner, Elizabeth loses her mother and her mother-surrogate, Alithea, but finds a father-figure whom she can also mother. Unlike Mathilda, these heroines do not rage against their filial status. They feel only love, not the concomitant resentment that would require or allow them to demand recognition as independent beings.

Again, in these late novels, the Promethean figures are either killed off (Lodore) or domesticated, even emasculated (Falkner) and drawn into a family idyll. The apotheosis of the family is an illusion in Frankenstein and Mathilda as well as in The Last Man, where it occupies a precarious position mid-book. In contrast, a happy family circle concludes Perkin Warbeck, Lodore, and Falkner. Relatedness supplants individuality as the ideal dominating Mary Shelley's final works. In The Last Man, moreover, we can see the transition between these diametrically opposed ideas of the self and its place in society.

The Last Man is a watershed in Mary Shelley's career, both politically and aesthetically. In this first novel written after Shelley's death, her feeling of engulfment by tragic events, her guilty apprehension of further "punishment" for living audaciously, cause her to resign her quest for self-knowledge. The order of things--in the family, the state, the universe--exacts submission rather than rebellion. Always before, the nature of life was a subject that prompted interrogation. In the original version of Mathilda, called The Fields of Fancy, the unhappy heroine is counselled by Diotima, instructress of Socrates, that human happiness "depends upon [one's] intellectual improvement . . ." in order to "become more like that beauty which I adore . . . ."[11] Mathilda's response to this Shelleyan idealism is an unanswered question: "If knowledge is the end of our being why are passions and feelings implanted in us that hurries [sic] us from wisdom to selfconcentrated misery and narrow selfish feeling?" (p. 99). In The Last Man, Mary Shelley schools herself in acceptance of the riddle of existence, without demanding an answer to it:

> What would become of us? O for some Delphic oracle, or Pythian maid, to utter the secrets of futurity! O for some OEdipus to solve the riddle of the cruel Sphynx! Such OEdipus was I to be-- not divining a word's juggle, but whose agonizing pangs, and sorrow-tainted life were to be the engines, wherewith to lay bare the secrets of destiny, and reveal the meaning of the enigma, whose explanation closed the history of the human race. (The Last Man, pp. 310-311)

This is no version of Keatsian negative capability, a conscious acceptance of the mystery, but really a withdrawal of the question posed in Mathilda.

After The Last Man, the protagonists in Mary Shelley's novels do not quarrel with their makers, nor does their author quarrel with herself. In the late novels, the egocentricity of the narrative point of view is reduced even as the Promethean protagonist is domesticated and reconciled, if not to the whole of society, at least to the microcosmic society of his family. Mary Shelley's conception of the self and its relation to society changes, and the narrative structure of her novels reflects this change.

The use of first-person narration conspicuously stops. (Falkner's first-person confession, I will suggest later, is the exception that validates the rule.) This signifies, I believe, a decision against the study of the consciousness of a single protagonist as he simultaneously reveals and makes himself. In its place we find the bilateral monologues and the dialogues--rather awkwardly executed--of the realistic <u>Perkin Warbeck</u>, <u>Lodore</u>, and <u>Falkner</u>. <u>The Last Man</u> reveals Mary Shelley's motivation for shifting from the "self-centered" to the objective in narrative modes.

In this novel, Lionel Verney speaks for the author through his aesthetic credo as well as his philosophical and political opinions. We must understand Verney's story--his survival of the plague that destroys not only civilization but (almost) the entire human species--and, more importantly, his attitude toward the telling of his story, in order to appreciate how and why Mary Shelley lost the liberal faith of her youth. Before analyzing <u>The Last Man</u> in closer detail, it will be important to explore the relationships Mary Shelley formed in her own life and those she represented in her novels in order to appreciate the significance of her apostasy.

* * * * *

The theme of the divided self is a primary one in Mary Shelley's fiction, from <u>Frankenstein</u> through <u>Falkner</u>. In real life, as well, she acknowledged (at least) two distinct identities. On the one hand, she was a devoted daughter, virtually in love with her philosopher-father, and subsequently an idolizing wife.[12] On the other hand, Mary Shelley was an <u>author</u> from childhood, as she tells us in her 1831 introduction to <u>Frankenstein</u>: "As a child I scribbled, and my favorite pastime during the hours given me for recreation was to 'write stories'" (<u>Frankenstein</u>, p. vii). Being a novelist meant being independent, self-sufficient, even omnipotent. Her preface to <u>Frankenstein</u> describes her view of the creative process:

> Invention, it must be humbly admitted, does not consist in creating out of void, but out of chaos; the materials must, in the first place, be afforded; it can give form to dark, shapeless substances but cannot bring into being the substance itself. . . . Invention consists in the capacity of seizing on the capabilities of a subject and in the power of moulding and fashioning ideas suggested to it. (p. x)

In the <u>Frankenstein</u> introduction, Mary Shelley implies that Shelley provided the fertilizing "substance" of her novel in his discussions with Byron and Dr. Polidori about new ways of creating life (p. 2). Her full description of the novel's genesis, however, clearly emphasizes the role of her own unconscious mind in the fertilization process. The subject for her "ghost story" came to her in a <u>dream</u>, and writing the novel was "making only a transcript of the grim terrors of my waking dream" (p. xi). Mary Shelley herself, then, supplied both the substance and the form given it.

Both creative functions--transcribing and imagining--are foreshadowed in her childhood pastimes of writing and "dreaming" ("the following up trains of thought, which had for their subject the formation of a succession of imaginary incidents," p. vii). Dreaming meant audacity and self-assertion; writing entailed conformity to other people's expectations:

> My dreams were at once more fantastic and agreeable than my writings. In the latter I was a close imitator--rather doing as others had done than putting down the suggestions of my own mind. What I wrote was intended at least for one other eye--my childhood's companion and friend; but my dreams were all my own; I accounted for them to nobody; they were my refuge when annoyed--my dearest pleasure when free. (p. vii)

Originality, liberation, independence: all are qualities she associates with dreaming. In dreams, the young Mary Shelley "was not confined to [her] own identity," her "common-place" child's life of constraint and powerlessness, we may imagine (p. viii). In "writing," however, the child was "a close imitator--rather doing as others had done . . . ." The dual impulses--dreaming and writing, fantasizing and organizing--are as integral to Mary Shelley's self-definition as to her fiction-writing.

The imitator in Mary Shelley wrote partly to please her father. (In 1817, she wrote Shelley of Godwin that "I know not whether it is early habit or affection but the idea of his silent quiet disapprobation makes me weep as it did in the days of my childhood."[13]) Godwin remained, with Shelley, her chief literary advisor, the person whom she trusted to edit and publish many of her manuscripts. (Not surprisingly, when Mary asked Godwin to find a publisher for Mathilda, he called the story "disgusting and detestable" and ignored her requests to have it printed.)[14] His influence was felt more implicitly in her use of themes borrowed from Political Justice and Caleb Williams. Clashing wills and patterns of flight and pursuit appear in Mary Shelley's first and last novels, Frankenstein and Falkner. (The title of the latter echoes the names of the heroes of Caleb Williams, Falkland, and of Godwin's closet drama, Faulkener. In the play the heroine joins her son in the kind of incestuous "mental union" sought by Mathilda and subsequent heroines of Mary Shelley's fiction.)

Besides Godwin's influence, Mary Wollstonecraft's novels were continually the subject of her daughter's study and suggested both thematic and formal elements. The first version of Mathilda, The Fields of Fancy, was written with a frame-tale structure owing something to Mary Wollstonecraft's unfinished tale, The Cave of Fancy. Indeed the plot of Mary Wollstonecraft's story--about a dead soul's "ill-fated love for a man whom she hopes to rejoin after her purgation is completed"--obviously foreshadows Mathilda's relationship with her father.

Again, Mary Shelley's ideas on the proper education of daughters reflect both parents' strictures on the importance of individual independence. In Lodore, she recasts Godwin's and Wollstonecraft's views, criticizing the hero for giving his daughter a "sexual education" conducive to passivity and urging: "A lofty sense of independence is, in man, the best privilege of his nature. It cannot be doubted, but that it were for the happiness of the other sex that she were taught more to rely on and act for herself."[16] Ideologically, then, Mary Shelley inherited many of her parents' values and freely borrowed from their literary examples.

Her fictive resemblance to her parents notwithstanding, Mary Shelley was by no means a wholly docile daughter. The excerpt quoted previously from the introduction to Frankenstein speaks of her childish self as rebellious, or at least strong-willed: ". . . my dreams were all my own; I accounted for them to nobody; they were my refuge when annoyed--my dearest pleasure when free" (p. vii). Her father documented this youthful independence in a letter to a friend about Mary:

"She is singularly bold, somewhat imperious, and active of mind. Her desire of knowledge is great, and her perseverance in everything she undertakes almost invincible."[17] His pride in her self-reliance signifies pleasure in his own handiwork, for his plan was that she "should be brought up like a philosopher, even like a cynic. It will add greatly to the strength and worth of her character."[18]

Godwin's educational principles evidently bore fruit. At 17, Mary Shelley would coolly tell her journal that she found her father unreasonable in his reaction to her relationship with Shelley: "Father wishes to see a copy of the codicil, because he thinks Shelley is acting rashly. All this is very odd and inconsistent; but I never quarrel with inconsistency; folks must change their minds."[19] Some of the same dependable rationality prompted her pragmatic reactions to Shelley's visionary states, as a wry journal entry suggests: "I go to bed soon, but Shelley and Jane sit up, and, for a wonder, do not frighten themselves" (Journal, p. 21, 18 October 1814). It must have seemed often that she was giving form or body to Shelley's otherworldliness.

Undoubtedly, Mary was not completely independent; she had from the first what she called a "woman's love of looking up, and being guided" (Journal, p. 205, 21 October 1838). Of her father, she wrote Jane Williams following Shelley's death, "Until I met Shelley I [could?] justly say that he was my God--and I remember many childish instances of the [ex]cess of attachment I bore for him."[20] In later life, Mary Shelley would suppress her own resentment at the dominance of her father and husband. (In the introduction to Frankenstein resentment breaks through her fulsome self-deprecation: "At this time [Shelley] desired that I should write, not so much with the idea that I could produce anything worthy of notice, but that he might himself judge how far I possessed the promise of better things hereafter" (p. viii). "Many and long were the conversations between Lord Byron and Shelley to which I was a devout but nearly silent listener" (p. x). Still, her adolescent impulse to worship philosopher-heroes can be seen clashing with her own imperious selfhood in her early fiction. The monster's rage against his indifferent, irresponsible creator; Mathilda's grief at her lost innocence--these tell of Mary Shelley's irrational anger at her own "makers," father and husband. Though the fictive rebellious offspring end in death, their expression of grief and resentment is in itself a declaration of independence.

What caused Mary Shelley's subsequent failure of will and muted her sense of rebellious anger? The answer seems to be the loss of belief in her own power to do, make, become something. Her education into fatalism was abrupt, exceedingly harsh, irreparably damaging to her inner security. Her early widowhood prematurely ended her quest for an identity. By robbing her of the primary relationship in her life, it undermined her desire to be independent. There was no one left whom she could define herself against and be independent of.

In <u>Falkner</u>, Mary Shelley writes a paean to adolescence, the threshold between the childhood and adult worlds. It seems steeped in nostalgia for a time when she felt her own powers strongly.

> If a time is to be named when the human heart is nearest to moral perfection, most alive and yet most innocent, aspiring to good, without a knowledge of evil, the period at which Elizabeth had arrived,--from 13 to 16,--is it. Vague forebodings are awakened; a sense of the opening drama of life, unaccompanied with any longing to enter on it--that feeling is reserved for the years that follow; but at fourteen and fifteen we only feel that we are

> emerging from childhood, and we rejoice, having yet a sense that as yet it is not fitting that we should make one of the real actors on the world's stage. A dreamy delicious period, when all is unknown; and yet we feel that all is soon to be unveiled. The first pang has not been felt; for we consider childhood's woes (real and frightful as those sometimes are,) as puerile, and no longer belonging to us. We look upon the menaced evils of life as a fiction.[21]

The "evils" of adult life, which precipitate the fall from innocence to experience, are the tragedies that the individual is powerless to prevent. Lost is the naive belief in one's ability to effect one's own destiny. In <u>Frankenstein</u> and <u>Mathilda</u>, the victimized monster and daughter are outraged at being neglected, hurt, or otherwise abused by their parents. Mathilda cries, "I lament now, I must ever lament, those few short months of Paradisaical bliss; I disobeyed no command, I ate no apple, and yet I was ruthlessly driven from it. Alas! my companion did, and I was precipitated in his fall" (<u>Mathilda</u>, p. 16). There is a striking difference between this and a more muted complaint in Mary Shelley's journal entry following Shelley's death: ". . . the courses of destiny having dragged me to that single resting-place, have left me. Father, mother, friend, husband, children--all made, as it were, the team that conducted me here; and now all, except you, my poor boy . . . all are gone, and I am left to fulfill my task. So be it" (<u>Journal</u>, p. 181, 2 October 1822). The revolution in Mary Shelley's life is indicated by the differing emotional tone of these laments. Mathilda's reproachful anger gives her force; Mary Shelley's grief is pathetic and impotent. It is as if she retreats to her pre-adolescent idolization of her male guardians, forgetting entirely the correlative anger. A formerly active love-hate becomes a monotone devotedness.

A widow, she consecrates herself to the dissemination of Shelley's fame and memory: "I would endeavour to consider myself a faint continuation of his being, and, as far as possible, the revelation to the earth of what he was. Yet, to become this, I must change much . . ." (Journal, p. 182, 7 October 1822). This dedication is a sad change from the bravely optimistic proposal she made to herself only the previous winter: ". . . above all, let me fearlessly descend into the remotest caverns of my own mind, carry the torch of self-knowledge into its dimmest recesses . . ." (Journal, p. 170, 25 Feb. 1822). Her pursuit of self-knowledge, her discovery of an identity, essentially end here.

For a brief period after Shelley's death, Mary's anguish enabled her to feel an exalted self-consciousness: "It is better to grieve than not to grieve. Grief at least tells me that I was not always what I am now. I was once selected for happiness; let the memory of that abide by me" (Journal, p. 185, 11 Nov. 1822). As the vividness of her loss pales, as the force of her relation to Shelley diminishes, she seems to panic. Four months after her return to England from Italy, she regrets leaving the scene of her tragic losses: "I thought of him with hope; my grief was active, striving, expectant. I was worth something then in the catalogue of beings. I could have written something, been something. Now, I am exiled from these beloved scenes . . ." (Journal, p. 191, 18 Jan. 1824). Feeling estranged from English society after her long, eventful stay in Italy only exacerbates her sense of loss: "Mine own Shelley . . . . To be here without you is to be doubly exiled, to be away from Italy is to lose you twice. Dearest, why is my spirit thus losing all energy?" (Journal, p. 193,

14 May 1824). This enervating double-exile tells on her ability to write.

Desperately lonely, Mary Shelley feels her failure to "become something" almost as acutely as she feels the loss of her husband: "Amidst all the depressing circumstances that weigh on me, none sinks deeper than the failure of my intellectual powers; nothing I write pleases me" (Journal, p. 192, 14 May 1824). In Italy, "Then I could think, and my imagination could invent and combine, and self became absorbed in the grandeur of the universe I created. Now, my mind is a blank, a gulf filled with formless mist" (Journal, p. 194, 14 May 1824). Town society oppresses her, she says (Journal, p. 194, 8 June 1824); alone, she communes with her own imaginings much as she did as a child and has an exalted sense of her own powers. The self capable of "being absorbed in the universe" is not obliterated; rather, it is enhanced.

Though she feels her creativity waning, Mary Shelley is at this time still emotionally inspired--by grief now, where formerly there were anger and rebelliousness. The "gulf filled with formless mist," like the "chaos" awaiting form that becomes Frankenstein, would eventually be given substance and shape. The very journal entry that records her despair at the failure of her imagination also contains the seed of her next novel: "The last man! Yes, I may well describe that solitary being's feelings, feeling myself as the last relic of a beloved race, my companions extinct before me" (Journal, p. 193, 14 May 1824). Mary Shelley uses the energizing emotions of grief and loneliness to make a final effort to "become something," to assert herself in the act of writing.

In *The Last Man*, Mary Shelley successfully drew upon the long-standing conflict between her desire to know herself independent and her desire to please others. It is her last novel to use first-person narration, in which the teller of the tale creates a self or persona in the process of telling it, where the narrative mode becomes an object of scrutiny in its own right. In the course of the novel, Lionel Verney's conception of his task undergoes a change that is symbolic of Mary Shelley's. Verney's definitions of himself, his relation to society, and his role as creator and historian represent the transformation of Mary Shelley's own roles.

In *The Last Man*, she chooses a narrator whose life history has less symbolic affinity with her own than the betrayed and disconsolate orphans of *Frankenstein* and *Mathilda*. Although both Mary Shelley and Lionel Verney are left widowed and childless, Verney does not express her sense of loss as well as the monster and Mathilda. Possibly Mary Shelley felt that a male observer would add versimilitude to the novel's depiction of political exchanges. At the same time, however, using a man as narrator distanced her from the experience described. In a sense, the maleness of the victimized hero may have intensified Mary Shelley's conflict--for she resented being left alone by male guardians as much as she mourned it.

* * * * *

In *Political Justice*, Godwin discriminated between right and wrongful kinds of personal freedom. He argued for intellectual, against social independence: "Natural independence, or freedom from all constraint except that of reason and argument presented to the understanding, is of the utmost importance to the welfare and improvement of mind. Moral independence on the contrary is always injurious." "The attachment that is felt by the present race of mankind to independence in this respect, the desire to act as they please without being accountable to the principles of reason, is highly detrimental to the general welfare."[22] As Godwin's hero Caleb Williams learns, man must feel himself free to act yet recognize his inability to survive morally and emotionally in isolation from his fellow man.

Intellectual freedom becomes an emotional burden in *The Last Man* because it entails exile from human fellowship. *The Last Man* depicts varieties of exile and gives both private and political causes for them. Ultimately, however, the root cause of all alienation is the insolubility of the metaphysical mystery, why do we live, if destined to die?, The novel asks, not "How live?" but "Why live at all?" The former question requires an answer in terms of personal choices, social responsibilities, political decisions. The latter, for Mary Shelley, proves unanswerable. Because she cannot teleologically justify why we live, the activity of living becomes an end in itself. This outcome, paradoxically, influences possible choices of how best to live.

Besides being the primary theme of *The Last Man*, exile is a fact confronted in the very narrative mode of the novel. That is, Lionel Verney's attitude toward his story--his conception of his role as narrator--is as much a revelation of the artist's role as of the relation of a single self to society. Mary Shelley depicts the artist's transformation from a (Romantic) sublime egotist, proudly superior to society if tragically alienated from it, into a (Victorian) scribe for whom writing becomes life-preserving, Carlylean _work_. This transition from a Romantic to a Victorian narrator is inextricably bound up with

Lionel Verney's discovery about the ultimate isolation of the self.

Verney's history, related in The Last Man, includes at least three distinct phases. As her modern editor points out, Mary Shelley ironically reverses the Wordsworthian triadic progression of innocent unity; experiential alienation; higher, maturer oneness with the universe. Instead, she "presents us with the pattern of a life beginning in alienation, temporarily achieving a sense of union, and then returning to an intensified isolation."[23] Verney's first and final states of isolation are different in kind as well as intensity. He undergoes a change from political to social exile, which is remediable, to existential exile, for which there is no solution. Through Verney's career, Mary Shelley demonstrates her new belief that political solutions to the problem of human unhappiness are not ineffectual but rather meaningless, a more radically pessimistic view of the human social condition.

Verney's initial social exile was brought on by his noble father's being exiled from the royal court for his recklessness and lack of self-control. The father's political sins being visited on the innocent child, Lionel grows up orphaned and neglected. He becomes rebellious and arrogant, conscious of some innate social superiority to his rustic friends: ". . . I knew I was different and superior to my protectors and companions, but I knew not how or wherefore" (The Last Man, p. 8). He is an incipient radical--"The sense of injury, associated with the name of king and noble, clung to me . . ." (p. 8)--angry at unjust or irresponsible authority figures who have deprived him of paternalistic nurturing. Exclusion from power brings about desire for illegitimate power: "I associated with others friendless like myself,

I formed them into a band, I was their chief and captain" (p. 8);
". . . finding that my chief superiority consisted in power, I soon persuaded myself that it was in power only that I was inferior to the chiefest potentates of the earth" (p. 9). The exiled boy, disinherited by the royal "father" and left orphaned by his real parents, represents the growth of disaffection in the childlike or primitive lower classes of a society whose leaders fail their subjects.

Mary Shelley does not recommend, as a solution to Verney's incipient rebelliousness and to popular unrest, a more humane and benevolent paternalism. Nor does she heroicize man in his natural, primitive condition and advocate complete self-rule. Instead, she gives Verney a friend, Adrian, himself a rebel against aristocratic tyranny in his own royal fmaily. Adrian (the novel's surrogate for Shelley) is a Platonist and a philanthropist. Eventually, he governs England in time of crisis as a philosopher-king. As a boy, his "active spirit of benevolence" (p. 18) wins a peaceful contest over Lionel's belligerence. Adrian's gentle personality converts Lionel to a political philosophy of good will: "'This,' I thought, 'is power! Not to be strong of limb, hard of heart, ferocious, and daring; but kind, compassionate and soft'" (p. 19). Showing the "'fervour of a new proselyte'" (p. 19), Verney feels transformed, "as much changed as if I had transmigrated into another form" (p. 21).

This internal revolution, a type of Godwinian intellectual change that must precede institutional change, produces admirable results--for a while. From social rebelliousness, Lionel Verney's energy is channeled into scholarship. As does Felix Holt, Verney exalts intellectual enlightenment over political activism. His scholarship takes a seemingly passive course. Books, he says, ". . . stood in the place of an active career, of ambition, and those palpable excitements necessary to the multitude. The collation of philosophical opinions, the study of historical facts, the acquirements of languages, were at once my recreation, and the serious aim of my life" (p. 112). Yet for Verney, knowledge represents power. His ardent enthusiasm makes him hope for a future of intellectual achievement: "Life is before me, and I rush into possession. Hope, glory, love, and blameless ambition are my guides, and my soul knows no dread. What has been, though sweet, is gone; the present is good only because it is about to change, and the to come is all my own. . . . my eyes seem to penetrate the cloudy midnight of time, and to discern within the depths of its darkness, the fruition of all my soul desires" (p. 25). With Wordsworthian (and Adamic) exultation, he anticipates constructing a brilliant future. He will become a ". . . citizen of the world, a candidate for immortal honors, an eager aspirant to the praise and sympathy of my fellow men" (p. 113). In thinking, Lionel conceives of himself--creating an identity as a scholar.

Verney's research, like Mary Shelley's autobiographical fiction, involves rescuing from obscurity and infamy "favourite historical characters, especially those whom I believed to have been traduced, or about whom clung obscurity and doubt" (p. 133). He sees himself as a heroic agent rather than as a transcriber of others' past deeds: "As my authorship increased . . . my point of sight was extended, and the inclinations and capacities of all human beings became deeply interesting to me. Kings have been called the fathers of their people. Suddenly I became as it were the father of all mankind. Posterity became my heirs. My thoughts were gems to enrich the treasure house of man's intellectual possessions . . ." (p. 133). Lionel's intellectual ambition is not destructive as was the Faustian drive of Victor Frankenstein. Without question, however, it is in his eyes a heroic and audacious activity. What he says about his sister Perdita's discovery of philosophy might be true of him as well: she was "questioning herself and her author, moulding every idea in a thousand ways, ardently desirous for the discovery of truth in every sentence" (p. 114). In short, the seemingly passive occupation of scholarship is, for Verney, a Promethean activity. Like Prometheus, he transmits wisdom to mankind, while at the same time "questioning . . . [his] author."

Verney's closest companions in a Promethean circle include Adrian and Raymond, both aristocrats with political interests that are, however, antagonistic. Adrian is a "philanthropist" who feels sympathy "with the universe of existence"; Raymond is a "politician" motivated by "self-gratification" and worldliness (p. 31). Both agree that England (a republic since 2073) is a nation of servile and vulgar citizens--"willing slaves, self-constituted subjects" (p. 41)--incapable of the "erect and manly" self-rule that would make the republic glorious. The chance to implement their different utopian visions comes to Raymond and Adrian by turns, with Mary Shelley demonstrating through them the benefits and limitations of political practice.

Raymond becomes Protector, chief governor of England, when the self-serving popular leader Ryland sells his candidacy for personal profit. Raymond's plan is to effect a utopia through the example of his own personality: ". . . men were not happy, not because they could not, but because they would not rouse themselves to vanquish self-raised obstacles. Raymond was to inspire them with his beneficial will, and the mechanism of society, once systematised according to faultless rules, would never again swerve into disorder" (p. 76). Unfortunately, Raymond's lack of self-rule makes it impossible for him to succeed politically, to provide an heroic example. He admits to being the "slave" of his own heart (p. 45), ruled by his passions (his love for Perdita; his fascination with Evadne, which precipitates his political ruin).

Mary Shelley implies that Raymond's political downfall stems from his disbelief in free will. He argues with Lionel and Adrian on this subject, insisting that our lives are determined both by nature and by nurture: "'. . . this cultivation, mingling with our innate disposition, is the soil in which our desires, passions, and motives grow'" (p. 47). Not feeling free to govern himself, Raymond ultimately cannot set the example of "beneficial will" that he hoped would inspire the people.

In contrast to the fatalistic Raymond, both Lionel and Adrian have faith in some degree of freedom of volition. Adrian enthusiastically believes in humanity's capacity to make the ideal real by willing it. Able to conquer his own passions, to rule himself as Raymond is not, Adrian overcomes his grief at Evadne's refusal to return his love and dedicates himself to humanitarian causes. He believes that man's ability to conceive of utopia ensures its realization, such is the power of the human mind: "'The choice is with us; let us will it, and our habitation becomes a paradise. For the will of man is omnipotent, blunting the arrows of death, soothing the bed of disease, and wiping away the tears of agony'" (p. 54). For Adrian (as for Shelley), nothing exists but as it is perceived. The ideal is more real (and more realizable) than what is actual.

Adrian is a pragmatic idealist, a philosopher-king who leaves the Platonic cave of philosophy to return to public service. His political ambition is vitiated by neither the greedy self-interest of the lower-class Ryland nor the aristocratic egotism of Raymond. Adrian is devoted to moral, aesthetic, and intellectual excellence. Despite his idealism, he does not aim at the establishment of an English utopia. He enters politics only in time of crisis and imperative public need, when the plague has devastated the citizenry and threatened to destroy civilization itself:

> "This is my post: I was born for this--to rule England in anarchy, to save her in danger--to devote myself for her. The blood of my forefathers cries aloud in my veins, and bids me be first among my countrymen. Or, if this mode of speech offend you, let me say, that my mother, the proud queen, instilled early into me a love of distinction. . . . I cannot, through intrigue and faithlessness, rear again the throne upon the wreck of English public spirit. But I can be the first to support and guard my country, now that terrific disasters and ruin have laid strong hands upon her." (p. 185)

Adrian's language is formal, abstract, remote from practical experience and application; it reveals Adrian's self-consciousness, more naive than self-interested. His failure to save England, despite his great talents and noble motives, proves the ultimate futility of heroism in politics.

Mary Shelley feels ambivalent about heroic individualism. On the one hand, pride of rank is artificial and "worse than foolish." "False was all this--false all but the affections of our nature. . . . There was but one good and one evil in the world--life and death"

(p. 212). But if pride based on birth, rank, wealth is fallacious, the loss of individual heroism wrought by the plague is lamentable:

> The pomp of rank, the assumption of power, the possessions of wealth vanished like morning mist. One living beggar had become of more worth than a national peerage of dead lords--alas the day! than of dead heroes, patriots, or men of genius. There was much of degradation in this: for even vice and virtue had lost their attributes--life--life--the continuation of our animal mechanism--was the Alpha and Omega of the desires, the prayers, the prostrate ambition of human [sic] race. (p. 212)

Mary Shelley regrets the passing not of aristocracy itself but of heroes--the individual patriots or philosophers or artists that the caste system is capable of producing. She sympathizes with an aristocracy of talent ("nature's true nobility," p. 161) and with the Promethean greatness that it makes possible.

Mary Shelley equates the anarchy caused by the plague that sweeps the entire earth with democratization. England is contaminated because of its increasingly unheroic mercantilism: "Our own distresses, though they were occasioned by the fictitious reciprocity of commerce, encreased in due proportion" (p. 169). In one description, the plague is explicitly likened to the French Revolution: "As at the conclusion of the eighteenth century, the English unlocked their hospitable store, for the relief of those driven from their homes by political revolution; so now they were not backward in affording aid to the victims of a more widespreading calamity" (p. 171). Mary Shelley regarded revolution in the social fabric with dread, even horror. In a letter inspired by the Revolution of 1848, she commented:

> . . . these are awful times. The total overthrow of law, the dislocation of the social system in France presents a fearful aspect. In Italy and in Germany the people aim at political rather than social change--but the French will spare no pains to inculcate their wicked and desolating principles--and to extend the power of their nefarious Provisional Government all over Europe. . . .

> their measures are so tyrannical--so ruinous that they must be looked upon as the worst engines of a bad system. There is no doubt that a French propaganda is spread among all nations--they are raising the Irish and even exciting the English Chartists. . . . I do believe that in England law and the orderly portion of the community will prevail. God grant it. God preserve us from the tyranny and lawlessness now oppressing France. . . .[24]

Even as early as 1826, when writing *The Last Man*, Mary Shelley echoed her father's fear of "social" revolution as opposed to political, institutional reform. She reacted to changes in the social fabric--relationships between people in the state or in the family--with outrage and fear. It was natural for her to advocate paternalistic custodianship of social bonds based on emotions.

Adrian's governing plan is benevolently paternalistic. The state will be governed like a well-ordered family unit. As his lieutenant, Lionel Verney decides that in rural England, "each small township [would be] directed by the elders and wise men . . . . Each village, however small, usually contains a leader, one among whom they venerate, whose advice they seek in difficulty, and whose good opinion they chiefly value" (p. 195). These "rustic archons," reminiscent of Wordsworth's wise solitaries, rule their tiny kingdoms like loving parents.

Like the nineteenth-century capitalist, the plague victim is advised to seek spiritual restoration in the bosom of his family. Lionel Verney's revulsion from public life, following his return from the war between the Greeks and Turks, sets a reactionary example: "I cannot describe the rapturous delight with which I turned from political brawls at home, and the physical evils of distant countries, to my own dear home, to the selected abode of goodness and love; to peace, and the interchange of every sacred sympathy" (p. 163). Lionel calls for retreat from the world, repudiation of political action altogether:

> How unwise had the wanderers been, who had deserted its shelter, entangled themselves in the web of society, and entered on what men of the world call "life,"--that labyrinth of evil, that scheme of mutual torture. To live, according to this sense of the word, we must not only observe and learn, we must also feel; we must not be mere spectators of action, we must act; we must not describe, but be subjects of description. Deep sorrow must have been the inmate of our bosoms; fraud must have lain in wait for us; the artful must have deceived us; sickening doubt and false hope must have chequered our days; hilarity and joy, that lap the sole in ecstacy, must at times have possessed us. Who that knows what "life" is, would pine for this feverish species of existence? . . . shut the door on the world, and build high the wall that is to separate me from the troubled scene enacted within its precincts. Let us live for each other and for happiness; let us seed peace in our dear home. . . . (p. 158)

The wall that Verney wants to erect between his family--his own little kingdom--and the larger world becomes a model for the organization of the state.

Adrian and Lionel exhort people to accept social order, including a hierarchic division of society, as the best means of controlling the spread of the plague: ". . . it became our part to fix deep the foundations, and raise high the barrier between contagion and the sane; to introduce such order as would conduct to the well-being of the survivors, and as would preserve hope and some portion of happiness to those who were spectators of the still renewed tragedy" (p. 195). The wall of separateness and order is a reactionary measure necessary to diffuse the power of political contagion.

Adrian's and Lionel's proposal is also conservative in that it is atavistic. It attempts to restore the lost harmony of the fabled Golden Age that was the object of much nostalgia in the increasingly industrialized eighteenth and nineteenth centuries. The devastation brought by the plague inspires paternalistic benevolence in other

aristocrats as well as in Adrian. Mary Shelley cites many modestly
heroic responses to anarchy:

> Among some these changes produced a devotion and sacrifice of self
> at once graceful and heroic. It was a sight for the lovers of the
> human race to enjoy; to behold as in ancient times, the patriarchal
> modes in which the variety of kindred and friendship fulfilled
> their duties and kindly offices. (p. 223)

Young noblemen perform rustic chores while noblewomen provide them with
"the simple and affectionate welcome known before only to the lowly
cottage--a clean hearth and bright fire. . ." (p. 223). The political
ideal is a pastoral idyll--peopled by happy children under a benevolent
guidance that is paternal (unlike the matriarchal utopias and four-
gated cities of Doris Lessing's fiction).

The domestic idyll briefly achieved in the home and in the
state proves an ineffectual antidote to anarchy. Mary Shelly, though
she may believe them possible or desirable in 1848, undercuts political
solutions in The Last Man. Because the plague does not merely symbol-
ize democratization and commercialism, political and social levelling,
no political solutions--radical or conservative--can forestall its
destructive advance.[25]

What the plague ultimately represents to Lionel Verney and Mary
Shelley can best be deduced from its effects. Its destructiveness is
so undiscriminating, so widespread, so irrevocable that survival
becomes the highest goal of every human being. Mere animal life comes
to have greater value than genius, moral worth, and other excellences
esteemed by civilized man:

> Now life is all that we covet; that this automaton of flesh should,
> with joints and springs in order, perform its functions, that this
> dwelling of the soul should be capable of containing its dweller.
> Our minds, late spread abroad through countless spheres and end-
> less combinations of thought, now retrenched themselves behind this

>wall of flesh, eager to preserve its well-being only. We were
>surely sufficiently degraded. (p. 230)

The plague represents, in essence, death: the metaphysical fact. "We were all equal now; but near at hand was an equality still more levelling, a state where beauty and strength, and wisdom, would be as vain as riches and birth. The grave yawned beneath us all. . ." (p. 231). Humanity, which had seemed a fertile "flood," "a vast perennial river," is now seen to progress toward "the ocean of death" (p. 300)--there is no greater end.

Death by plague comes to all, even to individuals who seek to isolate themselves for safety. The radical sectarians who follow a Methodistic "prophet" all succumb: "At length the plague, slow-footed, but sure in her noiseless advance, destroyed the illusion, invading the congregation of the elect, and showering promiscuous death among them" (p. 296). Justice is apparently served when the ranting religious despot is defeated. Yet the plague is not the instrument of an intelligible providence. It "promiscuously," indiscriminately, attacks benevolent as well as egocentric politicians and their dependents. It cruelly--or with indifference--kills children before their fond parents.

Perhaps worst of all, death in this virulent form seems <u>meaningless</u>. The human mind--Lionel Verney's, Mary Shelley's--cannot make sense of the effects of the plague: ". . . it appeared as if suddenly the motion of the earth was revealed to us--as if no longer we were ruled by ancient laws, but were turned adrift in an unknown region of space" (p. 270).

Lionel Verney's (and Adrian's) original brave faith in the human imagination is undercut by such unforeseeable, even unimaginable destruction. Verney had optimistically believed that the mind of man could effect anything it willed: "So true it is, that man's mind alone was the creator of all that was good or great to man, and that Nature herself was only his first minister" (p. 5). He had argued against Raymond's determinism: ". . . nature always presents to our eyes the appearance of a patient: while there is an active principle in man which is capable of ruling fortune, and at least of tacking against the gale, till it in some mode conquers it" (p. 46). Verney learns that man, individual or species, cannot conquer nature, at least nor the (natural) fact of death.

The illusion of human progress is undercut in public life and in private as well. Civilization is exposed as an evanescent fiction, a hopeful creation of man's imagination that has no substantial or absolute reality. "England, late birth-place of excellence and school of the wise, thy children are gone, thy glory faded! Thou, England, wert the triumph of man!" (p. 235). Without its heroes, the political and cultural glories of England are ephemeral.

One private illusion that the plague exposes is the natural though irrational faith of the parent that his children will survive to continue his life in theirs: ". . . we call ourselves lords of the creation, wielders of the elements, masters of life and death, and we allege in excuse of this arrogance, that though the individual is destroyed, man continues for ever" (p. 167). "Thus, losing our identity, that of which we are chiefly conscious, we glory in the continuity of our species, and learn to regard death without terror. But when any whole nation becomes the victim of the destructive powers of exterior agents, then indeed man shrinks into insignificance, he feels his tenure of life insecure, his inheritance on earth cut off" (p. 167). Lionel Verney is forced to realize, as he watches his children die before him, the delusion in his optimistic belief in posterity ("Willingly do I give place to thee, dear Alfred! advance, offspring of tender love, child of our hopes; advance a soldier on the road to which I have been the pioneer! I will make way for thee . . ." (p. 165). The blunt fact of death defeats this naive hope, as Mary Shelley learned when watching three of her own children die. In 1820 she wrote Leigh Hunt, ". . . you, my dear Hunt, never lost a child or the ideal immortality w[oul]d not suffice to your immagination [sic] as it naturally does thinking only of those whom you loved more from the overflowing of affection, than from their being the hope, the rest, the purpose, the support, and the recompense of life."[26]

Verney is progressively shorn of his human ties and props. With the death of his wife Idris, "the talisman of my existence" (p. 44), Lionel feels "as if all the visible universe had grown as soulless, inane, and comfortless as the clay-cold image beneath me. I felt for a moment the intolerable sense of struggle with, and detestation for, the laws which govern the world . . ." (p. 260). Lionel regains his resignation to fate, his hope that they will be reunited in an unearthly incarnation. But his response to Idris's death clearly emulates Mary's reaction to Shelley's. The world suddenly seems robbed of meaning. Even individual death (like Adrian's accidental drowning at the end of The Last Man) is senseless, random, absurd. Obviously it is not nature, in all its mutability and unpredictability, that is senseless or dead. It is man's mind that imbues the animate and inanimate universe with meaning; the "death" of the universe signifies the failure of man's imagination, its defeat by unbearable facts.

Lionel continues to hope--fantastically--that spiritually they can survive and continue to know each other: "We talked of what was beyond the tomb; and, man in his human shape being nearly extinct, we felt with certainty of faith, that other spirits, other minds, other perceptive beings, sightless to us, must people with thought and love this beauteous and imperishable universe" (p. 248). (Like Doris Lessing, Mary Shelley postulates a new race of survivors who will create a superior civilization; both give up on human contrivances--kinds of government and social structures--as remedies.) For a time, Lionel behaves as if this belief sustains him, retrieves his faith in the self-sufficient creativity of the human mind. He addresses the reader, for example, as one of this race of spiritually superior beings who have replaced humanity: "Patience, oh reader! whoever thou art, sprung from some surviving pair, thy nature will be human, thy habitation the earth . . ." (p. 291).

Really, however, Verney has no hope; the message that he wishes to transmit to this hypothetical posterity is negative: "Beware, tender offspring of the re-born world--beware, fair being, with human heart, yet untamed by care, and human brow, yet unploughed by time--beware, lest the cheerful current of thy blood be checked, thy golden locks turn grey . . ." (p. 318). "Seek a cypress grove, whose moaning boughs will be harmony befitting; seek some cave, deep embowered in the earth's dark entrails, where no light will penetrate, save that which struggles, red and flickering, through a single fissure. staining thy page with grimmest livery of death" (p. 318). Lionel advocates retreat from life--from the sun--to the depths of isolation and self-exploration.

The metaphor of the cave figures prominently in Mary Shelley's private and published writing for the depths of the individual mind. In Valperga, Euthanasia counsels Beatrice to seek "Content of Mind" by exploring the recesses of her subterranean mind.[27] As we have seen, in her journal Mary Shelley applies the metaphor to her own process of self-discovery: ". . . let me fearlessly descend into the remotest caverns of my own mind, carry the touch of self-knowledge into its dimmest recesses: But too happy if I dislodge any evil spirit or enshrine a new deity in some hitherto uninhabited nook."[28] In the author's "Introduction" to The Last Man the cave of the Cumaean sibyl is purported to be the source of the divinely inspired notes or "leaves" from which the editor compiled the novel. Throughout Mary Shelley's fiction, then, the cave symbolizes imagination, the unconscious depths of the mind from which arose inspiration or "dreams," the fertile "chaos" of her art. The dreams can be used for moral or immoral purposes, depending on how and why they are organized, but the primary goal is "content of mind," self-acceptance. This goal become secondary in The Last Man, however.

In advocating a retreat to a cave of solitude and self-communion, Lionel Verney is prescribing not self-discovery but quiescence, a passivity that is deathlike. In one particularly despairing mood, in fact, he advises his readers to seek rather than wait for death:

> Surely death is not death, and humanity not extinct; but merely
> passed into other shapes, unsubjected to our perceptions. Death is
> a vast portal, an high road to life: let us hasten to pass; let
> us exist no more in this living death, but die that we may live!
> (p. 310)

What must die is the illusory belief that not only man but also his fictions are indestructible, immortal, absolute.

Chief among man's fictions is his belief in free will and its power. When arguing against Raymond's fatalism, Lionel insists, "'There is much truth in what you say,' said I, 'and yet no man ever acts upon this theory. Who, when he makes a choice, says, Thus I choose, because I am necessitated? Does he not on the contrary feel a freedom of will within him, which, though you may call it fallacious, still actuates him as he decides?'" (p. 47). Man's feeling of free will is his chief weapon against death: ". . . in times of misery we must fight against our destinies, and strive not to be overcome by them" (p. 233). The impact of the plague is enervating; it saps the will of the survivors. The very fact that their dwindling number ensures greater wealth individually makes ambition unnecessary: ". . . there was no need of labour, no inquisitiveness, no restless desire to get on" (p. 279).

Confronting death forces the survivors to realize that the fictions by which they have lived are irrelevant to the mysterious laws of the universe. Action, even the act of willing, cannot prevent death; only resignation and submission to fate are possible:

> Would you read backwards the unchangeable laws of Necessity?
> Mother of the world! Servant of the Omnipotent! eternal,
> changeless Necessity! who with busy fingers sitting ever weaving
> the indissoluble chain of events!--I will not murmur at thy acts.
> If my human mind cannot acknowledge that all that is, is right;
> yet since what is, must be, I will sit amidst the ruins and smile.
> Truly we were not born to enjoy, but to submit, and to hope.
> (pp. 290-291)

At the last, living becomes an end in itself, a process of getting from point to point in time and space (just as Adrian leads his dwindling band of survivors across the Continent, believing that only endless motion will alleviate suffering and prolong life).

At the novel's end, Lionel Verney is the last man, and he longs for death. (It is most assuredly the "Friend" whom he adjures, "'Friend, come! I wait for thee!'" [p. 332].) He wants to die, either to rejoin his beloved friends or else simply to escape the enormous pain of being "alone of my race" (p. 324). At the same time, he has also, involuntarily, an imperative will to live. He survives the boating accident which kills Adrian and Clara because "instinctive love of life animated me, and feelings of contention, as if a hostile will combated with mine" (p. 323). Almost in spite of himself, Lionel is a survivor. Because of this strong will--"I, lord of myself"--he clings to life, half-resentful at his instinct for self-preservation (p. 323).

The achievements of the human will are ephemeral, but the will of individual man is tenacious. Lionel Verney turns this fundamental fact into its own justification. Like Tennyson's Ulysses, he voyages ceaselessly, having no goal beyond that of staving off despair and panic: "How dreadful it is, to emerge from the oblivion of slumber, and to receive as a good morrow the mute wailing of one's own hapless heart . . ." (p. 325); ". . . I would not believe that all was as it seemed--The world was not dead, but I was mad . . ." (p. 327). As for the Victorian Ulysses, Verney's travelling is an end in itself:

> . . . to endless time, decrepid and grey headed--youth already in the grave with those I love--the lone wanderer will still unfurl his sail, and clasp the tiller--and, still obeying the breezes of heaven, for ever round another and another promontory, anchoring in another and another bay, ploughing seedless ocean, leaving

> behind the verdant land of native Europe, adown the tawny shore of
> Africa, having weathered the fierce seas of the Cape, I may moor
> my worn skiff in a creek, shaded by spicy groves of the odorous
> islands of the far Indian ocean. (pp. 341-342)

The Romantic or Promethean hero has suffered a sea change into a Victorian. Work for its own sake, existence for its own sake, submission to the incomprehensible ways of a "dead," godless universe: all characterize Lionel Verney at the novel's end:

> I form no expectation of alteration for the better; but the monotonous present is intolerable to me. Neither hope nor joy are my pilots--restless despair and fierce desire of change lead me on. I long to grapple with danger, to be excited by fear, to have some task, however slight or voluntary, for each day's fulfilment. I shall witness all the variety of appearance, that the elements can assume--I shall read fair augury in the rainbow--menace in the cloud--some lesson or record dear to my heart in everything. (p. 342)

This endless motion for its own sake anticipates the last line of "Ulysses," with its goalless activity: "To strive, to seek, to find, and not to yield." Verbs without direct objects, actions that can have no satisfactory punctual end: the will to create a personality, a civilization, a universe, is subdued and reduced to sheer willing-ness.

This purposelessness is brought about not by exile or conscious, deliberate estrangement from society, but by solipsism. The novel closes with an image of intense isolation, with Lionel Verney's "tiny bark" dwarfed by an alien universe, neither malign nor benignant, only watchful:

> Thus round the shores of deserted earth, while the sun is high, and the moon waxes or wanes, angels, the spirits of the dead, and the ever-open eye of the Supreme will behold the tiny bark, freighted with Verney--the LAST MAN. (p. 342)

His initial social exile has been superseded by an existential isolation. Mary Shelley portrays Verney as the last survivor of a species, surrounded by alien beings and <u>watched</u>--not guided, protected, nurtured--by the Creator of this mystifying universe.

When the survivor of devastation undergoes transformation--encounters death and climbs back up from the cavern depths into the sunlight--there is no society left for him to rejoin. Nevertheless, Verney records his story for posterity. He counsels quiescence, resignation, submission to the incomprehensible ways of fate. Lionel Verney's life is, in essence, the lesson: it exemplifies the futility of exertion, the need for resignation. There is another message in Verney's story, too, besides the purposelessness of present action. Nostalgia for past glory--for the dead heroes and the lost treasures of civilization--is as strong as submissiveness. Verney presumes that his hypothetical readers will "seek to learn how beings so wondrous in their achievements, with imaginations infinite, and powers godlike, had departed from their home to an unknown country" (p. 339). Verney dedicates his history "To the Illustrious DEAD," bidding them, "Shadows, Arise and Read Your Fall!" (p. 339). In The Last Man, there is a Fall which precipitates man's exile from Paradise:

> Alas! to enumerate the adornments of humanity, shews, by what we have lost, how supremely great man was. It is all over now. He is solitary; like our first parents expelled from Paradise, he looks back towards the scene he has quitted. The high walls of the tomb, and the flaming sword of the plague, lie between it and him. Like to our first parents, the whole earth is before him, a wide desert. (p. 234).

Yet this fall is not sexual or social in nature. Not one human being's crime toward another, but the incontrovertible, morally neutral fact of death, brings the end of innocence--and with it, the end of hope, desire, will.

The destruction of civilization through the plague is an emblem for Mary Shelley's fear and outrage at political anarchy. The death of the heroic individual, the consequences of levelling revolutions in the social order, is similarly regretted. For Mary Shelley, however, the ineluctability of death is more terrifying than any political or social destruction. Her subject is as much the death of the human personality as it is the end of heroic individuality and civilized life. Hers is not the conservatism of T. S. Eliot, who held that "only those who have personality . . . know what it means to want to escape from" it. Escape into culture or other comforting fictions of and about the human mind eventually becomes impossible for Mary Shelley. Her imagination <u>cannot get beyond</u> the fact of death.

Yet it is not fear of her own death that makes Mary Shelley retreat to a conservative posture and console herself with society, in real life and in her novels.[29] Rather, death brings a terrible isolation, whose image is Verney's engulfment by the indifferent universe at the end of <u>The Last Man</u>. Shelley's death deprived Mary of her strongest social tie and, consequently, of a reflection of her own existence. There is no one, no event, no object to which Lionel Verney can feel himself bound, for good or ill. Unlike Frankenstein's monster and Mathilda, Lionel Verney cannot even complain to his Creator. Death is not crime, not an injustice; rather it is the quintessential fact of life.

Lionel Verney's response to this discovery is to retreat. He is not a coward withdrawing from a contest--in fact, he has lost his combatants; his ambition and will have no outlet. (In much the same way, Mary Shelley's pursuit of self-definition could not continue in a vacuum, in utter isolation.) Nevertheless, Lionel detaches himself from his own experience. This is clear in his attitude toward his role as narrator, which illuminates Mary Shelley's evolving conception of her own creative function.

The self-reflexive action of writing nullifies the pain of consciousness. As Lionel discovers while eulogizing his dead wife, mere articulation brings relief: "With ardent and overflowing eloquence, I relieved my heart from its burthen, and awoke to the sense of a new pleasure in life, as I poured forth the funeral eulogy" (p. 262). The act of writing the history, similarly, is anaesthetizing: "I had used this history as an opiate; while it described my beloved friends, fresh with life and glowing with hope; active assistants on the scene, I was soothed; there will be a more melancholy pleasure in painting the end of all" (p. 193). Like Lionel Verney, the author of The Last Man professes to find solace in the act of writing:

> Will my readers ask how I could find solace from the narration of misery and woeful change? This is one of the mysteries of our nature, which holds full sway over me, and from whose influence I cannot escape. I confess, that I have not been unmoved by the development of the tale; and that I have been depressed, nay, agonized, at some parts of the recital, which I have faithfully transcribed from my materials. Yet such is human nature, that the excitement of mind was dear to me, and that the imagination, painter of tempest and earthquake, or, worse, the stormy and ruin-fraught passions of man, softened my real sorrows and endless regrets, by clothing these fictitious ones in that ideality, which takes the mortal sting from pain. (p. 4)

Writing brings a distancing from pain rather than an engagement with it--even, paradoxically, when one is writing about the causes of that pain. Consolation comes from idealizing the past rather than contending with it. Lionel's role, as he defines it, is to organize reality into bearable form:

> All events, at the same time that they deeply interested me, arranged themselves in pictures before me. I gave the right place to every personage in the groupe [sic], the just balance to every sentiment. This undercurrent of thought, often soothed me amidst

> distress, and even agony. It gave ideality to that, from which, taken in naked truth, the soul would have revolted: it bestowed pictorial colours on misery and disease, and not unfrequently relieved me from despair in deplorable changes. (p. 126)

Later in his narrative he recurs to the idea that the act of giving form diminishes rather than augments reality:

> Time and experience have placed me on an height from which I can comprehend the past as a whole; and in this way I must describe it, bringing forward the leading incidents, and disposing light and shade so as to form a picture in whose very darkness there will be harmony. (pp. 192-193)

Lionel Verney's idealizing impulse contrasts with Mathilda's compulsion to confide even the most horrifying details of her past (notably, her father's confession of his incestuous love): "Perhaps a history such as mine had better die with me, but a feeling that I cannot define leads me on . . ." (Mathilda, p. 1). Unlike the Coleridgean narrator, who is inwardly compelled to tell the truth, however painful and horrific, Lionel Verney conceives of his narrator's duty as the idealization of the real.

Besides the consolation of the writer, narration has a second purpose in *The Last Man*, one that is equally centrifugal in its direction. The narrator's organizing function has been re-defined from Mary Shelley's earlier novels. The narrator of *Frankenstein* was an active artificer ("seizing on the capabilities of a subject and . . . moulding and fashioning ideas suggested to it") who sought to move his audience by manipulating the form of his materials. Narration in *The Last Man* has as its second goal the reduction of experience to static "pictures." Action is Victorianized aesthetically. Mary Shelley anticipates Matthew Arnold's dictum of *showing* right action rather than the workings of an individual mind. Her pictures of political and personal life also foreshadow George Eliot's *Felix Holt, the Radical*, where

Esther Lyon and Felix Holt are transformed by acquiring mental pictures that stand in place of action and experience. This impulse to show pictures rather than to tell stories prompts Mary Shelley's movement away from first-person, toward third-person, narration.

The solitary exiles who narrate Mary Shelley's earliest novels speak directly to their auditors and readers, more actively soliciting a response than subsequent characters whose stories are related in third-person narration or direct discourse. Paradoxically, despite their alienation, the first-person narrators reach out to their audience--like the Ancient Mariner, who is compelled to make an impact on his auditor. Unlike the correspondents in Frankenstein and Mathilda, who write to particular readers, Lionel Verney writes to an unknowable audience, an unembodied "posterity." And unlike Godwin, who wished to "write a tale, that shall constitute an epoch in the mind of the reader, that no one, after he has read it, shall ever be exactly the same man that he was before,"[31] Lionel Verney has no revolutionary intention. He doesn't aim at effecting psychologically radical change. Instead, for Verney, writing--like voyaging, striving, living--is an activity pursued for its own sake.

Frankenstein and Mathilda both center on individuals defined in separation from a group, society or the audience: the Promethean hero and the first-person narrator who creates his or her self in the process of telling his or her story. In The Last Man, however, the narrator who is "progenitor," who constitutes himself as subject in writing or talking, ceases to satisfy Mary Shelley. Instead, she returns to the third-person mode of Valperga, letting characters tell their stories to affect one another. Falkner's narration of his life story, for example, is circumscribed by his life with the orphan Elizabeth; it becomes a fact that other characters react to. In their responses to his tale, they show that they are humane and sensitive (Elizabeth and Gerard) or myopic and intolerant (Sir Boyvill). Their reactions to his narrative, rather than ours, constitute the significance of his history. We saw and felt Walton's reaction to the narratives in Frankenstein; in Falkner, characters merely talk about their responses. The meaning of the narrative, in short, resides in the social world of the novel and its mimesis of the real world.

Mary Shelley's interest passes from psychic doubling--the projection of emotionally conflicting aspects of her self--to relationships between protagonists. The constitution of the social group, the establishment of a happy family to compensate for a myriad of childhood deprivations, replaces the configuration of the single self as the primary object of Mary Shelley's fiction.

The conquest of the Promethean hero by death, marriage, or symbolic emasculation parallels the retrenchment from first-person narration. Static pictures of experience take the place of narrative complexity. From telling to showing; from self-realization to self-absorption; from imaginative isolation to assimilation: The Last Man enacts these transitions.

The Byronic hero's assimilation into society in Falkner sums up the thematic and structural evolution found in Mary Shelley's novels. The Promethean Falkner, after rebelling against authority in his home, his school, and the state, discovers that rebellion brings only suffering--destruction and subsequent guilt. (Falkner learns this painfully, having destroyed his beloved Alithea out of jealous passion and then being consumed by his own remorse.) Becoming guardian of the orphaned Elizabeth, he eventually receives from her the nurturing love he missed when a child. Though women are the victims of male aggression and ambition--Mathilda, Euthanasia, Beatrice, Katherine, Ethel, Alithea, and Elizabeth--it is women who must forgive and compensate for the destruction wrought by men. Mary Shelley ultimately advocates not anger and resentment but love as the antidote to male audacity and its fearful consequences. Unlike Mary Wollstonecraft, who criticized the tyranny of feminine weakness, Mary Shelley implicitly approves it as a latent power.

The feminization of (male) aggressiveness becomes a primary theme in Victorian social novels, whether aggression is private or public, psychological or political in nature. As is true for George Eliot, however, Mary Shelley's advocacy of "feminine" passiveness comes not from weakness but from her own feeling of audacious willfulness. Like Katherine in Perkin Warbeck, Mary Shelley witnessed the terrible cost of (masculine) overreaching in her own life and came to dread its consequences. Katherine survives her husband Richard, the rebel who sought to claim his rightful inheritance, and she gets the last word in the novel: "Permit this to be, unblamed--permit a heart whose sufferings have been, and are, so many and so bitter, to reap what joy it can from the strong necessity it feels to be sympathized with--to love."[32] Just as Katherine reconciles herself to living with her late husband's political enemies, Mary Shelley makes her peace with society. She finds consolation, if not a raison d'etre, in company. Her political sympathies are retrenched. At the end of her life, she is glad when her sole surviving son, Percy, renounces his parliamentary campaign in order to marry.[33] Yet for all this apparent comfortableness, her letters and journal entries become replete with more references to her "exile" than ever before.[34] As she moves further from the sources of her emotional life--anger at her father, resentment against Shelley, grief at his death--she seems to feel her own selfhood diminish. Accompanying this, as we see in The Last Man, is a decrease in the vitality of the roles of artist and narrator.

Recurring to the dual impulses of Mary Shelley's imagination, we might say that the active shaping of chaotic "dreams" is transmuted, de-emphasized, downplayed. The "imperious" child and adolescent becomes a submissive, dependent woman. Writing Maria Gisborne in 1835, Mary Shelley contrasted her character with her mother's:

> I know that however clever I may be there is in me a vacillation a weakness, a want of "eagle winged" resolution that appertains to my intellect as well as my moral character--and renders me what I am--one of broken purposes--failing thoughts and a heart all wounds-- My Mother had more energy of character--Still she had not sufficient fire of imagination--In short my belief is--whether there be sex in souls or not--that the sex of our material mechanism makes us quite different creatures--better though weaker but wanting in the higher grades of intellect.[35]

Mary Shelley left behind her girlhood rebelliousness and ambition, her audacity in emulating the "stupendous mechanism of the Creator of the world" ("Author's Introduction," Frankenstein). After her transformation by loneliness and grief, she embraces the passive, will-less identity of a "better though weaker" creative, as though reproaching her mother for excessive willfulness and lauding her own fertile imaginativeness.

In a sense, Mary Shelley's quarrel with her family becomes sublimated and transmuted into a tacit rebellion. Late in life, Mary Shelley would seem to apologize for not fulfilling the promise of her birth, alliances, and talents: "To hang back, as I do, brings a penalty. I was nursed and fed with a love of glory. To be something great and good was the precept given me by my Father: Shelley reiterated it."[36] This is corroborated by Claire's comment, quoted by Elizabeth Nitchie: "'In our family,' said Claire, 'if you cannot write an epic poem or novel, that by its originality knocks all other novels on the head, you are a despicable creature, not worth acknowledging.'"[37] Yet even as she reproaches herself and confesses to feeling guilty, Mary manages to accuse:

> Alone and poor, I could only be something by joining a party; and there was much in me--the woman's love of looking up, and being guided, and being willing to do anything if any one supported and brought me forward--which would have made me a good partisan. But Shelley died, and I was alone. My Father, from age and domestic circumstances, could not "me faire valoir."[38]

There is self-pity in this: "My total friendlessness, my horror of pushing, and inability to put myself forward unless led, cherished, and supported,--all this has sunk me in a state of loneliness no other human being ever before, I believe, endured--except Robinson Crusoe. How many tears and spasms of anguish this solitude has cost me, lies buried in my memory."[39] But there is also reproach of others.

The entire journal entry, in fact, is prompted by the impulse of self-justification. Mary Shelley explains--to herself as well as to posterity--her apostasy from her liberal heritage: "I have been so often abused by pretended friends for my lukewarmness in 'the good cause,' that, though I disdain to answer them, I shall put down here a few thoughts on this subject. I am much of a self-examiner. . . . I think my qualities (such as they are) not appreciated from unworthy causes."[40] With considerable dignity, she goes on to dissociate herself from her more radical relatives:

> Some have a passion for reforming the world; others do not cling to particular opinions. That my parents and Shelley were of the former class makes me respect it. . . . For myself, I earnestly desire the good and enlightenment of my fellow-creatures, and see all, in the present course, tending to the same, and rejoice; but I am not for violent extremes, which only bring on an injurious reaction.[41]

She next enumerates the "causes" for her not openly ("in writing") supporting liberalism:

> That I have not argumentative powers: I see things pretty clearly, but cannot demonstrate them. Besides, I feel the counter-arguments too strongly. I do not feel that I could say aught to support the cause efficiently; besides that, on some topics (especially with regard to my own sex), I am far from making up my mind. I believe we are sent here to educate ourselves, and that self-denial, and disappointment, and self-control, are a part of our education; that it is not by taking away all restraining law that our improvement is to be achieved; and, tho' many things need great amendment, I can by no means go so far as my friends would have me. When I feel that I can say what will benefit my fellow-creatures, I will speak: not before.[42]

The passage is rife with negatives and disclaimers of her own ability, yet even as she admits weakness, Mary Shelley defends her position. She replies to ". . . heavy accusations cast on me for not putting myself forward" by saying, "I <u>cannot</u> do that; it is against my nature. As well cast me from a precipice and rail at me for not flying."[43] She transforms negative qualities--shyness, passivity, reticence, indecision--into positive attributes: ". . . as I grow older I grow more fearless for myself--I become firmer in my opinions."[44]

In the end, Mary Shelley's defection from the liberalism of the Godwin circle represents her own version of "independence of mind." By allying herself with the orthodox social community rather than with the enclave of intellectual exiles (as Virginia Woolf would do in Bloomsbury), Mary Shelley chooses rather than accepts a superior authority. Deference is given, not owed; her role is selected, not inherited. The act of renouncing her intellectual and political inheritance brings with it a kind of self-acceptance. Yet there is a sad falling off, one felt and tacitly acknowledged by Mary Shelley herself, in this. Mary Shelley's political "independence" or apostasy really follows from her failure to achieve emotional independence. Imposed isolation removes the desire for self-sufficiency. The contentious, emotionally rebellious exile comes to identify herself as a follower, a party member, a dependent. More submissive than George Eliot, perhaps because her battle was with hostile circumstances rather than with her own conscience, Mary Shelley lacks Eliot's ambition to expand her private values into political programs. Instead, she retreats. Her protest against and interrogation of authority in the early novels lose their force when Mary Shelley loses her audience. In the end, apology conceals reproach; assimilation conceals the desire to "be something." These tactics make it possible for Mary Shelley to survive, but only at the expense of the self she once sought to fashion.

NOTES

[1] Rachel Brownstein, "Portrait of the Artist as a Young Woman: Mary Shelley," Book Forum, 2 (1976), 600.

[2] Patricia Meyer Spacks, Imagining a Self: Autobiography and Novel in Eighteenth-Century England (Cambridge: Harvard University Press, 1978), p. 78.

[3] Mary Shelley, "Author's Introduction," Frankenstein: Or, The Modern Prometheus (New York: The New American Library, 1965), p. viii. Subsequent references will be cited parenthetically in the text.

[4] U. C. Knoepflmacher, "Thoughts on the Aggression of Daughters," The Endurance of "Frankenstein": Essays on Mary Shelley's Novel, eds. George Levine and U. C. Knoepflmacher (Berkeley: University of California Press, 1979), p. 119.

[5] William Godwin, An Enquiry Concerning Political Justice and Its Influence on General Virtue and Happiness, ed. and abridged by Raymond A. Preston (New York: Alfred A. Knopf, 1926), II, 227.

[6] Ibid., p. 165.

[7] Mary Wollstonecraft, "Introduction" to "A Vindication of the Rights of Women," A Wollstonecraft Anthology, ed. Janet M. Todd (Bloomington: Indiana University Press, 1977), p. 87.

[8] Muriel Spark, in Child of Light: A Reassessment of Mary Wollstonecraft Shelley (Hadleigh, Essex: Tower Bridge Publications, 1951), posits a "state of strife between Mary's emotional and her intellectual lives; . . . her basically classical temperament . . . was not nurtured on its appropriate classical serenity but was fostered upon a setting of romantic turmoil" (p. 193). In Mary Shelley (New York: Twayne Publishers, Inc., 1972), William Walling speaks of "her fundamental conflict between intellectual liberalism and constitutional conservatism" (p. 99). In contrast to these biographer-critics, I maintain that Mary Shelley became increasingly conservative emotionally even as her politics diverged from the liberalism of her family circle.

[9] Mary Shelley, The Last Man, ed. Hugh J. Luke, Jr. (Lincoln: University of Nebraska Press, 1965), p. 290: "Mother of the World! Servant of the Omnipotent! eternal, changeless Necessity!" Subsequent references will be cited parenthetically.

[10] Mary Shelley, Mathilda, ed. Elizabeth Nitchie (Chapel Hill: The University of North Carolina Press, 1959), p. 19. Hereafter cited parenthetically in the text.

[11] Mary Shelley, The Fields of Fancy, in Mathilda, pp. 93, 98.

[12] The Letters of Mary W. Shelley, ed. Frederick L. Jones (Norman: University of Oklahoma Press, 1954), II, 88: on 30 October 1834 Mary Shelley wrote Maria Gisborne of her "excessive and romantic attachment to [her] Father." Elizabeth Nitchie quotes a letter to Jane Williams written in 1822: "Until I met Shelley I [could?] justly say that he was my God--& I remember many childish instances of the [ex]cess of attachment I bore for him." Mary Shelley: Author of "Frankenstein" (New Brunswick: Rutgers University Press, 1953), p. 89.

[13] Letters, I, 18 October 1817, 45.

[14] Elizabeth Nitchie, "Introduction," Mathilda, p. xi.

[15] Ibid., p. ix.

[16] Mary Shelley, Lodore (London: Richard Bentley, 1835), III, 21 and I, 40.

[17] William Godwin quoted in Eileen Bigland, Mary Shelley (London: Cassell, 1959), p. 29.

[18] Ibid., p. 30.

[19] Mary Shelley's Journal, 5 Feb. 1815, p. 37.

[20] Nitchie, Mary Shelley, p. 89.

[21] Mary Shelley, Falkner (London: Saunders and Otley, 1837), I, 169-170.

[22] Godwin, Political Justice, II, 264-265.

[23] Hugh J. Luke, Jr., "Introduction," The Last Man, p. xviii.

[24] Letters, II, 28 March 1848, 313-314.

[25] In "The Last Man: Anatomy of Failed Revolutions," Nineteenth-Century Fiction (1978), Lee Sterrenburg analyzes Mary Shelley's use of nature metaphors to render a "pessimistic and apocalyptic" view of a world where political reform and revolution are futile (p. 328). Sterrenburg says that The Last Man is "an antipolitical novel" (p. 328).

[26] Letters, I, 29 Dec. 1820, 122.

[27] Mary Shelley, Valperga, Or, the Life and Adventures of Castruccio, Prince of Lucca (London: G. & W. E. Whittaker, 1823), III, Ch. 5, p. 102.

[28] Mary Shelley's Journal, p. 170.

[29] In her journal on 21 Oct. 1838 Mary writes: "I like society; I believe all persons who have any talent (who are in good health) do. The soil that gives forth nothing, may lie ever fallow; but that which produces . . . needs cultivation, change of harvest, refreshing dews, and ripening sun. Books do much; but the living intercourse is the vital heat. Debarred from that, how have I pined and died!" (p. 205). In a letter to Maria Gisborne on 17 July 1832 Mary complained: ". . . I live in a silence and loneliness--not possible any where except in England where people are so islanded individually in habits-- I often languish for sympathy--and pine for social festivity" (Letters, II, 82). A negative view of her desire for society is taken by the editor of her Letters and Journal, Frederick L. Jones, in his "Appendix II" to Volume II of the Letters: "Mary had an insatiable desire to associate herself with people of talent and genius" (pp. 350-351); "Throughout Mary's whole life, her constant cry was for friendship. There is even something morbid in her desire for affection--a certain lack of self-confidence, of self-sufficiency" (p. 351).

[31] Godwin, 1832 Note to Fleetwood reprinted in Caleb Williams, (New York: Holt, Rinehart & Winston, 1967), p. xxvii.

[32] Mary Shelley, The Fortunes of Perkin Warbeck, a Romance by the Author of "Frankenstein" (London: Henry Colburn & Richard Bentley, 1830), III, p. 354.

[33] Letters, II, 30 June 1848, 318.

[34] See, for example, Letters, II, written 27 July 1828 (18); 17 July 1834 (82); 30 Oct. 1834 (87); 30 Aug. 1843 (193).

[35] Letters, II, 11 June 1835, 98.

[36] Mary Shelley's Journal, 21 Oct. 1838, p. 205.

[37] Elizabeth Nitchie, Mary Shelley, p. 141.

[38] Mary Shelley's Journal, 21 Oct. 1838, p. 205.

[39] Ibid.

[40] Ibid., p. 204.

[41] Ibid.

[42] Ibid.

[43] Ibid., p. 206

[44] Ibid.

Chapter 3

GEORGE ELIOT'S POLITICAL FICTION:
THE LEGACY OF THE FATHER

The assimilation of the individual into society is as important a drama in George Eliot's fiction as in Mary Shelley's. The collision between the individual and the general will must result in the individual's capitulation and this, rather than his heroic resistance, is what interests Eliot in a (tragic) subject:

> A tragedy has not to expound why the individual must give way to the general; it has to show that it is compelled to give way,--the tragedy consisting in the struggle involved, and often in the entirely calamitous issue in spite of a grand submission.[1]

Whether the individual's capitulation is enacted in private or in public, individual desire must give way before social duty: "The will of God is the same thing as the will of other men, compelling us to work and avoid what they have seen to be harmful to social existence."[2] Consequently, Maggie Tulliver is initiated into self-renunciation through painful experience; Dorothea Brooke must modify her ardent plans for social reform; and Lydgate's ambitious aims for medical reform are chastened.

Among the protagonists who have the greatest difficulty learning this lesson are those who are disenfranchised--women and workers--and those who are ambitious, particularly of social change. But whether the individual is a woman like Maggie Tulliver, submitting to her society's norms for feminine behavior, or a cruelly ambitious politician like Tito in Romola, she or he must submit to the collective will. Like Mary Shelley, George Eliot is critical of yet drawn to the rebel who seeks to improve life for himself and his fellow man. But such rebels are inevitably defeated in the collision with society's laws.

Eliot advocates self-perfection over social change, even though she depicts the mutual influence of individual energy and collective institutions. Raymond Williams points out in Culture and Society that Victorian intellectuals tended to stress the perfecting of one's self at the expense of social action.[3] Being or becoming was exalted over doing by Arnold, Newman, Pater and others as well as by George Eliot. Yet Eliot's resistance to change--especially change brought about by individual willfulness--takes particular shape from her experience as a woman.

Like Mary Shelley, George Eliot distrusts her own unfeminine egotism and will to power and suppresses their every manifestation in her life and fiction. Though political conservatism is not a necessary consequence of empiricism, Eliot's preference for inductive thought is related to her suppression of will. Not the intention of an individual agent but the cause of an event: to describe history in such terms is to discount the desire and will of the human beings who live it. Denial of the will results in a kind of conservatism that determines the plots of Eliot's novels, informs the voices of the narrator and the protagonists, and imbues the very syntax of her prose.

The primary plot of Eliot's fiction--the renunciation of the individual will--is recapitulated in dialogue, where Eliot distinctly prefers truth-telling to articulation of desire. The radicals who would willfully alter the structure of society speak a different language, use a different class of verbs, from the conservative reformers. The narrator whose voice tells us their history reveals her own conservative partisanship through her speech acts. Yet this partisanship is ambivalent; Eliot's sympathies are mixed. For while she substitutes self-perfection for political change, she at the same time reveals a latent skepticism about the passivity she apparently endorses. The painfully, vividly felt experience of Mrs. Transome in Felix Holt, the Radical is only one sign of Eliot's unconscious affinity with the Devil's party. The dissonance between brilliantly realized villains and insipid heroes in the novel stems from an ambiguity in Eliot's attitude toward the individual will. Ambition, the "most destroying, as it is the fruitful parent of" all her sins, is also the creative drive behind Eliot's fiction.[4] Her desire to win her readers' assent to her vision of truth underlies Eliot's scrupulosity as a truth-teller.

Eliot's suppressed sympathy with the power of the individual will stems from her own experience of conflict with and conformity to the collective (in this case, the patriarchal) will. In this chapter I will trace the links between the plot of Eliot's life and those of her novels, between the conservative elements of her politics and their articulation in her style. Eliot's partisanship, implicit in everything she wrote, is especially clear in her novels on political subjects, notably Felix Holt. There, as we shall see, Eliot quite explicitly connects egotism to political ambition.

In George Eliot's political thought, the individual's relation to the state is based upon the Burkean analogy: loyalty to one's father is the basis for political loyalties.[5] Prior to her creative period (the 1850s to the 1870s), Eliot rebelled against her father, against traditional religion, and against social norms for feminine behavior. She first became ardently Evangelical, then swung to the other extreme and left the Church altogether. At this time, Eliot felt strongly and rebelliously that the parent's duty (even God's) toward his offspring was much neglected. Discussing her views on patriarchal authority with a pupil, Eliot said that "There may be . . . conduct on the part of a parent which should exonerate his child from further obligation to him; but there cannot be action conceivable which should absolve the parent from obligation to serve his child . . . ."[6] In a sense, Eliot spent the rest of her life privately and publically suppressing such unfilial attitudes.

Eliot disapproved of any radicalism that sought to change England as she and her father knew it. The judicious tone in which she often discussed political remedies to social ills does not accurately reflect the depth of her fear of the power of the ungoverned masses. This reaction is not simply the typical nineteenth-century bourgeois fear of mob violence. It was dread of her own potential for rebellion that made Eliot a political conservative.

Like Comte, who thought of workers and women as the emotional, irrational class of society, George Eliot believed that the passional, willful aspect of human nature needed restraint by some authority principle.[7] Throughout Eliot's letters and early essays is an unselfconscious scorn for the lower classes. Her 1848 judgment on the English workers--"Here there is so much larger a proportion of selfish radicalism and unsatisfied brute sensuality . . . than of perception or desire of justice, that a revolutionary movement would be simply destructive, not constructive[8]--was repeated in 1856 when she indicted the German proletariat as "deserters of historical society" arrayed in "a terrible army."[9] When radical theorizers try to instruct the peasant, only further degradation results: "The coarse nature of the peasant has here been corrupted into bestiality by the disturbance of his instincts, while he is as yet incapable of principles . . . ."[10]

Eliot's low opinion of peasant and worker is not wholly founded on a Comtean natural history but is at bottom emotional. A brief reference in a letter of 1863 suggests that Eliot was upset by the disruption of sexual norms she found in working-class life. She castigates the lower class for sexual non-conformity: working women were especially prone to "those epicene queernesses that belong to the class."[11] Eliot's comments on the working class associate selfishness, sensuality and insurrection with the violation of sexual stereotypes. Especially abhorrent to her is women's abrogation of supposedly male appetites and aggressiveness, impulses that she sought to contain or deny in herself.

Eliot's private and public pronouncements about femininity are determinedly dutiful, as when she asserts that women are distinguished by an "exquisite type of gentleness, tenderness, possible maternity . . . ."[12] This sensibility did not, however, include instinctual submissiveness. Women submitted not because they were naturally more passive than men but because they were politically "Other" and had to submit. Consolation for this was to be found in knowledge, not in the relief of action. Women, said Eliot, "have never contemplated an independent delight in ideas as an experience which they could confess without being laughed at. Yet surely women need this sort of defence against passionate affliction even more than men."[13]

While Eliot endorsed intellectual expansion for both sexes, she was guarded in her support of women's petitions for educational and other rights. The primary career Eliot approved for women without reservation was that of the artist: "We went to see Rosa Bonheur's picture the other day. What power! That is the way women should assert their rights."[14] But even the impulse to write could seem too aggressive. Late in her career Eliot expressed doubt of the propriety of writing more fiction, despite the continued fertility of her imagination:

> The difficulty is to decide how far resolution should set in the direction of activity, rather than in the acceptance of a more negative state. Many conceptions of work to be carried out present themselves, but confidence in my own fitness to complete them worthily is all the more wanting, because it is reasonable to argue that I must have already done my best. In fact, my mind is embarrassed by the number and wide variety of subjects that attract me, and the enlarging vista that each brings with it.[15]

"Embarrassed" (in two senses) by her own ambition, Eliot waged a lifelong battle to curb her will. Yet unlike Virginia Woolf who distrusts and fears what she thinks of as the masculine will, George Eliot is drawn to it. Her conservatism stems in part from her recognition that she shares the potential rebellious assertiveness of Comte's third estate.

As a child and a young woman, Eliot wanted to be a law unto herself. At the age of twenty she remembered, "When I was quite a little child, I could not be satisfied with the things around me: I was constantly living in a world of my own creation, and was quite contented to have no companions, that I might be left to my own musings, and imagine scenes in which I was chief actress."[16] As she grew older, her desire for other beings to people this world grew also. In 1841 she lamented, ". . . I mean that I have no one who enters into my pleasures or my griefs, no one with whom I can pour out my soul, no one with the same yearnings, the same temptations, the same delights as myself."[17] Even at the end of her life, John Cross said, she was emotionally "ambitious":

> Very jealous in her affections, and easily moved to smiles or tears, she was of a nature capable of the keenest enjoyment and the keenest suffering, knowing "all the wealth and all the woe" of a pre-eminently exclusive disposition. She was affectionate, proud, and sensitive in the highest degree.[18]

The outlet for this egotism, which Eliot found as if by instinct, was writing. In 1848 her exuberance seemed uncontained: "It is necessary for me, not simply to be but to utter . . . ."[19] Some of her enormous longing for other human beings was expended in the self-reflexive love of her own language: "I am violently in love with the Italian fashion of repeating an adjective or adverb, and even noun, to give force to expression . . ." and ". . . I love words . . . ."[20] When Eliot began writing fiction in the 1850s, however, the self she created did not resemble the naive but sublime egotist of the previous decade. In its place was a careful, deliberate persona which set limits to her imaginative exuberance. The persona was not a completely successful means of unifying Eliot's public self, as it turned out.[21]

In her fiction. Eliot uttered and shaped a self in conformity with the expectations of her contemporary audience. Eliot strove for a sexlessness or rather androgyny in her prose style by adhering to the impersonality of scientific writing: "Science has no sex: the mere knowing and reasoning faculties, if they act correctly, must go through the same process, and arrive at the same result."[22] While Eliot goes on to deny that literature can be equally sex-free, her fictional empiricism is a step toward the androgyny of the scientific method. The voice she used, often identified with the "masculine" aspect of her persona, is the very means by which Eliot conformed to the passive stereotype of Victorian womanliness and denied full expression to her independent identity. There is a clear correspondence between Eliot's empiricism, as expressed in the form of her fiction, and her assimilation of patriarchal strictures about feminine behavior.

The egotism Eliot feared most was the spiritual pride that might lead her to set herself up in the Father's place as the end of feeling and action, answerable only to herself. Her anxiety was caused by a feeling not of impotence but of too much power. She seemed to fear what her creativity would be capable of without parental or divine or social sanctions. Immediately before her father's death, she was terrified by possibilities of what she might become or, more likely, might do: "What shall I be without my Father? It will seem as if a part of my moral nature were gone. I had a horrid vision of myself last night becoming earthly sensual and devilish for want of that purifying restraining influence."[23] Eliot's biographer Gordon Haight interprets this as an admission of lack of will, of inadequate self-control. He uses as a refrain Charles Bray's judgment, "She was not fitted to stand alone."[24] But perhaps it was not lack of will, rather an excess, that Eliot distrusted in herself. Her desires, both sensual and intellectual, seemed culpable because they were not proper in a woman.

Shortly after her father's death, Eliot wrote friends from Geneva that England

> looks to me like a land of gloom, of <u>ennui</u>, of platitude; but in the midst of all this it is the land of duty and affection, and the only ardent hope I have for my future life is to have given to me some woman's duty--some possibility of devoting myself where I may see a daily result of pure calm blessedness in the life of another.[25]

In 1859 she apologized to her hostess for her mood of youthful rebelliousness in her earlier visit abroad: "When I was at Geneva, I had not yet lost the attitude of antagonism which belongs to the renunciation of <u>any</u> belief; also, I was very unhappy, and in a state of discord and rebellion towards my own lot. Ten years of experience have wrought great changes in that inward self."[26] The key to her self-abnegation, her need to find "some woman's duty" before which to subjugate herself, lies in Eliot's fear of her potency operating without restraint from any paternalistic authority.

Once Eliot felt she had lost parental love and approval by rebelling, she unconsciously sought to regain that love by ever-increasing obedience to a Not-Self. There is a subtle masochism in the belief that "It is the very perception that the thing we renounce is precious, is something never to be compensated to us, which constitutes the beauty and heroism of renunciation."[27] The initial pleasure attendant upon the liberation from authority has been transmuted into pleasurable pain in the renunciation of the future.

When Eliot professed belief in "our total inability to find in our own natures a key to the Divine mystery" and rejected "a Theism which professes to explain the proceedings of God," she was perhaps turning her back on the mystery.[28] A scientific explanation of an uncaused mystery would be by definition impossible; but Eliot seemed reluctant to ask why she worshipped. Possibly behind the veil the mystery would have mirrored her own face. Whether the object of her worship was the particular memory of an individual or some abstraction like humanity or duty, her faith was not, as Martin Svaglic suggests, one of all works and no "religious emotions."[29] Whether or not Eliot actually spoke them, the words paraphrased by F. W. H. Myers capture the essence of her religious feeling. She spoke, he said, "the words God, Immortality, Duty--pronounced, with terrible earnestness, how inconceivable was the first, how unbelievable the second, and yet how peremptory and absolute the third."[30]

In Eliot's life, once the Father was rejected, the daughter refused to allow her own will to create a new world in accord with her ego. Instead of usurping her Father's place, she tried to deny its vacancy by focusing microscopically on the immediate foreground. The result is the carefully sustained, empirical rationalism of all her work.

What George Eliot represses is her instinctive desire to shape the future, the excessive subjectivity decried by Feuerbach. As Bernard J. Paris says, "In the doctrine of creation out of nothing man affirms 'the non-essentiality, the nothingness of the world' and the omnipotence, the independence, the unlimitedness of the will."[31] For Eliot and other empiricists, subjectivity is associated with deductive reasoning that presumes to know a priori truths without submitting first to experience. In the essay "The Future of German Philosophy," Eliot mocked metaphysics as "an attempt to poise the universe on one's head," suggesting not only the impracticality but the egocentricity of this approach.[32]

As one critic says, for Eliot and other empiricists, "the objective method--which bends the mind to the outward shows of things instead of ordering external existence according to the preconceptions or wishes of the mind--is the only path to truth."[33] Most of George Eliot's personal and public life was spent "bending" her mind into conformity and suppressing her strong drive to fashion her own final cause. Yet Jerome Thale points out, "The dilemma, to describe it in Schopenhauer's terms, is that the denial of the will involves an act of the will itself so that there is no escape from the prison of the active will."[34] Eliot's rationalism and objectivity are, in other words, grounded in an initial act of will, a repudiation of her own sublime egotism. Upon this initial choice she built up a superstructure of analytic thought, of explanation which seems simply to describe human behavior while actually bringing it about. The resulting dissonance between what Eliot says and what she does is the source of great tension in her work, particularly in her writing on politics.

Eliot's conservatism depends upon her distrust of metaphysics, which in turn depends upon her self-distrust. These interdependent choices are mirrored in Eliot's prose style, where the fundamental structure of her sentences is charged with resistance to change, even at times to action of any kind. The political rhetoric of Felix Holt can best be explained by reference to linguistic categories related to the philosophical split between metaphysics and empiricism.

Eliot is in the tradition of Mill and Comte whose atelic scientific method tries to explain the causes of things. Opposed to this is the idealist, teleological methodology, concerned not with the causes of actions but with their underlying intentions.[35] George Henrik Von Wright calls this practical reasoning and describes the Aristotelian syllogism on which it rests. A "major premise . . . mentions some wanted thing or end of action; the minor premise relates some action to this thing _roughly_ as a means to the end; the conclusion, finally, consists in use of this means to secure that end."[36] It is the independence of will implicit in the syllogism--A wants P and must decide whether or not to do Z in order to attain P--that George Eliot rejects for herself and her fictional characters. Instead of desire and will, she endorses belief and knowledge; instead of action, she favors passive comprehension; instead of practical reasoning, Eliot prefers empirical observation.

There is a correspondence between Eliot's empiricism and one set of characteristics of her syntax. Her scientific predilection leads her to use verbs related to knowing: explain, clarify, see, believe. In rejecting metaphysics she discards a vocabulary related to will and desire: hope, want, expect, and the imperative forms of must and will. The former set of words relate to knowledge, the latter to action.[37] In leaving behind Eliot's own metaphysics or structure of belief for her physics or fictional practice, we find a clear relation between her political vision and the primary modality of her language.

Eliot's preference for the language of knowing over that of doing, especially in association with political philosophy, appears as early as 1832 in the fragment "Edward Neville," published as an appendix to Gordon Haight's biography. Young Edward Neville is a supporter of Cromwell and, in his mind, "'an outcast from [the] society . . . I used to shine in an alien from my family a deserter, and a regicide . .

. .'" His uncle is both politically radical and morally licentious: "His temper was ungovernable and his hatred of royalty was only second to his detestation of religion . . . ." The belligerent dialogue between the two radicals is loaded with commands: "My . . . horse and my _will_ have brought me here said the young man . . . ." to which his uncle replies, " I _must_ I _will_ know what has brought you here . . . ."[38] When Eliot began to write fiction seriously in 1856, she was more sophisticated and temperate in expressing her religious and political prejudices--she didn't italicize them for emphasis--but she was fundamentally in agreement with her thirteen-year-old self.

In "Janet's Repentance," one of the Scenes of Clerical Life, Reverend Tryan is a good man but his motives are not unmixed. Like Savonarola in Romola, his preaching is sullied by latent egotism. These reforming saviors of mankind

> have earned faith and strength so far as they have done genuine work; but the rest is dry barren theory, blank prejudice, vague hearsay. Their insight is blended with mere opinion; their sympathy is perhaps confined in narrow conduits of doctrine, instead of flowing forth with the freedom of a stream that bless every weed in its course; obstinacy or self-assertion will often interfuse itself with their grandest impulses; and their very deeds of self-sacrifice are sometimes only the rebound of a passionate egoism.[39]

To the mind that deals exclusively with abstractions--"conservative-reforming intellect"--Eliot opposes the sympathetic feeling of the Tory imagination. The selfish intellect produces "endless diagrams, plans, elevations, and sections, but alas! no pictures. Mine, I fear, is not a well-regulated mind: it has an occasional tenderness for old abuses . . . ."[40]

In these early works Eliot's emotional tenderness explicitly underlies her political conservatism. In Adam Bede, Eliot reveres things as they are. She is like Adam Bede who is "not . . . a philosopher or a proletaire with democratic ideas, but simply a stout-limbed clever carpenter with a large fund of reverence in his nature, which inclined him to admit all established claims unless he saw very clear grounds for questioning them."[41] Adam's reverence, like George Eliot's, leads him to accept the status quo unquestioningly, as though the social order were a natural force.

A more sympathetic portrayal of the rebellious individual's clash with collective duty is found in The Mill on the Floss (1860). Eliot's most autobiographical novel, it shows most dramatically her ambivalence toward the suppression of the individual will. Maggie Tulliver is educated out of her youthful, self-centered martyrdom--her Thomas à Kempis phase (IV, iii). She acquires a more mature understanding of the need to live for others, to recognize the pressure of the collective will on her life. When she briefly succumbs to desire and floats downstream with Stephen Guest, her act is unwilled. She submits to *his* will: "Maggie was hardly conscious of having said or done anything decisive. All yielding is attended with a less vivid consciousness than our resistance; it is the partial sleep of thought; it is the submergence of our personality by another" (IV, xiii). But her inclination has misled her--Stephen's is not the will to which she should submit. The collective authority that binds her by memory, affection, and duty requires a different submission: "'Faithfulness and constancy mean something else besides doing whatever is opposed to the reliance others have in us . . .'" (VI, xiv).

It is her conscience (her superego) that impels her: "'We can't choose happiness either for ourselves or for another: we can't tell where that will lie. We can only choose whether we will indulge ourselves in the present moment, or whether we will renounce that, for the sake of obeying the divine voice within us--for the sake of being true to all the motives that sanctify our lives'" (VI, xiv). Maggie recognizes the emotional dependency on her of Lucy Deane and Philip Wakem and exalts their need over her own desires. Yet in another sense, she obeys the harsher rule represented by her brother Tom--a bond that is the strongest and oldest in her life.

Eliot criticizes Tom Tulliver for the prejudices that result from his "strength of will, conscious rectitude of purpose, narrowness of imagination and intellect, great power of self-control, and a disposition to exert control over others" (VI, xii). To his severe decisiveness, she clearly prefers "that complex, fragmentary, doubt-provoking knowledge which we call truth" (VI, xii). Yet this doubt (like that Maggie feels) is less intellectual than emotional: self-doubt and reliance on the will of another. Maggie's re-union with her brother at the novel's end suggests that she is merely conquered by Tom Tulliver rather than by Stephen Guest.

Even in renouncing Stephen, Maggie declares herself in the least assertive language possible:

> "No--not with my whole heart and soul, Stephen," she said, with timid resolution. "I have never consented to it with my whole mind. There are memories, and affections, and longings after perfect goodness, that have such a strong hold on me; they would never quit me for long; they would come back and be pain to me--repentance. I couldn't live in peace if I put the shadow of a wilful sin between myself and God. I have caused sorrow already . . . but I have never deliberately consented to it: I have never said, 'They shall suffer, that I may have joy.' It has never been my will to marry you: if you were to win consent from the momentary triumph of my feeling for you, you would not have my whole soul." (VI, xiv)

"I have never consented . . . . I have never said . . . . It has never been my will": Maggie's self-suppression infuses her speech. In subordinating her desires to the happiness of others, Maggie recognizes her emotional commitment to an authority outside herself. The possibility that this chosen authority is inadequate is merely broached by George Eliot; the novel's hasty conclusion allows her (and Maggie) no time to explore the idea. The very haste speaks of the urgency of the need to obey--in order to please.

The Mill on the Floss is particularly close to Eliot's own emotional history in its representation of Maggie's conflict between the desire to be happy and the need to please, especially to please her father and her even more intransigent brother. As a child, Maggie is often overcome by her anger and willfulness at the cost of peace between herself and Tom. As a woman, she is incapacitated by his disapproval and cannot please herself unless she pleases him. This emotional bind symbolizes Eliot's own estrangement from her brother Isaac Evans, who never relented and forgave her illicit relationship with George Henry Lewes. In the absence of the beloved masculine figures of her youth, Eliot became their spokeswoman--internalizing their voices and judging herself (and her protagonists) as they might. Eliot's difficulty was not so much to reconcile *her* desire with *their* idea of duty as to justify what she thought right without indulging herself. At times, she perhaps exaggerated the claims of outside authority in her scrupulous concern not merely to please herself. In her novels, it is always the rebels against the social status quo who have to yield, not the established order.

In Eliot's later works, the authority principle seems to supplant the historical father as a motive for obedience. Leaving behind the biologically necessary authority of parenthood for the authority of collective custom and law, Eliot's fiction becomes increasingly inflexible in preaching social conformity. In Romola, the heroine is shown in a series of ceremonial renunciations of self in the service of her father, her husband, her priest, and finally her fellow man. Eliot also moves further into the public sphere with a criticism of practical politics. Tito plays at politics, trusting to skill and luck rather than to inherited rights and duties for his success. Even Savonarola is tainted by desire for power: ". . . having once held that audience in his mastery, it was necessary to his nature--it was necessary for their welfare--that he should keep the mastery" (Ch. 25). His noble and passionate nature becomes subjected to the will of his mob of followers. The desire to lead seems to result only in degradation of one's noblest attributes: "No man ever struggled to retain power over a mixed multitude without suffering vitiation; his standard must be their lower needs and not his own best insight" (Ch. 25). As Nicholas Rance says in The Historical Novel and Popular Politics, "Savonarola, too, succumbs to the utilitarian pragmatism especially characteristic of politicians . . . ."[42] It is his own egotistic desire for mastery which led him to mix with the mob in the first place. Politics do not an egotist make; it is the other way around.

Again, in The Spanish Gypsy, Fedalma must renounce her love Don Silva and, with him, her own will. In marrying she had hoped to have her own way: "'Oh, I shall have much power as well as joy!/ Duchess Fedalma may do what she will'" (Bk. I). Instead she is forced to "wed" her gypsy heritage, "mastered" by her father's will in a melodramatic version of George Eliot's own case (Bk. I). Increasingly it seems Eliot's interest is no longer private memory but the more abstract, collective "Tradition" which must determine the course of an individual's life.

In novels where Eliot deals with Victorian political issues, notably Felix Holt, the Radical (1866), her conservatism supports the public good which turns out to be almost identical with the political status quo. Her distrust of revolutionary ideas and action persists, in less obvious forms than in "Edward Neville." Her heroes--Felix Holt and Daniel Deronda in particular--speak of social progress, but their rhetoric conceals a fundamentally conservative opposition to change. There is a contradiction between what Eliot appears to approve and what she actually desires. The divided nature of Eliot's political position is most striking in Felix Holt.

In Felix Holt, the relation between individual submission and the suppression of the entire working class is logical rather than merely symbolic. That is, Felix Holt does not simply stand for the ideal quiescence of the lower classes, his very speech acts characterize him as being of the party of passivity, a party to which Esther Lyon and the narrator also belong. The real schism in the novel is neither between radicals and conservatives nor between two types of radicals but rather between two kinds of speakers, those who assert facts and those who command or express desires.[43]

Eliot's syntax allies her with the linguistic conservatives who are also the most politically conservative, though nominally radical, characters in Felix Holt. Eliot seems as fond of Rufus Lyon of "illuminated thought, finely-divided speech . . . the choicer weapons of the divine armoury" (Ch. 15). Eliot's style has the stamp of truth-telling rather than world-shaping. She consistently uses existential assertions such as "it is" and "there is" to ground her observations of human nature in a quasi-scientific objectivity. "There is a sort of subjection which is the peculiar heritage of largeness and of love" (Ch. 6). "It is a fact perhaps kept a little too much in the background, that mothers have a self larger than their maternity" (Ch. 8). "There is no private life which has not been determined by a wider public life" (Ch. 3). Habitual use of "to be" verb forms with long noun and verbal complements suggests Eliot's concern with persuading us of the word-to-world fit, the descriptive truth, of her prose. She seems to guarantee the existence of the abstractions she names in the very act of asserting them: "To be right in great memorable moments is perhaps the thing we need most desire for ourselves" (Ch. 32).

Discriminating and defining are habits that characterize Eliot as a scientific user of language: "Strength is often only another name for willing bondage to irremediable weakness" (Ch. 6). "Perhaps the most delightful friendships are those in which there is much agreement, much disputation, and yet more personal liking" (Ch. 10). Eliot's own deliberateness and precision in defining abstractions make her a truth-teller, in a special sense. She is not so much creating a fictional analogue that mimetically portrays the real world as she is presenting (non-verifiable) facts within her fiction.

In Felix Holt, the contemplative author's sympathies are clearly not with the "men who are expected to apply" theories, of whom Harold Transome is the chief (and most sympathetic) example. Transome embodies all of the tendencies of a man of action: he has strong opinions about how things and people ought to appear and characteristically expresses these by means of the verbs "love" and "hate": "'I hate English wives; they want to give their opinion about everything'" (Ch. 1). "'. . . a woman ought to be a Tory, and graceful, and handsome, like you. I should hate a woman who took up my opinions, and talked for me'" (Ch. 8). He imperiously puts his mother in her place, emotionally and practically:

> "Women, very properly, don't change their views, but keep to the notions in which they have been brought up. It doesn't signify what they think--they are not called upon to judge or to act. You must really leave me to take my own course in these matters, which properly belong to men. Beyond that, I will gratify any wish you choose to mention." (Ch. 2)

Eliot uses such strongly desiderative speech to denote an egocentric philosophy.

Harold has his own private hedonistic calculus, "a way of virtually measuring the value of everything by the contribution it made to his own pleasure" (Ch. 43). He habitually pays attention to "'places and people--how they look and what can be done with them'" (Ch. 1), while showing "indifference to any impressions in others which did not further or impede his own purposes" (Ch. 1). Whether he is talking of marrying or of managing his property, Harold's will to have his own way is paramount. He tells Esther Lyon, while courting her, "'I am very fond of things that I can get. And I never longed much for anything out of my reach. Whatever I feel sure of getting I like all the better'" (Ch. 43). Taking his place as master of Transome Court, he informs his mother: "'Jermyn manages the estate badly, then. That will not last under _my_ reign'" (Ch. 1).

George Eliot ironically calls Harold's standing for Parliament as a Radical candidate "a good end." Transome's political intentions are, however, critically dissected by the author to show that his purpose is to have his own way in the public sphere, to add political power to personal. "The years had nourished an inclination to as much opposition as would enable him to assert his own independence and power . . ." (Ch. 8). "He was addicted at once to rebellion and to conformity. . . . The limit was not defined by theory, but was drawn in an irregular zigzag by early disposition and association . . ." (Ch. 8). As an M. P., Harold Transome would bring about whatever the "self-assertion of the majority peremptorily demanded" (Ch. 8). In a sense, as a radical Transome is still acting out of boyhood willfulness. (Soon after returning to England and to his home, he commands his mother, "'There shall be no further collision between us on subjects in which I must be master of my own actions'" [Ch. 1].) He distrusts the traditional institutions and established political parties of the country as he distrusted his wastrel older brother Durfey, the estate's original heir. Wanting to seize the power for himself that he would not have inherited in the natural course of things, Transome allies himself with the politically immature upstarts of the lower classes.

Transome is appropriately punished for his unfilial rebelliousness by the discovery that his real father is the unscrupulous lawyer Jermyn, whom he loathes. The upstart is defeated by this self-comparison; egotism is its own punishment. Eliot attributes the radicals' defeat to the inherent weaknesses of deductive reasoning:

> Fancy what a game at chess would be if all the chessmen had passions and intellects, more or less small and cunning; if you were not only uncertain about your adversary's men, but a little

> uncertain also about your own . . . . [y]ou might be the longest-headed of deductive reasoners, and yet you might be beaten by your own pawns. You would be especially likely to be beaten, if you depended arrogantly on your mathematical imagination, and regarded your passionate pieces with contempt. (Ch. 29)

The surface meaning of this passage is that men incapable of sympathy with others will be unable to imagine and to account for the desire and willfulness of anyone else; however, the message of the chess analogy is really that one should not play the game at all.

George Eliot does not wholly vilify Transome; she admits him to be, though an egotist, "a clever, frank, good-natured egotist" (Ch. 8). She reserves her real disapproval for the cast of mind that he represents:

> This determined aiming at something not easy but clearly possible, marked the direction in which Harold's nature was strong; he had the energetic will and muscle, the self-confidence, the quick perception, and the narrow imagination which made what is admiringly called the practical mind. (Ch. 8)

Transome's active determination to bring about the possible by means of his muscular will is evidently not admired by Eliot. For Eliot, the unrestrained will ironically makes its own narrow confines, a prison of the desires it cannot fulfill.

George Eliot conceives of practical reasoning as entailing the use of any means (however unscrupulous) to reach an often self-serving end: "A practical man must seek a good end by the only possible means" (Ch. 17). A practical man is unequipped to deal with a conflict between the desire to appear honorable and the desire to satisfy his wants. When faced with the news that evidence exists which will dispossess the Transomes in favor of an entailed heir, the tortuous calculations that pass through Harold's mind are mirrored linguistically: "In fact, what he would have done had the circumstances been different was much clearer than what he should choose to do or feel himself compelled to do in the actual crisis" (Ch. 38). The phrase "feel himself compelled to do" hints that Transome longs for a categorical imperative which will resolve his dilemma. For once his own will is inadequate to the situation. The complexity of the modal verbs in this passage suggests the intrinsic limitations and drawbacks of practical reasoning, which only a "clear" vision will resolve.

In contrast to the radicalism of Harold Transome, less a reasoned theory than an egotistic inclination to have his own way, is the conservative radicalism of Felix Holt. When he says, "'I want to go to some roots a good deal lower down than the franchise,'" he means he preaches spiritual enlightenment as the prerequisite to political activism (Ch. 27). Unlike Harold Transome, Felix displays the "habitual meditative abstraction from objects of mere personal vanity or desire, which is the peculiar stamp of culture" (Ch. 30). That is, he is too enlightened to act solely, even primarily, on the basis of his desires.

His education and his apprenticeship to an apothecary equip him to act decisively but negatively: he bans the sale of quack medicines, the family business. The son's scientific knowledge makes his father's folk learning obsolete: "'My father was ignorant,' said Felix, bluntly. 'He knew neither the complication of the human system, nor the way in which drugs counteract each other. Ignorance is not so damnable as humbug, but when it prescribes pills it may happen to do more harm. I know something about these things'" (Ch. 5). A broad knowledge of causes and effects makes action difficult, even undesirable.

Felix's conversion to a religion of humanity leaves him with this conviction: "'They may tell me I can't alter the world--that there must be a certain number of sneaks and robbers in it, and if I don't lie and filch somebody else will. Well, then, somebody else shall, for I won't'" (Ch. 5). In this novel, the hero's characteristic mental effort is to will-not to act. In his private life, Felix represses both desire and dissatisfaction: "'. . . I'll never love, if I can help it; and if I love, I'll bear it, and never marry'" (Ch. 10). He is a much more dutiful son than Harold Transome, who holds women in disesteem and denies their right to independence. Felix is more apparently reverential toward women. When tried by the pious complaints of his mother, he shows himself a true Wordsworthian, drawing on "the utmost exertion of patience, that required those little rill-like outflowings of goodness which in minds of great energy must be fed from the deep sources of thought and passionate devotedness" (Ch. 30). In Felix, patience is advocated as an end in itself: in the archaic sense of the word (sufferer), he is really a patient rather than an agent.

Though most of Felix's choices involve repudiation rather than assertion, still there is initially a willfulness in his nature that must be chastened. Reverend Lyon says that he is not really "'dreamy; rather, his excess lies in being too practical'" (Ch. 38). Felix inclines too much toward exercising his will: "'I want to be a demagogue of a new sort; an honest one, if possible'" (Ch. 27). In the election riot his "definite will and . . . energetic personality" (Ch. 33) influence lesser men whose "mental state was a mere medley of appetites and confused impressions" (Ch. 33). Eliot takes pains to suggest that Felix's misdeeds are to some extent merely the excesses of his virtues. "Nature never makes men who are at once energetically sympathetic and minutely calculating" (Ch. 33). Felix is above mere means-and-ends reasoning in his spontaneous impulse to control the rioters through his superior example. Still, his impulse leads him into the murky realm of practical purposes, where he cannot compete with the schemers he encounters there, "sharp-visaged men who loved the irrationality of riots for something else than its own sake," presumably for their private gain (Ch. 33). The result of the election riot, perhaps by implication of the entire electoral process, is that "the multitudinous small wickednesses of small selfish ends, really undirected towards any larger result, had issued in widely-shared mischief" (Ch. 33). Felix Holt learns through experience that outwitting selfish schemers is impossible; avoiding action seems to be the only alternative to "mischief."

For his willfulness, Felix is punished literally and figuratively by imprisonment. It is an experience that subdues him further and completes his education in self-control. Though Ester Lyon tells him, "'You are just the same'" (Ch. 45), Felix's language seems less imperious, less desiderative, more objective than before his prison stay. Felix's testimony at his trial for participating in the riot is couched in language that disclaims willfulness. He recounts "'. . . how I got entangled in the mob, how I came to attack the constable, and how I was led to take a course which seems rather mad to myself, now I look back upon it'" (Ch. 46). The cool detachment that accompanies retrospection enables Felix Holt to appreciate the need of governing his impulsiveness.

The syntax of his "truthful speech" (Ch. 46), which apparently documents Felix's passion for militantly defending truth and justice, is really the reverse of desirous:

> "I hold it blasphemy to say that a man ought not to fight against authority. . . . It would be impertinent for me to speak of this now if I did not need to say in my own defense that I should hold myself the worst sort of traitor if I put my hand either to fighting or disorder . . . if I were not urged to it by what I hold to be sacred feelings, making a sacred duty either to my own manhood or to my fellow-man." (Ch. 46)

Felix's speech acts are definitions, clarifications, qualifications ("'It would be impertinent for me to speak . . . if I did not need to say . . . that I should hold myself . . .'"). Not "A man ought to fight against unjust authority," but "I would hold it blasphemy . . . ." Felix Holt is concerned rather with what is permissible and with what truly *is* than with what he wants and what others desire or need. He comes to accede to Reverend Lyon's dictum: "'. . . the right to rebellion is the right to seek a higher rule, and not to wander in mere lawlessness . . .'" (Ch. 13).

Felix's realization that action is dangerous, its effects uncontrollable, leads him to advocate political quietism: "'If there's anything our people want convincing of, it is that there's some dignity and happiness for a man other than changing his station'" (Ch. 45). As a radical, Felix Holt is, like George Eliot, "'fonder of preaching than of practice'" because he wants to make men see the need for self-reform (Ch. 22). His rhetoric is calculated to quiet his auditors rather than to move or rouse them. Addressing a crowd of idle workers he assures them that, contrary to what the Union speakers say, "'if you go the right way to work you may get power sooner without votes'" (Ch. 30). Although Felix uses the language of moral obligation--"the right way"--

his message is not action but passivity. "'The way to get rid of folly is to get rid of vain expectations, and of thoughts that don't agree with the nature of things'" (Ch. 30). The equation of folly with desires and wants implies that wisdom is an assent to things as they are. Clearly the power that Felix is talking about is power over oneself: the ability to endure suffering because one apprehends its ancient causes in "'the nature of things.'"

When Felix justifies his political behavior to Esther, his language expresses a passivity out of keeping with his purported "energetic personality":

> "It is just because I'm a very ambitious fellow . . . that I have chosen to give up what people call worldly good. At least that has been one determining reason. It all depends on what a man gets into his consciousness--what life thrusts into his mind, so that it becomes present to him as remorse is present to the guilty, or a mechanical problem to an inventive genius." (Ch. 27)

The passage moves from an apparent choice (renunciation) to a retreat from so assertive a claim; from "I have chosen" to the ambiguity of "At least that has been one determining reason." The pattern of assertion and retraction is repeated: it seems first that a man forms his own mind ("what a man gets into his consciousness") but in reality "life thrusts" these ideas upon the passive observer. The seeming import of the speech--Felix's ambition--is at odds with the mood of his statements. "It is because I am ambitious" is an assertion of a truth--"it is"--not an avowal of intention or will. "I have chosen" signifies not only that "choosing" is a continuing activity rather than a punctual act, but also that "giving up" is a characteristic disposition of Felix's, a possession he "has." It is as if Felix corrects the ambiguous aggression his earlier phrase contained. Certainly the implied passive force of the verbs undercuts Felix's avowal of ambitiousness.

Felix's call for moral reform in place of political revolution stems from his secularized religious enthusiasm. He tells Esther, "'The old Catholics are right, with their higher rule and their lower. Some are called to subject themselves to a harder discipline, and renounce things voluntarily which are lawful to others'" (Ch. 27). Self-subjection to a "higher rule" means, for Felix, following his conscience. For Esther Lyon, the "higher rule" comes to mean Felix Holt's moral superiority.

The impulse that determines Esther's choice is not devotion to the divine will but a Miltonic devotedness to Felix Holt ("He for God only, she for God in him"). Felix introduces Esther to "the first religious experience of her life--the first self-questioning, the first voluntary subjection, the first longing to acquire the strength of great motives and obey the more strenuous rule . . ." (Ch. 27). As if becoming one of the relics of Felix's temple, Esther gives up a lively if selfish personality for the still unity of a sacred statue. She attains "fulness of perfection," (Ch. 44), her Arnoldian "best self" (Ch. 27), which is like some high plateau of rarified character development: "The higher mountain air, the passionate serenity of perfect love" (Ch. 44). Not motion but stasis--the arresting of life--is implicit in such perfection. Esther's self-sacrifice seems an entombment: "It is only in that freshness of our time that the choice is possible which gives unity to life, and makes the memory a temple where all relics and all votive offerings, all worship and all grateful joy, are an unbroken history sanctified by one religion" (Ch. 44). The passage reverberates with echoes of "Tintern Abbey": ". . . thy mind/

Shall be a mansion for all lovely forms,/ Thy memory be as a dwelling-place/ For all sweet sounds and harmonies . . ." (11. 139-142). Just as Wordsworth turns his sister's memory into a tomblike sanctuary, so George Eliot objectifies Esther's selflessness as a monument to a humanitarian religion.

Esther's new consciousness of "the best life" is "'that where one bears and does everything because of some great and strong feeling'" (Ch. 26). Characteristically, she thinks first of "bearing," then of "doing." It is an appropriately feminine activity, for Esther's submission is defined as a woman's: ". . . she was intensely of the feminine type, verging neither toward the saint nor the angel. She was 'a fair divided excellence, whose fulness of perfection' must be in marriage" (Ch. 44). Both Esther and the narrator assert that a woman cannot "make her own lot. . . . Her lot is made for her by the love she accepts" (Ch. 43). The perfecting of a woman's life in "a supreme love . . . is not to be had where and how she wills" (Ch. 49). Though Eliot asserts that perfection may necessitate "choosing what is difficult," the novel depicts Esther's decision as the reverse of a deliberate, intentional act. In her courtroom outburst on Felix's behalf, Esther does not consciously intend to speak out: "her feelings were growing into a necessity for action, rather than a resolve to act" (Ch. 46). Her involuntary impulse is rewarded; her "maidenly," "inspired ignorance" moves the "just spirited men and good fathers" in the courtroom to engineer Felix's release from prison.

Part of Esther's trial is to choose between the future (the potency of the wealthy estate entailed by her real father) and the past (represented by her spiritual father, Reverend Lyon). Esther's renunciation of a fortune, the <u>means</u> by which she could perform actions long dreamed of (both selfish and altruistic) thus involves a choice between two modes of being, the active, represented by Harold Transome, and the static, in the person of Felix Holt.

In truth, Esther does not so much choose as passively follow an impulse to obey. "What she desired to see with undisturbed clearness were things not present: the rest she needed was the rest of a final choice" (Ch. 49). Esther conceives of her decision as a cessation of conflict rather than as a positive assertion of herself that will precipitate further choices. Unlike George Eliot's other heroines, Romola and Maggie Tulliver, Esther is not borne away by a literal tide to a destiny of self-abnegation. A river does, however, figure in her submission. At the emotional crisis, she looks out of the window at the "for-ever running river" whose lack of apparent source or end soothes her and whose eternal drift implies a kind of immutability. She wants to escape from the teleological realm of process, to lose rather than to assert herself.

In order to achieve self-perfection, to become her best self, Esther needs Felix Holt's "better self." Without him, she would have "no strength to lean upon--no other better self to make a place for trust and joy" (Ch. 49). Esther's self-renunciation and Felix Holt's generous gift of moral strength and wisdom constitute a conservative model of sexual behavior. Esther embraces her duty for "modern" reasons--her religious feeling is directed toward humanity rather than another world--but her dutifulness is traditional. Similarly, Felix Holt is a political conservative in that he contains the rebellious energies of Esther as well as those of the unruly workers. He succeeds not because he is a powerful, dominant agent but because he incarnates the approved mode of feminine behavior: self-suppression.

Mrs. Transome, in <u>Felix Holt</u>, represents a woman whose willfulness brings her unhappiness, in her public life and in her private one. Socially, she is arrogant and domineering:

> She had that high-born imperious air which would have marked her as an object of hatred and reviling by a revolutionary mob. Her person was too typical of social distinctions to be passed by with indifference by any one: it would have fitted an empress in her own right, who had had to rule in spite of faction, to dare the violation of treaties and dread retributive invasions, to grasp after new territories, to be defiant in desperate circumstances, and to feel a woman's hunger of the heart forever unsatisfied. (Ch. 1)

She "liked every little sign of power her lot had left her" (Ch. 1). In her family role, she had also been ruled by her own imperious desires:

> The mother's early raptures had lasted but a short time, and even while they lasted there had grown up in the midst of them a hungry desire, like a black poisonous plant feeding in the sunlight,-- the desire that her first, rickety, ugly, imbecile child should die, and leave room for her darling, of whom she could be proud. Such desires make life a hideous lottery . . . . (Ch. 1)

In mildly comic counterpoint to this tragic willfulness is Mrs. Holt, Felix's mother, whose self-centered complaints and demands mask a really generous maternity: "Like many women who appear to others to have a masculine decisiveness of tone, and to themselves to have a masculine force of mind, and who come into severe collision with sons arrived at the masterful stage, she had the maternal cord vibrating strongly within her toward all tiny children" (Ch. 43). The connection between Mrs. Transome's aristocratic ruthlessness and her egocentric maternity implies that feminine submissiveness, maternal "suppression of self, and power of living in the experience of another" (Ch. 1), is connected with political obedience. Determination and insistence on action--"masculine" traits, in this novel at least--yield dangerous results. Innocent people and accomplices alike are victimized by willfulness.

Not only are they dangerous, selfish desires produce <u>ugly</u> consequences. Mrs. Transome's life is a grim, bleak, ultimately repulsive picture of the constriction of an existence through its own ambitions. Esther's revulsion from Mrs. Transome's life has an aesthetic basis, and it mirrors our own response.

> The dimly suggested tragedy of this woman's life, the dreary waste of years empty of sweet trust and affection, afflicted her even to horror. It seemed to have come as a last vision to urge her toward the life where the draughts of joy sprang from the unchanging fountains of reverence and devout love. (Ch. 50)

Earlier, Felix Holt was moved by two mental "pictures," one of the misery of the poor and the other of vulgar, "clerkly gentility" (Ch. 5), to renounce social ambition. In the same way, Esther is moved by Mrs. Transome's miserable lot to reject gratificiation of trivial desires in favor of resigning her will to a higher spiritual authority. Moral revulsion and aesthetic condemnation are manifestly interdependent in Eliot's politics, as in those of Virginia Woolf.

Eliot's style in <u>Felix Holt</u> makes use of two categories of adjectives and adverbs related to dimension, both categories associated throughout with willfulness and selflessness, with imperative versus truth-telling speech, and, consistently, with distinct moral judgments as well. When Eliot characterized Harold Transome as having the "energetic will and muscle, the self-confidence, the quick perception, and the narrow imagination which made what is admiringly called the practical mind," she employed a number of the adjectives associated with willfulness in the novel. Besides "narrow" and "quick," others include "sharp," "shallow," "petty," and "small."

On the day of the election riot, political agitators and trades union representatives all <u>look</u> as though they have "the practical mind": "Mingled with the more headlong and half-drunken crowd there were some sharp-visaged men who loved the irrationality of riots . . ." (Ch. 33). When Felix Holt succeeds the trades union speaker,

> The effect of his figure in relief against the stone background was unlike that of the previous speaker. He was considerably taller, his head and neck were more massive, and the expression of his mouth and eyes was something very different from the mere acuteness and rather hard-lipped antagonism of the trades-union man. Felix Holt's face had the look of habitual meditative abstraction from objects of mere personal vanity or desire which is the peculiar stamp of culture, and makes a very roughly cut face worthy to be called "the human face divine." (Ch. 30)

When Felix attempts to divert the mob's advance, "It was not a moment in which a spirit like his could calculate the effect of misunderstanding as to himself: nature never makes men who are at once energetically sympathetic and minutely calculating" (Ch. 33). In contrast to Felix's transcendence of mere "minute" personal ambitions, Harold Transome's charitable actions are narrowly self-reflexive:

> His very good nature was unsympathetic: it never came from any thorough understanding of deep respect for what was in the mind of the person he obliged or indulged; it was like his kindness to his mother--an arrangement of his for the happiness of others, which, if they were sensible, ought to succeed. (Ch. 43)

Esther Lyon's growth through the influence of Felix Holt enables her to avoid the moral claustrophobia that Mrs. Transome suffers. She exchanges life at Transome Court, "silken bondage that arrested all motive, and was nothing better than a well-cushioned despair" (Ch. 49), for a more beautiful sublimity--moral and aesthetic. Her wholeness of spiritual perfection comes through marriage with Felix Holt: "A supreme love, a motive that gives a sublime rhythm to a woman's life, and exalts habit into partnership with the soul's highest needs. . . . [is] a high initiation" (Ch. 49). The moral liberation attendant on self-perfection is described consistently, in this passage and throughout the novel, in dimensional adjectives like "wide," "broad," "deep," "slow," "high," and "sublime."

In the public sphere, narrow calculations designed to bring immediate benefits to the actors involved are as morally and aesthetically reprehensible as in private life. During the fatal election riot, "the multitudinous small wickednesses of small selfish ends, really undirected toward any larger result, had issued in widely shared mischief that might yet be hideous" (Ch. 33). The wise Reverend Lyon has a fuller, therefore a morally superior vision of "'the perplexed condition of human things, whereby even right action seems to bring evil consequences, if we have respect only to our own brief lives, and not to that larger rule whereby we are stewards of the eternal dealings, and not contrivers of our own success'" (Ch. 37).

Reverend Lyon's quaintly archaic locutions do not disguise the affinity between his speech and the narrative voice of George Eliot. The author's favorite honorific adjectives are "gradual, " "large," and "great"--in this novel and in others as well. Eliot the truth-teller describes truth as manifold and wide: "For what we call illusions are often, in truth, a wider vision of past and present realities--a willing movement of a man's soul with the larger sweep of the world's forces--a movement toward a more assured end than the chances of a single life" (Ch. 16). Eliot redefines selfishness and selflessness, making the latter seem attractive, the former repulsive:

> The stronger will always rule, say some. . . . But what is
> strength? Is it blind willfulness that sees no terrors, no many-
> linked consequences, no bruises and wounds of those whose cords it
> tightens? Is it the narrowness of a brain that conceives no needs
> differing from its own, and looks to no results beyond the bargains
> of today; that tugs with emphasis for every small purpose; and
> thinks it weakness to exercise the sublime power of resolved renun-
> ciation? There is a sort of subjection which is the peculiar heri-
> tage of largeness and of love; and strength is often only another
> name for willing bondage to irremediable weakness." (Ch. 6)

Willfulness is "blind," "narrow," "small," and "weak"; dependence and subjection are "sublime," "large," and, by implication, all-seeing.

A broad understanding of the truth about the far-ranging complexity of reality encompasses even the selfish and myopic theories of "practical" men and women: "none of our theories are quite large enough for all the disclosures of time" (Ch. 6). George Eliot's understanding takes in even her unattractively immoral characters: "At present, looking back on that day at Treby, it seems to me that the sadder illusion lay with Harold Transome, who was trusting in his own skill to shape the success of his own morrows, ignorant of what many yesterdays had determined for him beforehand" (Ch. 16). She is full of compassion for the suffering of Mrs. Transome, though it is the deserved consequence of her own early sins:

> If she had only been more haggard and less majestic, those who had
> glimpses of her outward life might have said she was a tyrannical,
> griping harridan, with a tongue like a razor. No one said
> exactly that; but they never said anything like the full truth about
> her, or divined what was hidden under that outward life--a woman's
> keen sensibility and dread, which lay screened behind all her petty
> habits and narrow notions, as some quivering thing with eyes and
> throbbing heart may lie crouching behind withered rubbish. (Ch. 1)

George Eliot's wide vision and deep compassion make it possible for her to understand the transgressions of even her most willful protagonists. The wider vision circumscribes the narrowly selfish one; the general truth supersedes the individual will; the greater dominates the lesser, both morally and aesthetically.

Eliot's rhetoric is less an end in itself, a truth, than a a means to the end of winning converts to her politics of selfless submission. The beauty of truth is brought into being not by passive observing but by active willing: by Eliot's own love of the truth. Ultimately, the truth Eliot tells is imposed upon her readers, for style is a manifestation of authorial will. Eliot's apparently neutral transcription of reality rests upon a prior willed commitment. Her empirical vision stems from a <u>need</u> to believe in its veracity. If we accept the premise underlying <u>Felix Holt</u>--that our greatest desire is to know the truth rather than to do what we want--we have been won over by the way it is phrased.

Less rhetorically persuasive than the novel, because more explicitly partisan, is the "Address to Working Men" written a year after the novel. There Felix Holt speaks for George Eliot when he recommends expansion of knowledge to the working classes in place of institutional reform. The idea that knowing the causes of events will nullify one's interest in bringing events about is the tacit assumption underlying the "Address." Felix Holt advises that increased "knowledge, ability, and honesty" are the only justifiable "means" to social reform.[44] Unfranchised members of society, those with no overt political power, still have a measure of control over the minds of their governors: "A majority has the power of creating a public opinion." "We could groan and hiss before we had the franchise: if we had groaned and hissed in the right place, if we have discerned better between good and evil . . . we should have made an audience that would have shamed the other classes out of their share in the national vices."[45] Espousing this belief makes the working class responsible for existent political and social evils without granting them power to change the status quo.

Perfecting himself is the only action that Eliot approves for a working man in the "Address." Perfecting society is disallowed. Felix Holt uses the analogy of the body politic to describe the interdependence of classes. Social injustice is like some transmitted social disease: ". . . when a man injures his constitution by a life of vicious excess, his children and grandchildren inherit diseased bodies and minds . . . ."[46] But no antidote to general social ills is offered in the "Address." Though present suffering may be the consequence of past sins inflicted on innocent heirs, the sufferer cannot take action to remedy it. Felix Holt counsels, "It is constantly the task of practical wisdom not to say, 'This is good, and I will have it,' but to say, 'This is the less of two unavoidable evils, and I will bear it.'"[47]

Alleviation comes to society as a whole; it cannot be willed. "The solution comes slowly, because men collectively can only be made to embrace principles, and to act on them, by the slow stupendous teaching of the world's events."[48] In her essay on "The Natural History of German Life," Eliot describes progress as "the gradual, consentaneous development" of man and society.[49] Her language shows up the absence of human agency from Eliot's conception of social and political life: "consent" seems the only action Eliot approves. Her idea of evolution grants more self-determinancy to the abstractions society and duty than to the individual agent.

Middlemarch, Eliot's finest novel, is an exception to the general rule in her fiction that action is subordinated to thought. In Middlemarch as in The Mill on the Floss, George Eliot implicitly criticizes women for being too ready to submit to an inappropriate "Other" that does not deserve their worship. In Middlemarch, of which U. C. Knoepflmacher has said that the only heroic character is the narrator, Eliot's irony illuminates Dorothea's erroneous choice of idols.[50] The selfishness of Casaubon is allied with his deductive method in scholarship; his theory "was not likely to bruise itself unawares against discoveries" (Ch. 48). Neither is he likely to accommodate his life to the real fact of Dorothea's existence. In Dorothea's second husband, Will Ladislaw, whose name suggests the force underlying all revolutionary planning, Eliot demonstrates the relative impotence of political practice (and action in general).[51]

Eliot has always deplored the tendency toward self-agnegation that is merely a version of martyrdom. Rev. Tryan and Savonarola are examples of the dangers implicit in voluntary suppression of self that is really a glorification of one's ego. In Middlemarch, however, Eliot makes it clear that Dorothea's passivity is partly to be blamed on the want of a "coherent social faith and order" in modern life ("Prelude"). Eliot deliberately leaves vague the connection between this general criticism and the ensuing story, in order not to reduce the novel to a narrow complaint. She recognizes that the conflict between self-assertion and self-denial cuts across sexual categories. But it is striking that Eliot originally ended the novel with even more explicit criticism of the social order for distorting and dissipating individual (female) energies.

The first edition, which Eliot hastily changed to suit public and critical opinion, read:

> Among the many remarks passed on her mistakes, it was never said in the neighbourhood of Middlemarch that such mistakes could not have happened if the society into which she was born had not smiled on propositions of marriage from a sickly man to a girl less than half his own age--on modes of education which make a woman's knowledge another name for motley ignorance--on rules of conduct which are in flat contradiction with its own loudly-asserted beliefs.[52]

Certainly this ending does not do as a summation of all of <u>Middlemarch</u>. It is not even adequate as a statement of the social rules Eliot criticizes: May-December marriages are a minor symptom of social sexual hypocrisy. But in a sense Eliot's original ending honestly addresses what she must have felt, perhaps half-consciously, was a root cause of not only Dorothea's problem but her own: the suppression and denial of the female will.

With <u>Daniel Deronda</u>, Eliot returns to the problem of the intransigent woman with less sympathy. The novel enacts the repudiation and final transcendence of the female will in an all-male marriage between patriarchal will and submissive temperament. The real wedding which takes place is metaphoric rather than practically possible since it occurs between the womanly man, Daniel Deronda, and the disembodied masculine will of Mordecai. It is the union of an abstraction and a ghost, a transcendental marriage of essences.[53]

Transcendence is found at every turn in the novel. Daniel Deronda achieves his identity and purpose in life only at the cost of turning his back on his disciple, Gwendolen Harleth. This rejection is paralleled by Eliot's rejection of the wasteland of present-day England for the vague possibility of a Palestine that is more a state of being than a geographical entity. Also transcended is Eliot's realistic aesthetic credo. Nowhere in her fiction does she create characters and situations more brilliantly, but this practice no longer seems to interest her. Singleness of purpose informs the novel, but the unification of Eliot's own personal imperatives does not yield the unity of an artifact. She achieves wholeness only by rejecting some parts of the fiction, and possibly aspects of her self as well.

As in Eliot's other novels, there is a carefully worked-out continuum of egotists and selfless characters, ranging from Grandcourt to Mirah at the two extremes. Among the egotists, the woman in particular are punished: Gwendolen's will is crushed by that of her sinister husband; the actress Alcharisi finds she is "'forced to obey my dead father'" and atone for youthful ambition (Ch. 51). Daniel Deronda is superior to his mother because "all the woman lacking in her was present in him . . ." (Ch. 51). He passively awaits a vocation and is rewarded by learning his ancestry: "He came back with what was better than freedom--with a duteous bond . . ." (Ch. 63). Deronda is the true vessel of the patriarchal will, transmitted from his grandfather Daniel Charisi through Mordecai to himself. He embraces submission and supplants the troublesome female altogether.

Mordecai is perhaps the sole willful character George Eliot presents uncritically in all her fiction. His is one of those "natures where a wise estimate of consequences is fused in the fires of that passionate belief which determines the consequences it believes in" (Ch. 41). His mind participates in "divine reason," which abbreviates the distance between idea and execution in social reform (Ch. 42). Creating Palestine as "'a neutral ground for the East as Belgium is for the West'" seems possible only by means of some miraculous divine fiat, by God's Word or the author's (Ch. 42).

Eliot's disinterest in practical politics, her impatience with means, is paralleled in <u>Daniel Deronda</u> by her diminishing interest in fictional realism. In place of the seductive yet sibylline persona of the earlier fiction is a narrator who is impatient, almost at times misanthropic. She repeatedly commands her readers to "Imagine" rather than showing them things (Chs. 32, 40). After meticulously depicting Grandcourt's appearance as Gwendolen first sees him, Eliot asks, "Attempts at description are stupid: who can all at once describe a human being?" (Ch. 11). In <u>Daniel Deronda</u>, Eliot jettisons the real in favor of the ideal. Her love of concrete, particular experience is channelled into generalized enthusiasm for the intangible. The novel becomes like the prayer Deronda hears in a Frankfurt synagogue, "the prayer which seeks for nothing special, but is a yearning to escape from the limitations of our own weakness and an invocation of all Good to enter and abide with us . . . ." (Ch. 32).

In this last novel, Eliot tries to escape from her own egotism, from the conflict between desire and duty which informs her art. She wants to make us feel that she is possessed by the spirit of truth, that we can be emotionally converted by a fiction which resembles Hebrew "chanted liturgies" in that its "strongest effect . . . is independent of detailed verbal meaning . . ." (Ch. 32). Paradoxically this impulse proves more isolationist and solipsistic than the imaginative, loving possessiveness of her earlier fiction. In works like <u>Adam Bede</u>, <u>The Mill on the Floss</u> and <u>Middlemarch</u>, it was the "massive egoism of [her] powerful personality" which made us believe in the reality of her imaginings.[54]

It is doubtful that Eliot expected her readers fully to follow and assent to the "passionate vision of possibilities" in this novel (Ch. 41). Privately she admitted, "Yes, I expected more aversion than I have found. But I was happily independent in material things, and felt no temptation to accommodate my writing to any standard except that of trying to do my best . . . ."[55] No longer solicitous about instructing her audience, Eliot turns to pleasing herself.

Underlying her support of Zionism in Daniel Deronda is the nostalgia Eliot reveals in "Looking Backward," an essay in Theophrastus Such: ". . . I often smile at my consciousness that certain conservative prepossessions have mingled themselves" in with childhood memories, Eliot writes.[56] She immerses herself in reconstructing life with her father, from whom she absorbed conservative political prejudices bound up with religious and moral scruples: ". . . I was accustomed to hear him utter the word 'government' in a tone that charged it with awe, and made it part of my effective religion, in contrast with the word 'rebel,' which seemed to carry the stamp of evil in its syllables, and, lit by the fact that Satan was the first rebel, made an argument dispensing with more detailed inquiry."[57] Since that unquestioning childish acceptance of her father's opinions, Eliot has made a more "detailed inquiry," but the end is the same.

As she wrote an old friend in 1879, "Imperative duties--such as leave us in no doubt as to what we shall do next--are the only condiion that makes life easy--though we ignorantly rebel against those benignant bonds while we still have them."[58] George Eliot renounces self-doubt along with self-determination in Daniel Deronda and other late writings. As U. C. Knoepflmacher has said, the novel marks a move "from the conditional to the categorical."[59]

Her novels show progressively greater conflict between Eliot's distrust of deductive reasoning and her own gradual movement toward deduction, aesthetically. In <u>Daniel Deronda</u> the movement toward romance implies a rejection of induction as well as of realism. Eliot seems to transcend the particular fact in favor of general truth. Like Deronda, she rejects the single self--Gwendolen and her egocentric demands--in favor of submission to a larger vision. Ironically, this transcendence results in something very like a (deductive) glorification of general theory over individual fact.

When Eliot subsumes the individual character or fact under the collective truth, logical and aesthetic contradictions result. Logically, there is a potential contradiction between Eliot's rejection of theory-making on the grounds of its implicit egotism and her à priori rejection of the individual will. Perhaps this tension between Eliot's denying her characters the will and means to shape their futures--in marriage, social reform, or other activities--and her own mimetic creation of a fictional world devoted to the past makes us feel that the creator of Maggie Tulliver and Gwendolen Harleth is being too severe with them.

Aesthetically, problems arise from the clash between the reader's preference for vividly-realized individuals (villains or victims) and the author's professed preference for heroic characters. This clash stems from Eliot's own ambivalence. She seems, we might say, to prefer her egotists emotionally and aesthetically, her heroes intellectually and morally. What she <u>should</u> love is at odds with what she actually prefers.

Eliot's conflicting impulses produce the formal contradictions we have seen in her novels on political subjects. The effort she makes to suppress her own unfeminine willfulness results in a conflict between the various voices of her fiction. Her narrator's political partisanship reflects Eliot's own need and desire; the self that was denied re-surfaces. The law of the father, which Virginia Woolf both despises and dreads, elicits a different (though equally contradictory) response from George Eliot. Her proselytizing for the patriarchy could not be so ardent if her potential rebelliousness were less strong.

NOTES

¹ George Eliot, "Notes on the Spanish Gypsy and Tragedy in General," in George Eliot's Life as Related in Her Letters and Journals, ed. John Cross (Edinburgh and London: W. Blackwood & Sons, 1885), III, 38.

² Ibid., p. 39.

³ Raymond Williams, Culture and Society 1780-1950 (New York: Columbia University Press, 1958), pp. 111, 167, 170-171, 190-192.

⁴ George Eliot, letter to Mrs. Samuel Evans, The Letters of George Eliot, ed. Gordon S. Haight (New Haven: Yale University Press, 1954), I, 19.

⁵ Burke asserted that "A spirit of innovation is generally the result of a selfish temper and confined views. People will not look forward to posterity, who never look backward to their ancestors," in Reflections on the Revolution in France (Garden City, NY: Doubleday & Co., Inc., 1961), p. 45.

⁶ Mrs. John Cash, "Appendix" to George Eliot's Life, ed. Cross, pp. 745-746.

⁷ W. F. T. Myers discusses the influence of Comte on Eliot in "Politics and Personality in Felix Holt," Renaissance and Modern Studies, 10 (1966), 5-33.

⁸ Letters, 8 March 1858, I, 254.

⁹ George Eliot, "The Natural History of German Life," The Essays of George Eliot, ed. Thomas Pinney (New York: Columbia University Press, 1963), p. 295.

¹⁰ Ibid., p. 285.

¹¹ Letters, 11 July 1863, IV, 92.

¹² Letters, 8 August 1868, VI, 486.

¹³ Letters, 8 July 1870, V, 107.

¹⁴ Letters, 19 August 1857, II, 377. John Cross said that Eliot told him of a "'not herself' which took possession of her" in writing (George Eliot's Life, p. 724), yet Jerome Beaty has shown how deliberate Eliot's method of working was. See his Middlemarch from

Notebook to Novel: A Study of George Eliot's Creative Method (Urbana: University of Illinois Press, 1960). Possibly Eliot needed to feel that her writing was not an egotistic impulse, that she submitted to both her own genius and society's will.

[15] George Eliot's Life, p. 669.

[16] Letters, March 1838, I, 22-23.

[17] Letters, 12 August 1841, I, 102.

[18] George Eliot's Life, p. 8.

[19] Letters, 8 March 1848, I, 255.

[20] Letters, 3 September 1841, I, 107.

[21] Eliot's readers and critics have long been troubled by the narrative voice in her fiction, sensing within it a conflict of emotional and intellectual interests. F. R. Leavis admires the (masculine) intellectual and criticizes the emotional woman in her persona, in The Great Tradition (Garden City, NY: Doubleday & Co., Inc., 1954), p. 105. He rightly sees, however, that these selves constitute no "simple antithesis" (p. 104). Virginia Woolf thought that Eliot's critics were chiefly men who found her deficient in feminine charm. See "George Eliot," The Common Reader (New York: Harcourt, Brace & World, Inc., 1953), p. 168. Avoiding sexual stereotyping, W. J. Harvey isolates two sorts of narrative intrusions: "commentary" and "analysis." He finds the former obtrusive; see Chapter 3 in The Art of George Eliot (London: Chatto & Windus, 1961). Synthesizing these critical tendencies is Ruby Redinger who distinguishes between "a strong and luxuriant imagination" and "a current of self-criticism" in the narrative. Her comments are found in George Eliot: The Emergent Self (New York: Alfred A. Knopf, 1975), pp. 60, 334. Possibly Eliot's self-criticism signifies that she assimilated patriarchal strictures about woman's duty into her fictional self. Self-indulgence and self-restraint both lie beneath her narrative persona.

[22] George Eliot, "Woman in France: Madame de Sable, " Essays, ed. Pinney, p. 56.

[23] Letters, 30 May 1849, I, 284.

[24] Gordon Haight, George Eliot: A Biography (New York: Oxford University Press, 1968), p. 51.

[25] Letters, 4 December 1849, I, 322.

[26] Letters, 6 December 1859, III, 230-231.

[27] George Eliot, "[Westward Ho! and Constance Herbert]," Essays, pp. 134-135.

[28] Letters, 15 November 1857, II, 403.

[29] Martin J. Svaglic, "Religion in the Novels of George Eliot," Journal of English and Germanic Philology, 53 (1954), 287.

[30] Haight, George Eliot, p. 464.

[31] Bernard J. Paris, Experiments in Life: George Eliot's Quest for Values (Detroit: Wayne State University Press, 1965), p. 85.

[32] George Eliot, "The Future of German Philosophy," Essays, p. 151.

[33] Bernard J. Paris, "George Eliot's Religion of Humanity," Journal of English Literary History, 29 (1962), rpt. in George Eliot: A Collection of Critical Essays, ed. George Creeger (Englewood Cliffs, NJ: Prentice-Hall, Inc., 1970), p. 20.

[34] Jerome Thale, The Novels of George Eliot (New York: Columbia University Press, 1959), p. 84.

[35] Georg Henrik Von Wright, Explanation and Understanding (Ithaca, NY: Cornell University Press, 1971), p. 30. For an excellent discussion of the role of the will in Eliot's ateleological universe, see Felicia Bonaparte, Will and Destiny: Morality and Tragedy in George Eliot's Novels (New York: New York University Press, 1975).

[36] Von Wright, p. 27.

[37] I am indebted for these terms to Professor Julian Boyd's work on modal theory. The reader may also refer to John Searle's Speech Acts: An Essay in the Philosophy of Language (Cambridge: Cambridge University Press, 1969), pp. 23, 30, 70.

[38] Haight, George Eliot, Appendix I, pp. 555-556.

[39] George Eliot, "Janet's Repentance," Scenes of Clerical Life (Edinburgh & London: W. Blackwood & Sons, Ltd., 1878), p. 341.

[40] George Eliot, "The Sad Fortunes of the Rev. Amos Barton," Scenes of Clerical Life, pp. 3-4.

[41] George Eliot, Adam Bede, in The Works of George Eliot, 24 vols. (Edinburgh & London: William Blackwood [n.d.], Chapter 16. Subsequent references to Eliot's novels will allude to this standard Cabinet Edition; chapters will be cited parenthetically in the text.

[42] Nicholas Rance, The Historical Novel and Popular Politics in Nineteenth-Century England (New York: Barnes & Noble Books, 1975), p. 116.

[43] Arnold Kettle defines the opposition as being between two types of Radicals, the Disraelian Tory Democrat and the actual working class radical. See "Felix Holt, the Radical," in Critical Essays on George

Eliot, ed. Barbara Hardy (London: Routledge and Kegan Paul, 1970), pp. 108-110. Linda Bamber, in "Self-Defeating Politics in George Eliot's Felix Holt," Victorian Studies (June 1975), pp. 419-435, corrects Kettle and argues that the novel's real conflict is between private and public morality. I would suggest that these views are not mutually exclusive. In Eliot's politics, the personal and public are interdependent.

[44] George Eliot, "Address to Working Men. By Felix Holt," in Essays, p. 417.

[45] Ibid., p. 416.

[46] Ibid., p. 418.

[47] Ibid., p. 425.

[48] Ibid., pp. 428-429.

[49] George Eliot, "The Natural History of German Life," Essays, p. 287.

[50] U. C. Knoepflmacher, Laughter and Despair: Readings in Ten Novels of the Victorian Era (Berkeley: University of California Press, 1971), p. 171.

[51] In The Appropriate Form: An Essay on the Novel (London: Athlone Press, 1964), Chapter 5, Barbara Hardy criticizes Will Ladislaw and Casaubon for another sort of impotence. Surely the diminished nature of their power is part of Eliot's larger point about the practical mind, the deductive reasoner.

[52] George Eliot, Middlemarch, ed. Gordon S. Haight (Cambridge: The Riverside Press, 1956), p. 612, editor's footnote.

[53] Critics as early as 1876 (Francillon) and as recently as 1960 (Robert Preyer) have called Daniel Deronda a romance rather than a realistic novel. Their discussions are found, respectively, in George Eliot: The Critical Heritage, ed. David Carroll (London: Routledge & Kegan Paul, 1971) and in "Beyond the Liberal Imagination: Vision and Unreality in Daniel Deronda," Victorian Studies 4 (1960), 33-54. See also U. C. Knoepflmacher, George Eliot's Early Novels: The Limits of Realism (Berkeley: University of California Press, 1969). He points out that Eliot's final novel transcends society and literary realism at the same time.

[54] John Cross, George Eliot's Life, p. 727.

[55] Letters, 29 October 1876, VI, 301.

[56] George Eliot, "Looking Backward," Impressions of Theophrastus Such, pp. 36-37.

⁵⁷ Ibid., p. 37.

⁵⁸ Letters, 25 November 1879, VII, 226.

⁵⁹ U. C. Knoepflmacher, Religious Humanism and the Victorian Novel: George Eliot, Walter Pater, and Samuel Butler (Princeton: Princeton University Press, 1965), p. 121.

Chapter 4

DOUBT AND "DELIBERATE FAILURE" IN THE YEARS

The most radical feature of Virginia Woolf's career is her contribution to the revolution in the novel form. The distinctive narrative voice in her works was a highly wrought innovation of style that enabled her to manipulate novelistic time and space. Her books were all experiments conceived against the form of the traditional novel. She called To the Lighthouse an "elegy," The Waves a "play-poem," and The Years an "essay-novel."[1] Yet like all novelists before her, Woolf took as her subject the relation of the individual to society, however idiosyncratically defined. In her fiction, Woolf explores selfhood in its essence and its social aspect. The Years is her most explicitly political novel, focused on the changes in English life from the Victorian era up to the growth of Fascism in Europe. A crisis with complexly tangled roots in Woolf's past and in contemporary English history shadows the novel, resulting in her strongest if not her clearest statement about the individual's relation to society. Not only the protagonists' lives but the overarching narrative consciousness is affected by events of this period. As it did in The Last Man and Felix Holt, the relation between self and society shapes the very form of The Years.

In the 1930s when Woolf agonized over the writing of The Years, her convictions about the relation of art and politics were unsettled. As a citizen (though not as a writer), Woolf essentially followed the tenets of feminist and socialist theory as they described the individual's relation to the social whole. Though she disliked political jargon, loathed "causes," and felt most theories of social reform were inadequate, Woolf periodically thought of herself as a political activist. She addressed envelopes in a Suffrage office, supported pacifists in World War I, journeyed to political meetings in Manchester, and was manifestly more than a political wife.[2] Her activism was chiefly expressed in writing, however, and she was celebrated for her tracts-- A Room of One's Own, Three Guineas, and a number of articles on the relation of politics and art. Woolf's political vision inevitably found articulation in her novels.

Like Mary Shelley and George Eliot, Woolf believes that the relation of the self to society entails the suppression of the ego in the service of some larger collective entity. What distinguishes Woolf from her nineteenth-century predecessors and allies her with Doris Lessing is the fact that ultimately not society but human subjectivity --not mankind but the collective unconscious mind--is to be served. For Woolf, the ego is an accident of history, a transitory phenomenon by turns inimical or irrelevant to the subterranean reality she once described as a "wedge-shaped core of darkness."[3] As Bernard says in The Waves, "'This is the truth'" (p. 376): "'This difference we make so much of, this identity we so feverishly cherish, [can be] overcome'" (p. 377).

For Woolf, the platonic-seeming truth that reality is one, undivided, absolute perhaps owes as much to Wordsworth as to G. E. Moore, whose Principia Ethica was Bloomsbury's bible.[4] That is, Woolf seems to imply that "our birth is but a sleep and a forgetting," that a child is born whole, perfect, and with enormous potential which suffers attrition or distortion in his or her progress through life in society. In flashes of perception, one can momentarily apprehend the reality that custom and convention blind us to: "'Immeasurably receptive, holding everything, trembling with fullness, yet clear, contained--so my being seems, now that desire urges it no more out and away; now that curiosity no longer dyes it a thousand colours. It lies deep, tideless, immune, now that he is dead, the man I called "Bernard" . . . .'" (Waves, p. 379). For Virginia Woolf's protagonists, the social identity--mother, father, hostess, businessman, teacher, philosopher, bureaucrat, soldier--is at best ephemeral, at worst a crippling deformation of the undivided being underneath. Like Bernard, Clarissa Dalloway, Mrs. Ramsay, Lucy Swithin and other characters are fleetingly gifted with insights which make intelligible if not bearable the facts of life in society.

Woolf apparently substitutes this impersonal realm, approachable only through the vision of an artist or vatic seer, for the social reality affirmed by Mary Shelley and George Eliot. The individual does not suppress his or her will in conformity to a moral duty, especially feminine duty as defined by a patriarchal society. The patriarchy, which Woolf attacks in her critical essays as well as her novels, seems unconnected with timeless, transcendent reality. And yet Woolf's "mythopoetic" realm perhaps could not exist without that timebound world.[5] Unity could not be posited in the absence of division, harmony in the absence of discord: just so, the ahistorical idea of intersubjectivity depends upon personal, historical experience.

If *The Waves* attempts to show "that in some vague way we are the same person, and not separate people," *The Years* portrays the seemingly inpenetrable walls between people in society.[6] *The Years* is a despairing admission (not wholly acknowledged by Woolf) that the oneness she believed in religiously was perhaps an illusion and the existence of social barriers, what was real and lasting. Human history rather than timeless subjectivity dominates *The Years*, suggesting that Woolf either doubts her vision or else demonstrates what would happen if she did.

As if to call attention to the departure that *The Years* represents, Woolf refers to it as a "novel of fact" and contrasts it with the non-realistic novel of "vision," a category that comprises *Mrs. Dalloway*, *To the Lighthouse*, and *The Waves*.[7] The alternation between fact and vision is one concrete manifestation of the dualism of Woolf's thought. Other terms include outer and inner; reason and imagination; criticism and creation; history and mysticism; egotism and selflessness; objectivity and subjectivity; "non-being" and "being"; and (in Woolf's lexicon) masculinity and femininity.[8] Within one novel, the artist sought to unify and harmonize these contradictory elements; in her career as a whole, Woolf saw herself oscillating between poles. For her, *The Years* was to liberate a store of facts and social criticism after the symbolic truth revealed in *The Waves*.[9]

But something went wrong. Woolf had difficulty defining her task and struggled throughout the writing of the book. (*The Years* was originally to be an "essay-novel" but the essay portion was deleted.) The novel itself has generally been viewed by critics as a falling off in her vision. The cause of this failure is difficult to define. I would suggest that it is not the realistic novel form per se--"masculine" or not--that inhibited Woolf.[10] Nor was it Woolf's loathing of partisanship and patriarchy that caused the crisis, the supposed failure to reconcile art and politics. Perhaps one might say that fact and vision, social history and mythic truth, were not so easy to discriminate as formerly. That is, the fundamental impersonal subjectivity Woolf wanted to believe in--untouched by the accidents of everyday life--seemed less separate from those accidents. The vision was contaminated by historical consciousness, which filtered into the purity of its "truth."

Briefly, for reasons buried deep in childhood experiences, Woolf seems to have identified the social self with sexual stereotypes. In the quotidian world, the male ego constantly tries to dominate the passive female. The unconscious, however, is sexless. In <u>A Room of One's Own</u> (1929), Woolf cited Coleridge's idea "that a great mind is androgynous" (p. 97). Much earlier (1906) she elaborated her theory of art to friends in letters: "But my present feeling is that this vague and dream like world, without love, or heart, or passion, or sex, is the world I really care about, and find interesting. For, though they are dreams to you, and I cant express them at all adequately, these things are perfectly real to me."[11] To another friend Woolf explained her idea that art transcends merely personal experience: ". . . it is a theory of mine that happiness and sorrow are equally good, and beautiful, if you can only find the form for them, because that tickles, supplies, the sense which is above the reach of these accidents."[12] At this same period, when she was writing her first novel and formulating her aesthetic credo, she wrote Clive Bell: ". . . I should choose my writing to be judged as a chiselled block, unconnected with my hand entirely."[13]

In a memoir written shortly before her death, Woolf reaffirmed this faith. The artist, she wrote, takes events that occur in ordinary life and synthesizes them in a meaningful pattern: each event

> is a token of some real thing behind appearances; and I make it real by putting it into words. It is only by putting it into words that I make it whole; this wholeness means that it has lost its power to hurt me; it gives me, perhaps because by doing so I take away the pain, a great delight to put the severed parts together. Perhaps this is the strongest pleasure known to me. It is the rapture I get when in writing I seem to be discovering what belongs to what; making a scene come right; making a character come together. From this I reach what I might call a philosophy . . . that behind the cotton wool is hidden a pattern; that we--I mean all human beings--are connected with this; that the whole world is a work of art; that we are parts of the work of art. ("A Sketch of the Past," p. 72)

Woolf tries in her writing to evoke total apprehension of this meaning, the feeling she says she knew as a child "that poetry was coming true" --of reading "words when they cease to be words and become so intensified that one seems to experience them . . ." ("A Sketch of the Past," p. 93). Like the words themselves, the artist's personality is effaced in these epiphanic moments of "being":

> <u>Hamlet</u> or a Beethoven quartet is the truth about this vast mass that we call the world. But there is no Shakespeare, there is no Beethoven; certainly and emphatically there is no God; we are the words; we are the music; we are the thing itself. And I see this when I have a shock. ("A Sketch of the Past," p. 72)

Woolf upheld the theory of the impersonality of art throughout her career.[14] But by the 1930s her faith was unwavering. The etiology of this would be impossible to describe definitively, yet it may be Woolf was having to consider that the truth beneath these "accidents" was not sex-free but specifically female. That is, perhaps escape from selfhood did not mean leaving behind both male and female sex roles prescribed by society. If visionary reality is to be equated with femininity, then Mrs. Ramsay does not so much escape from the Victorian matriarch's role with its immense emotional power but virtual lack of authority as she does carry self-suppression to an extreme. As we will see, the subconscious in Woolf's work does not appear to be a third thing, transcending masculine and feminine traits in a greater unity. Instead impersonality entails loss of self: the half that is aggressive, egotistic, <u>male</u>.

Why should Virginia Woolf's faith in the transcendence of art have wavered at the period when she wrote <u>The Years</u>? Perhaps she felt her own genius no longer capable of the sustained effort needed to unify the accidents of personal experience. Certainly the political climate of the 1930s exacerbated her fear that what is worst in social life could intrude upon pure subjectivity. At the same time, Woolf felt defensive about her reputation as a Bloomsbury aesthete. Perhaps Woolf was also troubled by latent and long-suppressed resentment against the family and its mirror image, society. Woolf thought she had made her peace with her family long before, that she had laid to rest her parents' ghosts in writing <u>To the Lighthouse</u>: ". . . I was obsessed by them both, unhealthily; and writing of them was a necessary act."[15] But recently critics have stressed the autobiographical nature of <u>The Years</u>, a family chronicle which locates the origin of private and public aggression in the patriarchal family. Mitchell Leaska points out that the time span of the novel virtually coincides with that of Woolf's life; that she deletes from the chronicles the years in which her greatest personal traumas occurred; and that "through this deliberately elliptical novel, this aesthetic confession, all her suffering loomed up before her in the Present and became transformed in her mind as punishment for the past."[16]

Whatever the causes of Woolf's crisis, it seems bound up with her concern about the oppression of the independent self. The Years makes an implicit statement about her notion of impersonal genius and her belief that the self was oppressed by society. Both ideas are influenced by Woolf's relation to her parents and her definition of the role of the artist. For, like Mary Shelley and George Eliot, Virginia Woolf identifies herself as a writer at least in part to escape from or mediate between limiting social roles.

Her parents gave Virginia Woolf her sense of available roles that were both positive and negative. Enthusiasm and discrimination, associated respectively with her mother and father, constitute the primary impulses of her psyche, the parentage of her writing. But this marriage of impulses was as volatile psychologically as it was in the Stephen household. From Julia Stephen, Woolf inherited her love of society:

> This social side is very genuine in me. Nor do I think it reprehensible. It is a piece of jewelry I inherit from my mother--a joy in laughter, something that is stimulated, not selfishly wholly or vainly, by contact with my friends. And then ideas leap in me.[17]

She wrote Ethel Smyth, answering the charge that she was sexually frigid:

> And I reply (I think often while holding their hands, and getting exquisite pleasure from contact with either male or female body) "But what I want of you is illusion--to make the world dance." More than that, I cannot get any sense of unity and coherency and all that makes me wish to write the Lighthouse etc. unless I am perpetually stimulated. Its no good sitting in a garden with a book; or collecting facts. There must be this fanning and drumming. . . . Where people mistake, as I think, is in perpetually narrowing and naming these immensely composite and wide flung passions--driving stakes through them, herding them between screens.[18]

In the same vein, another letter links love and imagination: "Take away my love for my friends & my burning & pressing sense of the importance & lovability & curiosity of human life & I should be nothing but a membrane, a fibre, uncoloured, lifeless to be thrown away like any other excreta."[19] The asexual passion was associated with her mother's gift for unifying the discords in family and social groups. In "A Sketch of the Past," Woolf wrote, "She was the whole thing. . . . She was keeping what I call in my shorthand the panoply of life--that which we all lived in common--in being" (p. 83).

Woolf's version of "feminine" creativity was the act of writing: ". . . these efforts of mine to communicate with people are partly childlessness, and the horror that sometimes overcomes me."[20] She wrote another correspondent: ". . . one tries to imagine oneself in contact, in sympathy; one tries vainly to put off this interminable--what is the word I want?--something between maze and catacomb--of the flesh. And all one achieves is a grimace. And so one is driven to write books . . . ."[21] To communicate is to escape the limits of the body, to transcend one's single mortality in an activity like parenting. Writing did not wholly take the place of having children, Woolf always admitted; but apparently she felt her creativity was distinctly feminine.[22]

Femininity in its maternal form is not unambiguously laudable in Woolf's fiction; even Lily Briscoe sees Mrs. Ramsay's faults. Woolf's private opinion, no doubt tinged with envy, was expressed to her sister Vanessa: ". . . I slightly distrust or suspect the maternal passion. It is obviously immeasurable and unscrupulous. . . . I don't like profound instincts--not in human relationships."[23] But Woolf's dislike of family bonds and obligations was generalized and is traceable to her relation with her father as well.

Her ambivalence toward "profound instincts . . . in human relationships" owes a great deal to the demands made by Leslie Stephen. When Ethel Smyth pursued her, Woolf explained her resentment by alluding to her youthful subservience to her father.

> Your extreme susceptibility to criticism and your vast . . . need of sympathy inevitably make one feel that one cannot be at ones ease, and free, and careless with you as with other people. . . . One therefore feels that one is limiting oneself, being simpler, cruder and less communicative than is natural. The same thing has happened to me twice before--once with my father whom I adored.

"Limiting oneself" to the role exacted by another person in a relation: this was abhorrent to Woolf. And yet she acknowledged all that Leslie Stephen endowed her with. Her genius and vocation, for one thing: "If my father didn't leave me pearls, this was by way of a makeshift."[25] Her sureness of taste, her coolly ironical judgments, reflect her admiration for Stephen's intellectual honesty. In many ways, he was the model on which she patterned herself.

The combination of profound feeling with discernment is found early in Woolf's private expressions of her intellectual values. She criticized Leslie Stephen's Quaker sister, whose kindness irritated the daughter as much as it had the father: "Also I disagree entirely with her whole system of toleration and resignation, and general benignity, which does seem to me so woolly."[26] In another letter she continued, "I mean you criticised me, certainly; which I dont mind, because I think criticism is the only sound basis of appreciation . . . ."[27] Much later (1930) in a letter to Ethel Smyth, Woolf referred to these two impulses in a definition of genius: "And enthusiasm . . . is not enough. No, nor discrimination either. It is the rare and blessed combination that I find truly imaginative--and I grant that having been born within the Polar region of Cambridge I tend by education not instinct to frigidity."[28] The Cambridge atmosphere is that in which she was raised; the education begun in Leslie Stephen's study was reinforced by Bloomsbury.

On Leslie Stephen's birthday in 1928, Woolf wrote in her diary, "His life would have entirely ended mine. What would have happened? No writing, no books;--inconceivable."[29] If it is true that his death made her writing possible by putting an end to his moral judgment, his emotional demands, his potential criticism of her work, it is equally true that his life made her writing possible.

The madness which became the source of her art was deeply connected with Woolf's feelings about both parents.[30] She seems to have unconsciously regarded her breakdowns as deserved punishments for wrongs done them. Immediately after Leslie Stephen's death, her guilt was strongest: "The dreadful thing is that I never did enough for him all those years. . . . If he had only lived we could have been so happy. But it is all gone."[31] This intense, self-pitying reproach was muted following Woolf's breakdown. And with the grief, her egotism was subdued (at least temporarily): "I do think I may emerge less selfish and cocksure than I went in and with greater understanding of the troubles of others."[32]

It has been suggested that Julia Stephen's death prompted more lasting guilt because Woolf had less sympathy for her mother than her father and because Julia's death occurred at a critical period of Woolf's adolescence.[33] Having wished both parents dead so that she could live, Woolf would be plagued by guilt after every self-assertive act of writing and publishing. In her biography, Phyllis Rose speculates that Woolf felt guilty at "deny[ing] a certain female role they [her parents] sought, or she felt they sought, to impose on her."[34] Woolf denied this role by becoming a writer, but her postpartum suffering after she finished each novel may have resulted from the "enormously aggressive act of writing a book," usurping a masculine role.[35] Yet, as I have suggested, Woolf's own description of her creativity stresses its feminine component. It is this which Woolf felt was threatened by aggressiveness in "masculine" society in the 1930s. To appreciate Woolf's reaction to this threat, we must first understand her theory of androgynous genius and its importance for her.

Despite the obvious connection between filial resentment and guilt, and her breakdowns, Woolf regarded her madness as in a sense uncaused, unconnected with such "accidents" as family relationships and social roles. She would tell E. M. Forster, "Not that I haven't picked up something from my insanities and all the rest. Indeed, I suspect they've done instead of religion."[36] Later she was even more explicit with Ethel Smyth: "As an experience, madness is terrific I can assure you, and not to be sniffed at; and in its lava I still find most of the things I write about.[37] The wholeness of the vision proceeds from the wholeness of the artist's unconscious mind, its faculties working toward one end. As a reader or critic of her own work or others', Woolf acknowledged the censorship of a number of inner phantoms, particularly the Angel in the House and the Victorian patriarch.[38] Woolf always insisted, however, that in creation her mind was incandescent and sexless, free of social identity. In writing, "one must become externalised; very, very concentrated, all at one point, not having to draw upon the scattered parts of one's character, living in the brain. Sydney comes & I'm Virginia, but only when I'm scattered & various & gregarious. Now . . . I'd like to be only a sensibility."[39] Ten years later she reaffirmed her "philosophy of anonymity": "I will not be 'famous,' 'great.' I will go on adventuring, changing, opening my mind and my eyes, refusing to be stamped and stereotyped. The thing is to free one's self: to let it find its dimensions, not be impeded."[40] Madness and its legacy, genius, put one _outside_ the conventional roles.[41]

The anonymous sensibility of the artist produces "impersonal works" such as Woolf's novels where multiple characters speak in one voice[42]; where subjectivity knows no sex, however individual characters are constrained by sexually defined roles; where felt duration replaces clock-time; where sensitivity is measured by empathy, the imaginative ability to become another person and so transcend one's social identity. In Woolf's novels, the artist-figure perhaps best embodies this androgynous empathy.

In the original manuscript of _Between the Acts_, called "Pointz Hall," Woolf wrote of "This nameless spirit then, who is not 'we' nor 'I,' nor the novelist either" which creates a fictive analogue of the reality that "is not mind or body, not surface or depths, but a common element in which the perishable is preserved and the separate become one."[43] Miss La Trobe (_Between the Acts_) is an unromantic version of Lily Briscoe (_To the Lighthouse_): both emulate the "nameless spirit." Bernard, in _The Waves_, best articulates Woolf's position. His final monologue describes the difficulty of the artist's task: to convey abstract reality that is beneath and prior to human contact and even self-consciousness: "'But how describe the world seen without a self? There are no words'" (The Waves, p. 376). He asks, "'What is the phrase for the moon? And the phrase for love? By what name are we to call death? I do not know. I need a little language such as lovers use, words of one syllable such as children speak. . . . a howl; a cry. . . . None of those resonances and lovely echoes . . ." (pp. 281-282).

Both Bernard and Virginia Woolf want to portray the "truth" that precedes the artist's rendering. Like Lily Briscoe's painting, Woolf's novels attempt to suggest the feeling "that beauty . . . is only got by the failure to get it; by grinding all the flints together; by facing what must be humiliation--the things one can't do . . . ."[44] Woolf wrote Vita Sackville-West that

> the main thing in beginning a novel is to feel, not that you can write it, but that it exists on the far side of a gulf, which words can't cross: that its to be pulled through only in a breathless anguish.[45]

This very failure to describe the ineffable is what Woolf hopes to convey: Lily's and Bernard's frustration is modelled on her own. She told T. S. Eliot her work was "'futile. Negligible. One goes on because of an illusion.' He told me that I talked like that without meaning it. Yet I do mean it."[46] Woolf's dilemma is not the linguistic crisis which Doris Lessing faces--that words seem no longer to connect with solid objects. Rather, Woolf tries to suggest the pre-verbal reality--whether one calls it "truth," intersubjectivity, collective unconsciousness--of which words can give only partial and imperfect glimpses.

The act of writing alone evokes what is just beyond the reach of the pen, prior to the word. Writing means gestation, giving birth to artifacts that are versions of one's self. The "illusions," as Bernard calls them, are manifold, in Woolf's novels and in her own private world of myth.[47] There is the myth of her childhood: "Why am I so incredibly & incurably romantic about Cornwall? One's past, I suppose: I see children running in the garden. . . . well, Leonard, & almost 40 years of life, all built on that, permeated by that: how much so I could never explain."[48] There is the romance of herself (like Mr. Ramsay) as stoic sufferer: ". . . forging ahead, alone, through the night: of suffering inwardly, stoically; of blazing my way through to the end--and so forth."[49] And of course, the myth of her vatic madness: ". . . this elemental fact--what a crazy piece of work I am--like a cracked looking glass in a fair. Only, as I write this, it strikes me that as usual I am romancing, led on irresistibly by the lure of some phrase; and that in fact Virginia is so simple, so simple, so simple: just give her things to play with, like a child."[50] Paradoxically, these personal romances, wordspun illusions, are the only means of getting at the truth of the world "without a self."

If there is a figure that the artist pursues down the corridors of memory, it seems feminine. The "truth" of this undivided reality partakes of the maternal more than the androgynous. Bernard's epiphany suggests that "feminine" intuition leads to his insight: "'The old nurse who turns the pages of the picture-book had stopped and had said, "Look. This is the truth"'" (<u>The Waves</u>, p. 376). It is Woolf's own image for the transcendence of the social identity, for the escape from anxieties of the personal and timebound. She told Ethel Smyth that her maternal affection gave her "protection":

> Its the child crying for the nurses hand in the dark. You do it by being so uninhibited: so magnificently unself-conscious. This is what people pay ₤ 20 a sitting to get from Psycho-analysts--liberation from their own egotism. . . . I think you're right--we all cry for nurses hand.[51]

Writing represents a like return to that mythic childhood realm of absolute security, where one's identity need not be defined or defended. The guide who leads one back to this state seems to be, in Woolf's sexual mythos, feminine: the muse is maternal, as we will see is true for Doris Lessing. Being a writer, Woolf is simultaneously mother and child--creating and receiving form. Her conception of the androgynous imagination, it appears, verges on the passive, self-effacing ideal of Victorian femininity.[52]

Woolf felt that reasoning power was a specifically masculine ability to accommodate rather than run away from unpleasant reality. She admired her husband's ability to sift facts and deduce from them an explanation or solution of a problem:

> L. has been telling me about Germany, & reparations, how money is paid. Lord what a weak brain I have--like an unused muscle. He talks; & the facts come in, & I can't deal with them. But by dint of very painful brain exercises, perhaps I understand a little more than Nelly of the International situation. And L. understands it all--picks up all these points out of the daily paper absolutely instantly, has them connected, ready to produce. Sometimes I think my brain & his are of different orders.[53]

Deprecating her understanding of her own work, she welcomed G. L. Dickinson's appreciation of The Waves as a reasoned statement of her aims in the novel:

> What you say you felt about the Waves is exactly what I wanted to convey. Many people say that it is hopelessly sad--but I didn't mean that. I did want somehow to make out if only for my own satisfaction a reason for things. That of course is putting it more definitely than I have a right to, for my reasons are only general conceptions, that strike me as I walk about London and then

> I try to fit my little figures in. . . . What the significance is, heaven knows I cant guess; but there is significance--that I feel overwhelmingly. Perhaps for me--with my limitations,--I mean lack of reasoning power and so on--all I can do is to make an artistic whole; and leave it at that.[54]

The artist perceives unity, the critic categorizes and divides to find "reasons." It is this unifying function--accounting for the way things cohere--that Woolf came to feel herself incapable of performing. In the decade when she wrote The Years, when Europe faced a political crisis that threatened individual liberty, the task of identifying and explaining the causes of human unhappiness overwhelmed her.

Perceiving significance behind apparently random events was important to Woolf from the very first. In "A Sketch of the Past," Woolf describes three childhood "shocks" that lastingly impressed her. One was fighting with her brother Thoby; another, seeing a flower as part of a whole "ring" including the earth it was rooted in; the last, hearing of the suicide of a family friend. Woolf described the effect of these "shocks" on her: ". . . many of these exceptional moments brought with them a peculiar horror and a physical collapse; they seemed dominant; myself passive" (p. 72). Her explanation of why only the middle moment--perceiving the flower as a whole--seemed satisfactory was that "in the case of the flower I found a reason; and thus was able to deal with the sensation" (p. 72). The other two moments, which made her feel despair, were inexplicable at the time: ". . . I was quite unable to deal with the pain of discovering that people hurt each other; that a man I had seen had killed himself. The sense of horror held me powerless" (p. 72). Woolf seemed to believe that "horror" came from apparent senselessness and inexplicability; if reasons could be found for aggressive, destructive behavior, then even such "shocks" became a "revelation of some order" (p. 72). It seems more likely, however, that violence, aggression, and self-destruction were peculiarly horrible to her. Their connection to the "masculine" order of society is clear. The passive "feminine" sensibility which seeks pattern and order and beauty can be defeated by such "shocks." This, I would suggest, is what happened to Virginia Woolf in the 1930s.

The unconscious sensibility Woolf drew upon when writing was threatened in the 1930s. There are personal reasons for this: the deaths of a number of close friends including Lytton Strachey (in 1932) and Roger Fry (1934). Recurrence of congenital ill-health must be considered, the tendency toward insanity that she quite possibly inherited.[55] Then, too, Woolf's role as an "outsider" and rebel against Victorian and Edwardian conventions, both social and literary, was now being challenged by a newer generation for whom she represented the Establishment.[56] Finally, the political climate of the 1930s would have exacerbated such private despair about the value of creating beautiful artifacts in the face of the breakdown of civilized society. Personal and public chaos made order seem more and more illusory.

Woolf was especially preoccupied with politics in this decade, more intensely than with suffrage or socialism, pacifism or passive resistance. The threat to the individual psyche by the tyrannical father became external and hugely symbolic. As Woolf wrote in Three Guineas, "Society it seems was a father . . . ."[57] The Victorian patriarch was stronger than ever in the Fascist dictator who carried domestic tyranny to public extremes.[58] The nightmare, it seemed, was not personal but historically universal. Not merely her individual identity but the sanctity of aesthetic freedom was jeopardized: not only the artist, but art as well.

The individual soul could be threatened by violation; her horror at this prospect recurs throughout Woolf's novels and personal writings. Septimus Smith in <u>Mrs. Dalloway</u> dreaded the "conversion" offered by Doctors Holmes and Bradshaw. Woolf described religious and political conversion in terms of rape; like Septimus, she felt susceptible to violation by the will of male authority:

> Now about Causes. Of course . . . I'm not such a pacifist as to deny that practical evils must be put to the sword: I admit fighting to the death for votes, wages, peace, and so on: what I can't abide is the man who wishes to convert other men's minds; that tampering with beliefs seems to me impertinent, insolent, corrupt beyond measure. I never pass through Hyde Park without cursing separately every God inventor there. This is partly because . . . some cousins in particular, the daughters of Fitzjames, rasped and agonised us as children by perpetual attempts at conversion. As they were ugly women, who sweated, I conceived a greater hatred for them than ever for anyone. And even now, when no one tries, I still draw in and shiver at the suspicion--he's got a finger in my mind.[59]

Whether the tyrant takes the shape of dictator, Harley Street physician, or elderly cousin, Woolf's response to oppression is horror.

This response is in part an aesthetic one. Her revulsion against political jargon and partisanship has a similar basis. After a campaign trip to Manchester with Leonard, she described the political meeting in her diary as having no "surface brilliancy; not a scrap of romance."[60] Suffrage meetings elicited the same ambivalence--sympathy for the cause and revulsion against the political platitudes she heard:

> The hall was fairly well filled; the audience almost wholly women, as the speakers were too. The pure essence of either sex is a little disheartening. . . . I get one satisfactory thrill from the sense of the multitude; then become disillusioned, finally bored & unable to listen to a word. . . . I . . . thought very badly of this form of art.[61]

Woolf's distaste for "ugly" behavior extended to her own life; she

preferred remaining outside the fray to engaging in (egotistic) self-
assertion. She advised Ethel Smyth, impractically, to cease complaining about the discrimination she suffered as a woman composer and

> to furbish up some orchestra and run the things on your own. This
> I did--oh yes, in a modest way, when the publishers told me to
> write what they liked. I said No. I'll publish myself and write
> what I like.[62]

If the facts are ugly, repudiate them: establish an identity outside
society and its norms.

Woolf was not an aesthete who abhorred what she found mediocre
or idiosyncratic in people whose class differed from hers. Nor did she
dislike mankind in the mass, regardless of class, sex, or political
affiliation. Her attitude seems not so much contradictory as paradoxical. The special beauty of the discrete--word or personality--is what
she cherished. It is what paradoxically made perceptible the greater
unity in which differences dissolved. One could only find (so she
felt) one's own route to this experience. The dilemma was that the
ugliness that proscribed or inhibited perception of beauty could be
unresponsive to the individual vision.

Because she dissociated genius and political partisanship,
because in her view the creative artist transcended and was "outside"
society, Woolf was especially vulnerable when her vision was
threatened by the persistence of ugly facts. I would suggest that in
the 1930s Woolf came to doubt her vision; what had seemed absolute
might be accidental and transitory. The historical fact--the endurance of social oppression--seemed more real. Ugliness, divisiveness,
randomness, and deadening repetition threatened to overtake society.
Pursuit of the truth became an illusion, truth conceived as undivided,

absolute, beautiful and superior to accidents of class, sex and other such distinctions. As I have suggested, this truth may have been peculiarly "feminine" and therefore especially liable to oppression by the symbolic patriarch--society as a whole.

Writing in the 1930s, Woolf was preoccupied with defining the relationship, as she then perceived it, between politics and literature. In the 1937 broadcast entitled "Craftmanship," she asserted that "words never make anything that is useful; and words are the only things that tell the truth and nothing but the truth."[63] Coercing words, intending them to carry information, is destructive of the subconscious associations which enrich them. Literature must evidently be pure: such motives and uses are illegitimate in art. Consciousness of utility intrudes upon creativity; and part of that practical consciousness is political thought.

The value of any creation is a function of its author's "freedom of mind, security of person, and immunity from practical affairs," Woolf wrote in another essay.[64] In "The Leaning Tower," she indicted political turmoil as a cause of obscurity, ugliness and egotism in modern fiction. Writers in stable societies were luckier: "That unconsciousness was an immense advantage."[65] Virginia Woolf believed that excessive awareness of social, economic and political crises fosters excessive self-consciousness. When the artist's ego takes over, his work becomes the vehicle of opinions, an abuse of the art form.

Despite the assurance of such pronouncements in essays, Virginia Woolf was troubled by her own helplessness in the face of the crises of the 1930s. She believed in passive resistance; she doubted the efficacy of political and social reforms to change humanity; and she felt, as an "outsider," cut off from the problems.[66] Privately, however, the uncertainty of this position tormented her. Her diary reveals a tentativeness lacking in her public statements. For example: ". . . non-resistance. . . . That should be our view. But then if society is in its present state?" (AWD, p. 247). Significantly, in this same diary entry she records that Leonard "says that politics ought to be separate from art"; she does not tell what *she* said. Instead, The Years is her statement, her political contribution.

In Three Guineas she ironically wrote that turning Antigone into "anti-Fascist propaganda" would be "mutilation."[67] The Years is a fiction which has suffered such mutilation. It is the product of the very conditions Woolf said would destroy art: anxiety and confusion about the political future, the breakdown of community, and the loss of social and aesthetic decorums. These preoccupations inhibit the artist and prevent her escaping from the burden of self-consciousness. The result is a novel that turns in on itself.

Though it is the preaching of an unbeliever, we might call The Years an exemplum which demonstrates the impossibility (Woolf felt) of writing visionary fiction under conditions of repression and suffering. Whether or not Woolf consciously calculated upon this outcome, we know she imposed conditions upon her writing with the deliberateness of a scientist conducting an experiment. There is even an admission that this was (in part) her intention in The Years: "the point is that I myself know why it's a failure, and that its failure is deliberate" (AWD, p. 267). Yet Woolf's recognition comes after her achievement; she realizes what she must have intended when she sees the outcome in her novel. It was unlikely, perhaps even impossible, that Woolf ever would have consciously admitted to herself and published her doubts about the transcendent purity of art.

The Years fails to render a vision of unity and harmony persisting through the ugly, violent accidents of history. But this is not to say that rendering such a vision was Woolf's purpose. The Years is an anti-visionary novel--and to some extent was intended to be, though Virginia Woolf's imagination was severely strained by the effort of writing such a work. It is Woolf's resistance to the implications of her own pessimism that yields contradiction and confusion within the novel.

The depressing style of The Years, which has been called Woolf's worst novel, has inspired eloquent criticism. W. H. Mellers grudgingly admires her skill in conveying "a quality of passive desolation which is comparable with the neurasthenic weariness and fatigue" of Kurt Weill's music.[68] Josephine O'Brien Schaefer captures the "almost Swiftean revulsion from the human flesh" that characterizes the style of the novel.[69] Critics have not, however, generally accounted for the scope, nature, and especially function of such flaws. I would like to explore the possibility that Woolf sought, though unconsciously, to write an anti-visionary novel, one that would admit the vulnerability of her own aesthetic.

A Writer's Diary attests to Woolf's deep skepticism in the 1930s about the communicability of her vision of truth and even about the possibility of literary creation itself. The Years seems a necessary result of the convergence of particular social forces and aesthetic values. It is both an unconscious product of and a deliberate protest against conditions that Woolf deplored in essays throughout that decade. The contradictions in her achievement come from the irreconcilability of Woolf's professed aims in the novel.

Woolf says of The Years that it is "a creative, a constructive book" (AWD, p. 268) but also that "it's a failure, and that its failure is deliberate" (AWD, p. 267). To help us interpret Woolf's contradictory attitude toward the novel, we may turn to an early review, one that Woolf herself applauded. Basil de Selincourt's article in The Observer convinced her "that my intention in The Years may be not so entirely muted and obscured as I feared" (AWD, p. 268). De Selincourt finds that the novel "drives toward disjunction."[70] Motifs such as deaths and unsuccessful dinner parties contribute to social disintegration on the level of the plot. More abstractly, on the level of what he calls "poetry," de Selincourt characterizes The Years as a "kaleidoscope" of "tiny cubes" of consciousness, each inevitably isolated from the others. Though he thinks Virginia Woolf has sought to overcome separateness between minds by objectifying it in fiction, de Selincourt feels the quest is paradoxical. In Woolf's representation of consciousness, the poetic image calls attention to itself in a way that ultimately isolates the apprehending mind--inside and outside of the fiction. It is a self-contradictory technique used in a self-defeating quest.

Other contemporary reviewers found in The Years a radical skepticism about human communication. John Hawley Roberts thought that "to write a novel demonstrating that there is no chance of understanding ourselves or our neighbors is almost perverse"; Woolf is "cutting off the flow of fiction at its source."[71] Roberts and de Selincourt see that The Years is a complex work examining the very possibility of literary creation and communication. Virginia Woolf herself recommends that we approach The Years in this way.

Entries in A Writer's Diary record her states of mind in writing and her working plans for the novel. Reconstructing the context in which Woolf wrote the novel is important, for it has been perhaps too convenient to ascribe its "failure" to a lapse in creative power or to menopausal tensions.[72] While it is finally impossible to prove subconscious motives and influences, it may be that Woolf was right to insist that The Years is not merely "a tired book, a last effort" (AWD, p. 266).

During the three years when Woolf was chiefly occupied in writing The Years (1932-1935), her diary entries reveal extremes of pessimism and exhilaration, a manic-depressive rhythm that Woolf desired to capture in the book. Her own state of mind--"all I know, feel, laugh at, despise, like, admire, hate and so on"--was to be reflected (AWD, p. 191). As well as this flux of feelings, the novel would contain "satire, comedy, poetry, narrative" (AWD, p. 191). But taken singly, none of these genres would provide an adequate form for her purposes; Woolf wondered, "What form is to hold them all together?" (AWD, p. 191). Clearly The Years began as a conscious departure from traditional novel form. We shall see that it became a departure from her own vision as well.

Woolf originally conceived of The Years as a paradoxical composite of "propaganda" and fiction (AWD, p. 236), a "novel of fact" (AWD, p. 184), more radically, "an Essay-Novel" (AWD, p. 183). Her original goal was to alternate chapters of essay and fiction in order to create a hybrid of (potentially conflicting) ends and means. But ultimately she saw that the potency of the work required her "leaving out the interchapters--compacting them in the text" (AWD, p. 189). The novel itself would embody her argument. Nevertheless, setting aside the essay did not resolve her problems with form; as late as 1935 she recorded that "a kind of form is, I hope, imposing itself" (AWD, p. 248). By this time, Woolf appeared to feel that the novel was not fully under her control. Perhaps it might be truer to say she seemed reluctant to acknowledge consciously the implications of what she was writing.

Critics usually hold that formal symmetry was never realized in The Years because the author failed to synthesize fact and vision.[74] Her diary, however, suggests that Woolf may have deliberately restrained the unifying impulse in herself that would have made the book, formally, a single thing. At times she willfully resisted both the "tug to vision" (AWD, p. 184) and the full presentation of background facts (AWD, p. 276). Some part of her being evidently willed this uneasy compromise as the set of conditions from which The Years was to evolve. The conflict which impeded her writing is not necessarily then between fact and vision but perhaps between writing and revising. For Woolf wrote fairly fluently from 1932 until about 1935, when problems of "architecting" began to trouble her (AWD, p. 238). Perhaps it was in the revision process that she had to confront the implications of form or lack of it in The Years.

Rewriting was always "the chillest part of the whole business of writing, the most depressing--exacting" (AWD, p. 70). In earlier books, Woolf conceived the form first (Jacob's Room; To the Lighthouse; The Waves), and revision had taken the direction of unifying and harmonizing. She rewrote Mrs. Dalloway as "one works with a wet brush over the whole, and joins parts separately composed and gone dry" (AWD, p. 68). She aimed at "one consecutive writing of The Waves etc.--the interludes--so as to work it into one" (AWD, p. 158). In that novel, her goal was "a saturated unchopped completeness" (AWD, p. 160). But just as Woolf worked on The Years without a clear, controlling idea of form, so revision also involved a departure from her usual practice:

> The thing is to contract: each scene to be a scene: much drama-
> tised: contrasted: each to be carefully dominated by one
> interest: some generalised. (AWD, p. 224)

This comment, with its colons and lack of subordination, actually imitates the effect of independent, juxtaposed units that her design for The Years embraced. The diary further reveals that Woolf sought an effect of discontinuity "by breaking up, the use of thought skipping and parentheses" (AWD, p. 233). This fragmenting of voice and thought seems to have been inimical to her genius, contrary to her deepest creative instincts: the instinct to perceive flower and earth in a ring, as a coherent whole.

Woolf's method of deliberate disruptiveness yielded obscurity in The Years, where intelligible patterning is difficult to perceive. The weather interludes that preface the chapters, for example, seem to announce a structure that is not to be found. There is no single temporal relationship between interlude and narrative; not even any absolute correspondence between the length of a preface and that of the succeeding story; and no apparent consistency in the duration of either interludes or narratives. Other patterns, especially imagistic, suggest themselves. Echoes between images repeated in the interludes and in the text necessarily signal important correspondences, the reader thinks. But these are false clues: images whose recurrence gives only an illusion of meaning; pseudo-symbols with no ultimate resonance; and purposeless, self-duplicating actions.

Lack of significant patterning makes The Years difficult to read, but even more mystifying is the monotonous repetitiveness which characterizes the novel. The Years is a labyrinth in which there are a number of stylistic blind alleys. Images, actions, thoughts, dialogue, and other units of meaning are repeated and induce us to look for some underlying principle. In The Years, we wonder with Eleanor, "Does everything then come over again a little differently? . . . If so, is there a pattern; a theme, recurring, like music; half remembered, half foreseen?" (p. 369). This question remains unanswered; the desired pattern is withheld. What should be a narrative technique for unifying a fictional world apparently usurps the author's control. But this effect of chaos may be deliberate. It is achieved through two types of calculated repetition. The first involves repetition of thought, speech, and gesture by the characters in the novel. The second sort is repetition of images, phrases, and events by the author. Both types coalesce in the final section, "Present Day," where the characters assemble to confront the chaos of their lives, and where an answer to Eleanor's question should be forthcoming.

Critics often blame the disunity of The Years of the inadequacies of its characters. Eleanor Pargeter is the chief target of such criticism by Charles Hoffman, for example: "too much of a burden is placed on Eleanor's interrupted and often discursive vision. . . ."[74] Hoffman and others believe Woolf wanted Eleanor to be a successful unifying force within the novel, like Clarissa Dalloway or Mrs. Ramsay.

But there is evidence in her diary that Woolf deliberately weakened the visionary powers of her character, to caricature the great unifiers in her other novels.[75] Eleanor cannot create experiences that will endure as revivifying memories. Instead of renewing themselves by reliving experience meaningfully, characters like Eleanor merely re-enact their pasts.

Efforts to comprehend and control life in The Years yield only deformation. Cliché behavior dominates the Pargiters' lives, and with the repetition of thoughts, speeches, and gestures, life turns into grotesque caricature. Abel Pargiter's daughters Delia and Rose, among others, become obsessed with private fictions as they grow older. Delia, full of passionate rebellion in "1880," despises her father's hypocritical grief at his wife's death (p. 47). When she next appears in the novel, however, her own life has become merely a performance. Like a character actress, Delia perpetually plays the role of the "harum-scarum Irish hostess" (p. 365). Her sister Rose continues to inhabit the mythic world of childhood, pretending that she is "Pargiter of Pargiter's Horse." While her upright bearing contributes to her storybook heroism, it also betrays an inner rigidity. The encounter with an exhibitionist at age ten obviously terrified her so much that, thirty years later, her manner still reveals its repression. Questioning Maggie in "1910" about drunken men following her at night, Rose armors herself against masculine attack, pinning and buttoning herself together "as if she were making ready" (p. 173). The psychological background of repressed sexual fear is masked by the "Pargiter's Horse" romance; consequently, her own existence shrinks to the dimensions of an oft-told tale. Perhaps her deafness is the ultimate symbol of this withdrawal into a private world of memories and fancies.

The sterility of repeated action is evoked through habits and features handed down from one Pargiter to another. The inheritance of nervous tics and other unproductive behavior--the fumbling with the tea kettle wick in "1880" and "1908"--implies that a crazy sort of determinism operates in the novel. Unconsciously and unwillingly repeated by generations of Pargiters, such actions acquire the general status of myths or rituals but are devoid of spiritual purpose.

As well as action, thought is controlled by insidious clichés. The smoke that dominates the landscape in the preface to "1891" becomes literal smoke from Eugenie's bonfire. To Abel Pargiter, it symbolizes the passing of his youth and the departure of his children (p. 128). This uncharacteristic sentimentality is determined by a mental operation of which the Colonel is unaware: the smoky rooms have brought to mind the truism, "one must burn one's own smoke" (pp. 127-128). His poignant insight--"perhaps he never would tell anybody anything"--is reduced by association to the level of cliché. Only the reader perceives the ironic aptness of this judgment on the Colone's life--and on everyone else's.

Words can actually dictate thought processes. One can trace the genealogy of the word "poppy-cock," for example. Eleanor first hears it used at Renny's party in "1917" (p. 286) by Nicholas, who probably passes it on to his friend Sally. She includes it in a letter to North, who adopts the word and recalls it twice at the final party. The first time he is consciously trying to add it to his vocabulary; the second use is unconscious--it has dictated his thoughts. War is "poppy-cock," politics is "poppy-cock"--the ineffectuality of the word, seemingly the Pargiters' only tool against such threats, is shown by its occurrence during World War I and during the Fascist buildup of power. Minds thus trapped linguistically, whose thoughts are dictated by single words, fail utterly to master the world around them.

These instances of cliché behavior proliferate, all sharing certain traits: (1) origin in a verbal construct; (2) failure to result in either catharsis or productive action; (3) perpetual, compulsive repetition. Human beings are controlled by fictions, instead of using them to confront reality.

We must further recall that the Pargiters' fiction-dominated lives are circumscribed by the larger fiction of the novel. Woolf enforces the feeling that they repeat themselves in speech and thought by using stylistic repetition. Recurring objects become the focus for different pairs of eyes. The pigeons' cooing echoes like a refrain throughout the book and is heard in turn by Kitty in "1880," by Eleanor in "1891" and "1910," and by the whole family assembled in "Present Day." An empty repetition, however, it does not serve to join multiple minds by connecting thought processes as do the plane and clock chimes in Mrs. Dalloway. The portrait of Rose Pargiter is a more effective link between minds; its symbolic importance lies in the history of its neglect. In "1880" the portrait depicts a red-haired girl who bears no resemblance to the dying mother. In subsequent years it becomes clouded with dirt. Martin finds in "1908" that "it had ceased to be his mother; it had become a work of art" (p. 149). In "Present Day" Eleanor has the picture restored, but she cannot overcome the schism between representation and reality: Peggy repudiates the family resemblance between her grandmother and herself (p. 325). In The Years, characters either do not perceive or do not wish to acknowledge links through such solid objects to other human beings.

Still another sort of repetition cannot be explained by reference to the round of life in which the Pargiters are fixed. The repetition of adverbs is an idiosyncrasy of style in this novel which demands recognition as a conscious, deliberate device. Their occurrence is of several conspicuous sorts.

The amount of reported dialogue in The Years is extraordinary for a Woolf novel (if we except The Waves, where the soliloquies were not meant to emulate lifelike dialogue). The overuse of adverbs in The Years seems flagrant and denotes not lack of skill or carelessness so much as despair. Woolf uses adverbial modifiers to sum up characterization in single words. Some people never change; for example, Kitty's gruffness merely intensifies. In "1880," she speaks "briefly" and "rather sharply"; in "1914," "brusquely" and "perfunctorily"; and in "Present Day," "rather fiercely" (perhaps thinking of her unhappy youth).

On the other hand, adverbs may convey the evolution of personality. In "1880" the rebellious Delia speaks "severely," "irritably," "tentatively," "boldly," "abruptly," "suddenly," "briefly," "wildly" and "dully." Resigned to her fate, in "Present Day" she talks "rather shortly," "dryly" and "quite simply." Through such adverbial shorthand, characterization is reduced to caricature. Though the technique itself is not comic, it is used deliberately to undermine the seriousness of the drama unfolding.

An extraordinary number of adverbs occur at moments of emotional crisis in the plot. The preponderance of adverbs may mean that

Virginia Woolf is imitating the tension felt by the characters, but the effect is that of deflecting our absorption in the events of the novel to her own artifice. At the Pargiter tea table in "1880," Delia talks "idly," then "irritably"; Milly answers "severely"; Rose, "grumpily." Martin turns away "sharply," Milly exclaims "warningly" as the Colonel enters and looks at them "fiercely." He drinks tea "perfunctorily" and addresses them "sharply, but not unkindly." Delia speaks "tentatively," then "boldly," only to be answered "surlily." As the party ends, the Colonel "imperiously" sends Martin away (pp. 10-15). The scene is full of "suppressed emotion" (p. 44) which cannot be conveyed through speech, only through gesture and manner. Yet it seems that Virginia Woolf has temporarily suspended what she called "the appalling effort of saying what I meant."[76] To tell "how" and "how much" characters feel she lapses into adverbial prose, which clearly cannot carry the weight of her meaning.

The use of such modifiers to describe Kitty's trip to Scotland in "1914" actually undercuts the visionary content. The passage invites reading as a lyrical description of Kitty's escape into the natural world after the stifling atmosphere of London society. The chapter ends in a vision of union with the land comparable to several such moments in <u>Orlando</u>. In the morning on the terrace, Kitty "saunter(s) slowly," looking at the library which appears "more than usually stately, its proportions seemly," whose books "exist silently, with dignity, by themselves, for themselves." On the hillside which rises "sharply," she "suddenly" sees the sky "extraordinarily blue." The land, she thinks, is "existing by itself, for itself," the land itself, singing to itself." However tempting, it is impossible to read this passage as totally affirmative, because of the self-consciousness of the style. Though this description is perhaps the best approximation in The Years of what Virginia Woolf called the "'beautiful writing'" of her other fiction (AWD, p. 218), there are reasons to interpret the passage as a parody of that writing style, one which finally resists serious interpretation:

Virginia Woolf deliberately eschewed her usual style in The Years: it was to have "no 'beautiful writing,'" as she wrote in her diary (p. 218). The Scotland passage is suspect, therefore, by virtue of its anomalous character.

The multiplicity of adverbs throughout The Years puts the modifiers in this passage, whether adverbs, or nouns and adjectives ending in "-y," in a dubious light.

The repetition of "-y" and "-ly" sounds suggests that not the mind of Kitty, who is unpolished and abrupt, but that of the author, is the source of the voice in this section. And the author's mind appears to be caught up by the sonorous sounds until meaning becomes of secondary importance.

The repetition of "by themselves, for themselves," "by itself, for itself," "to itself" undercuts the visionary experience that is being presented. That is, the author forces the words to mean more than they ordinarily do; she asserts her will by repeating them until her meaning is exhausted.

Rhythmic repetition of course distinguishes most of Virginia Woolf's fiction.[77] A stylized trait, it often signals a creative capacity whether in the author or in her characters. In The Years, however, such exaggeration in feeling and speech is suspect. Like his father (p. 210), Martin Pargiter enjoys Eugenie's propensity for exaggeration while Eleanor is suspicious of it (p. 151). His exclamation, "'We can't tell a lie to save our souls,'" shows the poverty of a life without such free imaginative play. Again, "emotion out of all proportion to its object" is variously attributed to Col. Pargiter (p. 122); to Martin (p. 264); and to North (p. 393). Does Virginia Woolf make such judgments ironically as the mock-spokesman for a repressive society? Or does she feign to suffer herself from comparable repression? In either case, she decorously restricts her vocabulary to a stock of adverbs, putting herself in the place of her characters. The inadequacy of this conventionalized vocabulary to convey emotion and to communicate meaning is demonstrated by the "collaboration."

In "Present Day," Virginia Woolf identifies herself with characters who are composing fictions, weaving an especially complex tissue of role-playing. Critics generally agree that Virginia Woolf tries and fails to show the redemptive power of memory in the last chapter of The Years, where there is "a series of echoes that have no significance beyond the fact that they refer back to the years preceding the evening of the party."[78] Josephine O'Brien Schaefer bases this evaluation on a diary comment by the author about "Present Day": "the last chapters must be so rich, so resuming, so weaving together. . . . What I want is to enrich and stabilise" (AWD, p. 212). Perhaps it is inaccurate to assume an honorific function for those words. Though Virginia Woolf did mean to bring together all the images and themes of the book in the party scene, "enrichment" through repetition (as we have seen) does not necessitate that the images be beautiful, that the moments of communal feeling succeed, or that the book render a completed vision.

One important clue given us by Woolf in the diary entry of May 22, 1934 is the information that she did not care to plot image patterns and repetitions carefully: "I shan't, I think, re-read; I shall summon it back . . . from my memory" (AWD, p. 212). The chapter would embody a test of the power of her memory and synthetic imagination as well as those of her characters. In other words, she intended to reveal the gropings of her imagination, to render the fiction-making process visible. This decision resulted in a chapter that talks about its own origins and limitations. At the same time that North, Peggy, and Eleanor are trying to make sense of their lives, Virginia Woolf is trying to reconstruct their lives fictionally. Their obsession with fiction-making reflects her own immediate task. "Present Day" becomes a chapter about how to construct just such a chapter, rather than a visionary affirmation.

Characters in "Present Day" make up their own fictions, trying to harmonize their experience. North and Eleanor are particularly obsessed with reducing the world to order. North may end up a writer of "little books" as Peggy scornfully predicts (p. 390). In social gatherings, however, his comprehension of people is limited. Thinking that "he knew the type," North soon finds his portrait of Kitty inaccurate (pp. 393-394, 400). He also tries to construct a portrait of Sally based on appearances, "as if he were writing a novel" (p. 317). Yet while North is proved wrong, The Years presents us with just such "little snapshot pictures of people" and invites us to deduce from them their motivations (p. 317). Perhaps we are also invited to wonder if Virginia Woolf is questioning her own aesthetic along with North's.

Eleanor obligingly tries to reconstruct her life history for Peggy, but proves even less successful at portraiture than North. "Atoms danced apart and massed themselves. But how did they compose what people called a life? . . . thing followed thing, scene obliterated scene" (pp. 366-367). Like Virginia Woolf, Eleanor wants to "enrich the present day with echoes from the past." Like the Mrs. Ramsays of Woolf's other fiction, she wants to "enclose the present moment; to make it stay; to fill it fuller, with the past, the present and the future, until it shone, whole, bright, deep with understanding" (p. 428). Eleanor, however, gives up the pursuit.

Instead of a vision, she sees only "the endless night" (p. 428). Suddenly, "thinking of the dark, something baffled her; in fact it was growing light" (p. 428). The introduction of a literal dawn has almost the effect of a pun. An appropriate dissatisfaction with this climax perhaps inspired Josephine O'Brien Schaefer's criticism of "aesthetic complacency."[79] But perhaps Virginia Woolf did not aim to rescue Eleanor from her plight through poetic justice. A similar intervention succeeds in To the Lighthouse, where Lily's longing for Mrs. Ramsay results in her vision. The sleight of hand does not work in The Years, however, nor is it intended to. Virginia Woolf shows us how she does her magic trick in order to destroy the illusion.

In the first place, the spiritual correspondence to the dawn-metaphor is lacking. We are left with literal daylight, not with the transporting illumination that Eleanor has sought. Then, the end of the novel gives Eleanor the chance to share her vision with the assembled Pargiters. She spots the taxi and the young couple who echo Delia's vision in "1880" (p. 19). The satisfaction that Eleanor evidently feels at this completion provokes the exclamation, "there." However, nothing is conveyed by the repetition of this demonstrative beyond her feeling that something is summed up. If the taxi cab becomes a symbol in The Years, it is a solipsistic one. To the community of readers, as perhaps to the Pargiters, it is baffling.

Eleanor's last words--"and now?"--denote expectancy; but the repetition, echoing her earlier question "And then?" practically answers her. We know what to expect from the future, for the novel has shown us that this cycle of lives will simply repeat itself. The feeling of entrapment in an inexorable process which has neither outlet nor end is our final experience of the novel.[80] The last words then do not connote "calm of mind, all passion spent." The "extraordinary beauty, simplicity and peace" of the dawn link it to the sunset of the preface (p. 435). These circumscribing passages comment ironically upon the conflicts between characters and upon their groping efforts to make life intelligible. The scenic decorum imitates a serenity of mind utterly alien to the novel. It is as if Virginia Woolf were parodying her own fictional endings, those great moments of fulfillment at the end of Mrs. Dalloway and To the Lighthouse. Or rather, perhaps she is parodying the sense that such an abortive fiction can have an end. A pseudo-ending is only the crowning measure by which Virginia Woolf seeks to deceive us into believing this a coherent fictional world. Instead of being such a world, with order and rules of its own, The Years is an anti-novel.

In A Writer's Diary, Virginia Woolf once compared The Years to her historical fantasy: "in truth The Pargiters is first cousin to Orlando . . . Orlando taught me the trick of it" (AWD, p. 185). It is usually thought that Woolf refers to history-writing as the lesson she learned in Orlando, but another interpretation is possible as well. A diary entry underscores her intention in the earlier book: "My own lyric vein is to be satirised. Everything mocked" (AWD, p. 104). As we have seen, The Years undercuts lyricism, if with less mocking exuberance than Orlando. In place of the unifying personality of Orlando's Carlylean "Biographer," The Years presents a seemingly random multiplicity of styles. At times the novel seems utterly out of the control of its author.

The author's self-consciousness about her own failure keeps us from accepting the novel as a transcription of either imaginative or exterior reality. Virginia Woolf will not allow us to believe in the literary illusion, because she herself no longer can believe in it. The violation of her vision is difficult for Woolf to accept, however, and The Years reflects her struggle.

The Years is a nightmarish negative image of subjective harmony and beauty. Woolf had always recognized the threat to human happiness and fellowship posed by what in her early novels might have been called Fate: Jacob Flanders' death in World War I has only slightly more reason in history than Rachel Vinrace's in The Voyage Out (1915). Andrew and Prue Ramsay in To the Lighthouse seem victims of an incomprehensible destructive principle rather than of a patriarchal system, though he dies in the war and she in "some illness related to childbirth" (p. 199). Mrs. Dalloway is perhaps Woolf's first novel to locate the death force in society: Septimus Smith is clearly a victim of World War I, which is in turn the result of aggression and inhumanity fostered by society. Yet in Mrs. Dalloway, as in To the

Lighthouse and The Waves, Woolf presents subjectivity as eternal in the face of the passing accidents of human history. Mrs. Ramsay survives in memory and Lily Briscoe's painting; The Waves celebrates "one character," the stable and universal element that persists despite changes in human history.

The Years overturns such positive visions. Nothing lasts except all that Woolf abhors: ugliness, antagonism, disharmony, meaninglessness. Not some eternal layer of unconscious life but the "cripped" historical self is what persists through change. Between the Acts (1941) seems a less despairing and less bleak look at this possibility than The Years. Yet it can be read as undercutting belief in all ideals--in the idea of the pastoral; in the literary tradition (the chief version of history with which Woolf felt sympathy); in the continuity of civilization.[81] In a sense the vitality of the book comes from the "unscrupulous" instinctive passions that Woolf always distrusted: aggression, lust, greed. These will endure, it seems. At the novel's end, husband and wife confront each other, alone and silent; but this place beyond words scarcely resembles the harmonious spaces of pure subjectivity described in Woolf's other novels: "Alone, enmity was bared; also love. Before they slept, they must fight; after they had fought, they would embrace. From that embrace another life might be born. But first they must fight, as the dog fox fights with the vixen, in the heart of darkness, in the fields of night" (Between the Acts, p. 219). It would be romanticizing Woolf's own life story (as she herself might have done) to see this last novel, written when her final major illness was setting in, as an energetic affirmation. Still, one thinks of Septimus Smith's vigorous final gesture: "'I'll give it you!'" he cries, as he jumps (<u>Mrs</u>. <u>Dalloway</u>, p. 226). Bafflement at human beings (Septimus asks, "What did <u>they</u> want?") and love of life: these form the central polarity of Woolf's art.

When she was writing <u>The Years</u>, Woolf's historical identity seems to have engulfed her "sensibility," that unself-conscious creator who evoked illusions suggestive of what was for her the "truth." In part, there was a loss of self-confidence, a shift in external conditions that imbalanced her tenuous self-belief. Her vision seemed inadequate to the task of showing "significance," the "reason for things." Woolf's understanding of human history seems to have altered as well. Her faith that social change could improve human relations and reform crippling conditions seems undermined. In 1918 she had written Margaret Llewelyn Davies,

> . . . there's something about a mind which hasn't been used at all which makes one shudder at the degradation of human beings. In fact I believe the only hope for the world is to put all children of all countries together on an island and let them start fresh without knowing what a hideous system we have invented here.[82]

Yet even this optimism is qualified, for the letter continues, "Or would they hark back to the same ways of their own accord?" Doris Lessing asks the same question in <u>The Four-Gated City</u> and her answer there is a science-fictional solution. Failing a genetic mutation of the sort Lessing offers, however, the children's republic may not lastingly improve upon civilization in its present form. Indeed, Woolf's pessimism may have been exacerbated by seeing the "children" repeat the errors of their parents: her nephew Julian was killed in the Spanish Civil War; the newest generation of writers and poets was more militant in its anti-Fascism than the pacifists of early Bloomsbury had been in their opposition to the First World War.

While for Doris Lessing human nature itself would have to change radically before social change could occur, Woolf believed in a substratum of consciousness somehow independent of historical reality. In *The Years*, the independence of these two orders was called into question. Art and its vision of oneness came to seem a maternal consolation threatened on a large scale by society, the tyrannical father. The vehemence with which Woolf denounces the patriarchal system in *Three Guineas* is telling. Why should her anger have received its strongest public expression in 1938 (especially in view of the personal exorcism achieved in *To the Lighthouse*)? It seems that Woolf was gradually feeling the full import of her idea that "society was a father." The corollary was that her imaginative vision was somehow feminine and thus susceptible to aggressive incursions from historical reality. In a sense, art was not an androgynous escape from political oppression but perhaps dependent upon it. As we will see in Lessing's work, the not-self that Woolf opposed to the accidents of social life was ultimately a consolatory illusion. The realm she imagined beyond the anxieties and pressures suffered by the historical self proved to be vulnerable to violation, because in its essence it could not transcend history.

NOTES

[1] Virginia Woolf, A Writer's Diary, ed. Leonard Woolf (New York: Harcourt Brace Jovanovich, 1954), pp. 78, 107, 183.

[2] In his "Afterword" to The Novels of Virginia Woolf: From Beginning to End by Mitchell A. Leaska (New York: The John Jay Press, 1977), John Lehmann says: "Virginia Woolf . . . called herself a Socialist mainly, I think, because Leonard was a Socialist" (p. 241). This judgment sounds more disparaging than it may have been meant to, for Lehmann continues, Woolf "believed passionately in the emancipation of women, [but] was not fundamentally a believer in progress" (p. 241). While Woolf had little faith in theory per se (whether political or psychoanalytical), I would agree with Phyllis Rose that Woolf had at intervals a strong interest in politics. Rose says "Her political consciousness--and feminism was her only true politics--ebbed and flowed . . . ." See Woman of Letters: A Life of Virginia Woolf (New York: Oxford University Press, 1978), p. 257. I found Rose's biography extremely interesting on the topic of the relation between Woolf's art and her politics, though many of my conclusions differ from Rose's.

[3] Virginia Woolf, To the Lighthouse (New York: Harcourt, Brace & World, 1927), p. 95. Subsequent references will be cited parenthetically in the chapter. Other editions of works by Virginia Woolf to be cited include: Mrs. Dalloway (New York: Harcourt, Brace & World, 1925); A Room of One's Own (1925; rpt. London: Penguin Books, 1970); The Waves (New York: Harcourt, Brace & World, Inc., 1939); and Between the Acts (New York: Harcourt, Brace Jovanovich, Inc., 1941).

[4] Rose, p. 39.

[5] Jean O. Love, in Worlds in Consciousness: Mythopoetic Thought in the Novels of Virginia Woolf (Berkeley: University of California Press, 1970), stresses the myth-making tendency in Woolf's art.

[6] The Letters of Virginia Woolf, Vol. IV (1929-1931), ed. Nigel Nicolson and Joanne Trautmann (London: The Hogarth Press, 1978), 27 October 1931, p. 397.

[7] A Writer's Diary, p. 184.

[8] Woolf defines the terms "being" and "non-being" in her memoir, "A Sketch of the Past," in Moments of Being: Unpublished Autobiographical Writings, ed. Jeanne Schulkind (New York: Harcourt Brace Jovanovich, 1976), p. 70. "Non-being" refers to the "great part of every day [that] is not lived consciously"; moments of "being" are charged with great significance.

For a discussion of these opposing states of consciousness and their role in Woolf's theory of creativity, see Rose, p. 139.

[9] A Writer's Diary, p. 184.

[10] Rose suggests that the "tradition of fictional form was, or was perceived by Woolf to be, masculine" (p. 94) and that writing in this mode was inhibiting to Woolf.

[11] Letters, I (1882-1912), June (?) 1906, 227.

[12] Letters, I, 22 September, 1907, 310.

[13] Letters, I, 15 April 1908, 325.

[14] Rose points out that Woolf "would later become conscious of having reached in 1935 a stage of hating personality, desiring anonymity in writers, but in fact this 'standpoint' . . . was evident rather earlier" (pp. 207-208).

[15] A Writer's Diary, p. 125.

[16] Mitchell A. Leaska, "Virginia Woolf, the Pargeter: A Reading of The Years," Bulletin of the New York Public Library, 80, No. 2 (1977), 210, 207.

[17] The Diary of Virginia Woolf, Vol. II (1920-1924), ed. Anne Olivier Bell (New York: Harcourt Brace Jovanovich, 1978), p. 250.

[18] Letters, IV, 15 August 1930, 200.

[19] Letters, IV, 19 August 1930, 202-203.

[20] Letters, III (1923-1928), 11 March 1925, 172.

[21] Letters, IV, 4 October 1929, 97.

[22] Diary, II, 221. An entry written 2 January 1923 shows Woolf taking stock of her own motives and feelings, assessing her achievements in the "one confessional where I need not boast. Years & years ago . . . I said to myself . . . never pretend that the things you haven't got are not worth having; good advice I think. At least it often comes back to me. Never pretend that children, for instance, can be replaced by other things."

[23] Letters, III, 21 April 1927, 366.

[24] Letters, IV, 4 July 1931, 353.

[25] Letters, III, 6 March 1927, 344.

[26] Letters, I, 24 October 1904, 146.

[27] *Letters*, *I*, 11 December 1904, 165.

[28] *Letters*, *IV*, 16 October 1930, 230.

[29] *A Writer's Diary*, p. 135.

[30] Woolf's manic-depression has been analyzed in terms of these parental roles, her mania associated with the "feminine" pursuit of unification, her depression with the "masculine," scientific view of life as flux. See Nancy Topping Bazin, *Virginia Woolf and the Androgynous Vision* (New Brunswick, NJ: Rutgers University Press, 1973), p. 17. Phyllis Rose suggests that the "voices" Woolf heard during her breakdowns echo those of Leslie and Julia Stephen. The naked King Edward shouting obscenities in the rhododendrons suggests the symbolic father: "With the king, the very symbol of patriarchal authority, the potential for threat--the threat of male lust and male power--is clearer. It seems that conscious life penetrated her underlife as well. But what was her mother saying on that horrible morning in 1915 when Virginia suddenly saw her by her bedside and began a nonstop response?" (Rose, p. 265).

[31] *Letters*, *I*, 28 February 1904, 130.

[32] *Letters*, *I*, 26 September 1904, 143.

[33] Rose, p. 111.

[34] Rose, p. 161.

[35] Rose, p. 168.

[36] *Letters*, *II*, 21 January 1922, 499.

[37] *Letters*, *IV*, 22 June 1930, 180.

[38] Phyllis Rose discusses the impact of the Angel in the House and of Leslie Stephen's influence as well, p. 161.

[39] *Diary*, *II*, 193.

[40] *A Writer's Diary*, p. 206.

[41] We might compare Woolf's "outsider" notion with Doris Lessing's use of the idea, shared with R. D. Laing, that madness may be a kind of social protest. According to Anne Olivier Bell, editor of Woolf's diary, she may have been influenced by Leonard Woolf's interest in Tolstoi's "sillies," visionaries who cannot function within society. See note #5, p. 266, *Diary*, *II*.

[42] J. Hillis Miller, "Virginia Woolf's All Soul's Day: The Omniscient Narrator in *Mrs. Dalloway*," in *The Shaken Realist: Essays in Modern Literature in Honor of Frederick J. Hoffman*, eds. Melvin J. Friedman and John B. Vickery (Baton Rouge: Louisiana State University Press, 1970), p. 105.

[43] Quoted in Harvena Richter, *Virginia Woolf: The Inward Voyage* (Princeton: Princeton University Press, 1970), p. 138.

[44] *Letters*, *II*, 25 December 1922, 599.

[45] *Letters*, *III*, 8 September 1928, 529.

[46] *Diary*, *II*, 104.

[47] Rose discusses a number of Woolf's autobiographical myths on pp. 18, 24 and 40.

[48] *Diary*, *II*, 103.

[49] *Diary*, *II*, 221.

[50] *Letters*, *IV*, 19 August 1930, 203.

[51] *Letters*, *IV*, 1 April 1931, 302-303.

[52] Phyllis Rose maintains that as Woolf's "talent was feminine," she had to devise a new novel form predicated on "tenuousness of self" (pp. 94, 156). More critical of Woolf's theory of androgyny are Elaine Showalter and Marilyn R. Farwell, who argue that Woolf's androgynous mind is not unified but partial, that it represents denial of or escape from the feminine. See Showalter, "Killing the Angel in the House: The Autonomy of Women Writers," *Antioch Review*, 32 (1973), 341; and see also Farwell, "Virginia Woolf and Androgyny," *Contemporary Literature*, 16 (1975), 436.

[53] *Diary*, *II*, 309.

[54] *Letters*, *IV*, 27 October 1931, 397.

[55] Rose stresses a connection between Woolf's breakdowns and her guilt at the self-assertion implicit in publishing, but she admits the possibility of a "genetic tendency toward some form of insanity which seems to have run through the Stephen family, [and] the possibly pathogenic effect of childhood experiences" (p. 169).

[56] Rose, p. 196.

[57] Virginia Woolf, *Three Guineas* (New York: Harcourt, Brace & World, 1963), p. 135.

[58] *Three Guineas*, p. 142.

[59] *Letters*, *IV*, 18 May 1931, 333.

[60] *Diary*, *II*, 102.

[61] *Diary*, *I*, 125.

⁶² *Letters*, *IV*, 27 June 1931, 348.

⁶³ Virginia Woolf, "Craftsmanship," *The Death of the Moth* (New York: Harcourt Brace Jovanovich, 1970), p. 198.

⁶⁴ Virginia Woolf, "The Artist and Politics," *The Moment and Other Essays* (New York: Harcourt Brace Jovanovich, 1964), pp. 180-183.

⁶⁵ Virginia Woolf, "The Leaning Tower," *The Moment and Other Essays*, p. 109.

⁶⁶ *Three Guineas*, p. 107.

⁶⁷ *Three Guineas*, p. 169.

⁶⁸ W. H. Mellers, "Mrs. Woolf and Life," rpt. in *The Importance of Scrutiny*, ed. Eric Bentley (New York: George W. Stewart, 1948), p. 381.

⁶⁹ Josephine O'Brien Schaefer, *The Three-Fold Nature of Reality in the Novels of Virginia Woolf* (The Hague: Mouton, 1965), p. 184.

⁷⁰ Basil de Selincourt, "Infinity in Experience: Virginia Woolf's New Novel," *The Observer*, March 14, 1937, p. 5.

⁷¹ John Hawley Roberts, "The End of the English Novel?" *Virginia Quarterly Review*, 13 (1937), 439, 437.

⁷² Quentin Bell implies this in *Virginia Woolf: A Biography*, II (New York: Harcourt Brace Jovanovich, 1972), 197.

⁷³ See Jean Guiguet, *Virginia Woolf and Her Works*, trans. Jean Stewart (New York: Harcourt, Brace & World, 1966), p. 312. See also Charles G. Hoffman, "Virginia Woolf's Manuscript Revisions of *The Years*," *PMLA*, 84 (1969), 79-89.

⁷⁴ Hoffmann, p. 89.

⁷⁵ Woolf seems to have split the original visionary character, "Elvira," into Eleanor and Sally; she feared that Elvira was becoming "too dominant" (*AWD*, p. 191). Elvira was first to be the spokeswoman for the author (*AWD*, p. 189). At that time she resembled Sally: see references to "Elvira in bed" (p. 190) and to "Bobby and Elvira" meeting at St. Paul's (p. 205); "Elvira & George, or John, talking in her room" appear to be Sally and North (p. 211). But then Elvira as Eleanor goes out of the house with knot in handkerchief and coppers in hand (p. 214). By January 23, 1935, Woolf has separated "my Sarah and Elvira" (p. 230). Hoffmann's article suggests that Woolf tried to diminish Eleanor's authority further by focusing on the rebel Delia in "1880" rather than on Eleanor, the "unifier." (See Hoffman, p. 87.) Eleanor, mild and discursive, and Sally, the Cassandra-like prophetess of doom, share the visionary role.

[76] Virginia Woolf, "Mr. Bennett and Mrs. Brown," in The Captain's Death Bed and Other Essays (New York: Harcourt Brace Jovanovich, 1950), p. 112.

[77] See the chapter entitled "Repetition and Rhythm" in Allen McLaurin's Virginia Woolf: The Echoes Enslaved (Cambridge: The University Press, 1973), and his chapter on The Years. See also Irma Rantavaara's comments on repetition and rhythm in Virginia Woolf's "The Waves" (Port Washington, NY: Kennikat Press, 1960).

[78] Schaefer, p. 181.

[79] Schaefer, p. 181.

[80] In Three Guineas, Woolf wrote "It seems as if there were no progress in the human race, but only repetition" (p. 66).

[81] Alex Zwerdling, "Between the Acts and the Coming of War," Novel, 10 (1976), 223, 226-227, 229.

[82] Letters, II, 2 January 1918, 208.

Chapter 5

DORIS LESSING'S CHILD OF VIOLENCE

Born (in 1919) into a world that recognized women's political power as legitimate, Doris Lessing has found it easier than her predecessors to act decisively to shape her own life and to influence the structure of the society she lives in. Lessing's legal rights are enhanced by intellectual support for the woman's right to assert herself and exercise political power. Modern psychological and political theories criticize the deformation inflicted on the individual by the family, by repressive institutions and laws, and by their representatives within the psyche. For Doris Lessing, however, knowing that the bourgeois family breeds neurotic children ultimately neither brings consolation nor suggests remedies. Lessing's autobiographical heroine Martha Quest is forthright in her criticism of her upbringing and of the racially and economically oppressive culture around her. But Martha is no more successful than the protagonists of Mary Shelley, George Eliot and Virginia Woolf in combatting the inner allies of external repression. Martha pursues a long series of panaceas for the deprivation she feels. In The Four-Gated City, her final consolation is the fantastic hope that a new breed of children will save the world as former children have not been able to save it--or themselves.

Martha's faith, apparently unreligious, derives from the religious impulse Freud wrote of in The Future of an Illusion:

> And so a rich store of ideas is formed, born of the need to make
> tolerable the helplessness of man, and built out of the material
> offered by memories of the helplessness of his own childhood and
> the childhood of the human race. It is easy to see that these
> ideas protect man in two directions; against the dangers of nature
> and fate, and against the evils of human society itself.[1]

Freud concludes (hopefully) that man's reason will triumph over his instinctual neediness--that individual man and the human race will eventually grow up:

> He will have to confess his utter helplessness and his insignificant part in the working of the universe; he will have to confess that he is no longer the centre of creation, no longer the object of the tender care of a benevolent providence. He will be in the same position as the child who has left the home where he was so warm and comfortable. But, after all, is it not the destiny of childishness to be overcome?[2]

Doris Lessing asks the same question--are we never to become responsible for our own destinies, never to cease complaining about suffering inflicted by our families and society at large? Her answer is implicitly that we should transcend "childishness"; yet her novels are more eloquent about deprivation and need than about overcoming them. Martha Quest seeks a satisfying relationship to society through personal relations, political commitments, and psychic exploration. But her quest ultimately diverges from individuation back toward "the home where [she] was so warm and comfortable." Correspondingly, Lessing's novels stop short of offering political and other practical solutions to the problems they describe. They nostalgically recommend transcendence of this troubling social world altogether.

It is difficult to be sure precisely how far Lessing's own experience parallels that of her heroines, since there is far less biographical evidence available about Lessing than about Mary Shelley, George Eliot and Virginia Woolf. Lessing's attitude toward her parents is, in her non-fiction, affectionate, ironic but understanding. *In Pursuit of the English* begins with wry retrospection:

> I wouldn't like to say that I brooded over [my father's] character . . . but I certainly spent a good part of my childhood coming to terms with it. I must confess, to be done with confessions right at the start, that I concluded at the age of about six my father was mad. This did not upset me. For a variety of reasons . . . the quintessential eccentricity of the human race was borne in upon me from the beginning.[3]

In this memoir Lessing's father's "splendidly pathological character" is made amusingly representative of the "English" type (p. 6). The picture of her father's idiosyncrasies--his code of honor, his theories about racial purity and minerals and politics--is darker in the essay "My Father." There Lessing's point is that "this naturally vigorous, sensuous being was killed in 1914, 1915, 1916. I think the best of my father died in that war, that his spirit was crippled by it."[4] Lessing shows how political reality--World War I; the intolerant and intolerable straitness of the British social system--made her father unhappy and spurred his exile to Southern Rhodesia. Lessing portrays her real father more fully in these pages than most fathers in her fiction. The novels dwell rather more on wives and mothers of exiled men than the memoirs, which present only a brief, sympathetic sketch of her gregarious, bourgeois mother:

> But it was my mother who suffered. After a period of neurotic illness, which was a protest against her situation, she became brave and resourceful. But she never saw that her husband was not living in a real world, that he had made a captive of her common sense. ("My Father," p. 91)

Lessing's tolerant portrait of her parents--two unhappy people, insecure and exiled from their homeland--suggests that Lessing is a daughter who has, so to speak, left home. She understands and forgives what she may have suffered as a child. She even apologizes: ". . . it occurs to me that I was not always there for my father" ("My Father," p. 83).

Lessing's heroines, however, are depicted in the throes of unresolved conflicts with their parents and with their parents' voice, the conscience or superego. Lessing generally maintains that she is not to be identified with the women in her fiction:

> I got angry over the reviews of The Golden Notebook. They thought it was personal--it was, in parts. But it was a very highly structured book, carefully planned. . . . But the book they tried to turn it into was: The Confessions of Doris Lessing.[5]

In the autobiographical Bildungsroman series Children of Violence, Lessing frequently distances herself from her heroine, for example, calling Martha "the type of woman who can never be, as they are likely to put it, 'themselves' with anyone but the man to whom they have permanently or not given their hearts."[6] Lessing's detachment from her protagonists does not, however, extend further than her giving an anatomy of their unhappiness. The distance between Lessing and her heroines (never immense or absolute) dissolves at the next stage, when she describes the outcome of their quest. What Martha should do, what she should be, is less clear than what has been done to and made of her. There is a blind spot about the self that eludes even the penetrating vision of a woman equipped with sophisticated theories about need and fulfillment, about how to know one's self and one's place in society.

Doris Lessing does not have to struggle against the outworn creeds of her society in quite the way that Mary Shelley, George Eliot and Virginia Woolf had to. With no stable faith imposed upon her, she freely chooses the ideology or ideologies by which she may explain and validate her life and that of her epoch. Marx and Freud (or Jung) are two patriarchs whose theories influence Lessing's exploration of the individual's relation to the collective. In her early work, the first four volumes of <u>Children of Violence</u> in particular (the plan of which was sketched in the early 1950s),[7] both the political content of the novels and the realistic form they take reflect a Marxist interpretation of how fiction emerges from historical reality. The writing of <u>The Golden Notebook</u> was a watershed in Lessing's ideological transformation. In this novel, as in <u>The Four-Gated City</u>, Lessing's ideas and their fictional embodiment are increasingly influenced by psychoanalytic theory, with its emphasis on the psyche's self-confrontation. Eventually, Lessing's interest in Jung's and R. D. Laing's thought has been succeeded by her preoccupation with Sufism and other mystical philosophies, a change reflected in <u>The Four-Gated City</u> and <u>The Memoirs of a Survivor</u>. Many of Lessing's readers interpret this movement as a disillusionment with political solutions and an embracing of psychological ones, which is both a reasonable and a convincing description. It is possible, however, that it describes the effects rather than the causes of her change of heart and mind. Indeed, Lessing seems to describe the symptoms of human unhappiness and their antidotes as first political, then psychological. Beneath this diversity of solutions, however, there is one problem that has persistently troubled Lessing from the very first: the status of the individual self. This preoccupation lies beneath all the various "isms" that Lessing has embraced.

Underlying Lessing's attraction to various ideological patriarchs--Marx, Jung, R. D. Laing, Idries Shah (the Sufi teacher)--is, ironically, a quest for mothering. That is, Martha Quest, Lessing's autobiographical heroine, seeks an emotional and intellectual surrogate for the mother she feels she never had. Without reducing the complexity and seriousness of Lessing's political and philosophical searches, I think it can be argued that they share this single, psychological end.

Lessing's fiction has consistently dealt with political causes and correctives of social problems. Outside her fiction, Lessing's political commitment has been constant as well. Though she is no longer a Communist Party member,[8] Lessing remains sympathetic to left-wing ideology. In her 1969 interview with Jonah Raskin she emphasizes this: "'I'm concerned with the preservation of liberties. I realize that to you that sounds like an old-fashioned liberal bleat, but I've seen liberties destroyed and left-wing people suppressed too often.'"[9] In her 1971 preface to The Golden Notebook (1963), she reiterates her concern with the individual's relation to the collective entity:

> The way to deal with the problem of "subjectivity," that shocking business of being preoccupied with the tiny individual who is at the same time caught up in such an explosion of terrible and marvellous possibilities, is to see him as a microcosm and in this way to break through the personal, the subjective, making the personal general, as indeed life always does, transforming a private experience . . . into something much larger: growing up is after all only the understanding that one's unique and incredible experience is what everyone shares.[10]

Lessing's world view has not changed, then, in the sense that she retains a humanistic concern for the individual against all types of oppression and yet sees the individual's life always in relation to a larger social whole.

If her politics have remained liberal, her aesthetic credo has gradually diverged from traditional realism. Much of her work, through the first four volumes of Children of Violence, exemplifies a number of the tenets of the Marxist critic Georg Lukács, especially the use of the <u>Bildungsroman</u> to explore the individual's relation to his or her community.[11] Lessing further shares Lukács' belief that "it is just the opposition between a man and his environment that determines the development of his personality."[12] Again, in the tradition of bourgeois and socialist realism alike, Lessing conceives of her characters as simultaneously unique and typical of a historically determined group.[13] In her article on <u>The Golden Notebook</u>, she insists that the experience of individuals in the novel is typical as well as unique and private:

> . . . you could put names to them like those in the old Morality Plays: Mr. Dogma and Mr. I-Am-Free-Because-I-Belong-Nowhere, Miss I-Must-Have-Love-and-Happiness and Mrs. I-Have-To-Be-Good-At-Everything-I-Do, Mr. Where-Is-A-Real-Woman? and Miss Where-Is-A-Real-Man?, Mr. I'm-Mad-Because-They-Say-I-Am, and Miss Life-Through-Experiencing-Everything, Mr. I-Make-Revolution-And-Therefore-I-Am, and Mr. and Mrs. If-We-Deal-Very-Well-With-This-Small-Problem-Then-Perhaps-We-Can-Forget-We-Daren't-Look-At-The-Big-Ones.[14]

Again, in <u>Children of Violence</u>, Martha Quest is at once a typical adolescent of the 1930s, a typical realistic heroine seeking her destiny in a diminished world (much like Maggie Tulliver), and an original character whose inner life becomes a new landscape in literary psychology. The <u>Children of Violence</u> series is indeed such a novel as Lucien Goldmann describes: "The story of a degraded search for authentic values in an inauthentic world," and thus "necessarily both a biography and a social chronicle."[15]

Not all the <u>Children of Violence</u> novels, however, remain faithful to the tenets of Marxist literary theory. As Martha Quest rejects the limits on her personal freedom imposed first by her family, then by her ordinary middle-class marriage, and finally by the fruitlessness of

Communist Party activities in Africa, the novel's form moves beyond that of the conventional Bildungsroman toward an experimental structure in The Four-Gated City (1969). Accompanying Lessing's (and Martha's) political apostasy has been a revolution in her aesthetic. Lessing's belief about the relation between the individual and the institutions of civilization appears to have undergone a change. Her acceptance of the sufficiency of traditional narrative forms has wavered along with her faith in strictly political solutions to social problems.

The fiction that has evolved from Lessing's crisis is the non-realistic "inner space fiction" or "historical fantasy" of Lessing's recent years.[16] In The Memoirs of a Survivor (1975), the citizens of a decaying bureaucratic regime make their escape from impending chaos, not by willing or acting to win their freedom, but by being led beyond the walls that constrain them by a female figure resembling Shelley's Intellectual Beauty. In the "Appendix" to The Four-Gated City, a race of "new children" is being born whose moral and emotional capacities, altered by the effects of nuclear radioactivity, perhaps will forge a new "future for our race."[17] These works document the individual's powerlessness to effect his destiny, to shape the reality in which he finds himself. This powerlessness, I will attempt to show, is a function of Lessing's anxiety about the individual.

Lessing's movement away from political solutions, toward Sufism and other suprarational philosophies, has been widely noted. Marion Vlastos, in particular, sees Lessing rejecting an Orwellian belief in the need for social change in favor of emphasis on inner, personal transformation. It is not so much that Lessing has become discouraged about the efficacy of individual action in the face of nuclear catastrophe, global famine, and other imminent cataclysms. Rather, Vlastos suggests, Lessing's world view now is one of "metaphysical" rather than "economic" determinism.[18]

Still, whether Lessing's fiction shows the influence of Marxist or psychoanalytic or mystic thought, it may be said to reject the ego for a higher (unconscious) collectivity. In this respect, Lessing's ideological allegiances represent responses to one fundamental problem: that of the individual's self-definition.[19] Her philosophical crisis is related to how we know the world and our place in it. Specifically, Lessing is preoccupied with the individual self as the source of the meaning, even the very structure, of reality itself. In a sense, the individual user of language does not refer to reality but in fact may be said to create it.

Lessing's response to this "discovery" has been, I think, to give up trying to write fiction that defines and, by defining, __establishes__ the relation between an individual self and the reality beyond it (whether this reality is political or mystical). This change in Lessing's thought has influenced the shape of her recent fictions. Lessing reverses Lukács' maxim, "The novelist's ethic becomes an aesthetic problem of the work."[20] Instead, Lessing's aesthetic--her view of the relation between literature and society, her idea of the ordering capacities of language--becomes a problem in the ethical and political vision of her fiction. The crisis and its implications have caused her, I would suggest, to withdraw from the difficult task of describing the relation between self and society.

In __Martha Quest__ (1952), the heroine has an epiphany on the African veld, an experience that symbolizes the relation of the individual to the cosmos that Martha and Lessing's other heroines continually seek. Martha is both giving birth and being born: ". . . what she had been waiting for like a revelation was a pain, not a happiness; what she remembered, always, was the exultation and the achievement, what she forgot was this difficult birth into a state of mind which words like <u>ecstasy</u>, <u>illumination</u>, and so on could not describe, because they suggest joy" (p. 61). Like a laboring mother, "She felt the rivers under the ground forcing themselves painfully along her veins, swelling them in an unbearable pressure; her flesh was the earth, and suffered growth like a ferment. . . . Not for one second longer . . . could she have borne it; but then, with a sudden movement forwards and out, the whole process stopped . . ." (p. 62). What she learns in this process is "her smallness, the unimportance of humanity" in the "inhuman" movement of the spheres (p. 62). The new growth "demanding conception, with her flesh as host, as if it were a necessity," entails the dissolution of self in the chaos--the giving up of "her own ideas of herself and her place" (p. 62).

In this "lodestone" (p. 220) experience, the only completely authentic experience of Martha's life, she learns the essential insignificance of her individual self. She is merely one particle in the cosmic "dissolution of dancing atoms" (p. 62). This experience, which Martha says constitutes her "conscience" (p. 220), will determine her eventual disenchantment with politics, familial and sexual relationships, psychoanalysis, and even philosophical systems. Though apparently collective experiences, these prove egocentric and divisive (of the self and of society in general).

Lessing's conception of the rational and conscious processes of the mind as divisive, aggressive, and destructive leads her to decry egotism and individualism in personal and social life. The quest for identity in her novels is supplanted by a longing for the dissolution of personality, for being rather than for selfhood. Analysis of the individual's relation to the collective in Lessing's novels suggests, however, that her heroines have an unachieved selfhood whose development is thwarted, without their realizing this, in its first stages.

The impulse toward self-definition is complexly tied up with Lessing's notion of the "self-hater" (4GC, p. 536). According to Lessing, a self-hating impulse is universally, collectively unconscious (4GC, pp. 518-519). By recognizing and acknowledging the "self-hater," Martha thinks she achieves a wholeness of self previously unknown to her. In reality, however, Martha never really comes to grips with the source of her self-hatred. Martha does not defeat "the Devil" within, she suppresses him: he recedes into the "sea of sound" (4GC, p. 556). This suppression occurs because Martha mistakenly identifies the "self-hater" as an inherent, universal element of subconscious life. Actually, he represents others' hatred of, or failure to love, her.

Martha's subconscious self-hating stems from her having internalized others' evaluations of and reactions to her. Instead of seeing these reactions as learned, acquired from others' responses, Martha assumes they are innate and therefore necessary. Self-hatred, the negative image of self-approbation, lies beneath the hostile aggression which causes the failure of Martha's attempts to love others. The implication is, one must love oneself first to be able to love others. Or it might be truer to say, one must love others in order to love oneself. That is, fascination with some other-than-self leads to fascination with the image of oneself-as-other. Both kinds of loving identification are prerequisites to selfhood. Because Martha (like Lessing's heroines in general) is denied love by others from the first, and not permitted to identify completely with them, she has no positive image of a whole self to assimilate. She feels only hostility and rejection, describing this as a reaction originating in herself rather than attributing it to the reactions of others.

Though Martha regards her epiphany as revealed truth, it imparts partial rather than total knowledge of the self's relationship to the cosmos. Martha and Lessing's other heroines long for such dissolution, not as a final state of rest but as the first stage in a process of attaining selfhood. Because she is rejected by her mother, Martha seeks dissolution of self in a compensatory experience (Communism, sexual ecstasy, madness, mysticism). These experiences are not forms of one final stage in Martha's development; rather, they are means to a single end: selfhood. Before Martha can have autonomy of being, she must feel that she securely belongs to some group or collective experience, whether political, psychological or mystical. Only after belonging to and identifying completely with this Other can Martha identify herself as a separate and complete self. In a sense, Martha Quest's ultimate rejection of the egocentric self can be seen as a reaction against the frustration and difficulty of the process of establishing that self, not as a repudiation of selfhood as narrow or partial. Underlying Utopian fantasies like Martha's four-gated city in Children of Violence is the individual's essential need for self-definition and self-knowledge. Such fantasies are projections of the subject that seeks reunion with the Other, rather than remain (necessarily) partial, alienated and unsatisfied.

Just as the subject can never regain his primal sense of wholeness and unity with the Other, so his words will not revert or refer to any absolute, transcendent referent. There is an unbridgeable gap between word and referent, as between self and Other. Language is a dialectical system of relatedness, not achieved signification. Language does not describe reality; a word is not the sign of a specific object or perception. Meaning is rather a momentary coalescence of the fluid relations between (what continental linguistics calls) "signifier" and "signified," dependent on the subject's intention for its meaningfulness.

As Michel Foucault demonstrated in The Order of Things: An Archaeology of the Human Sciences, "we no longer have that primary, that absolutely initial, word upon which the infinite movement of discourse was founded and by which it was limited . . . ."[21] Meaning is the responsibility of the individual subject, not guaranteed by the transcendent Logos. The implications of this relativistic view of meaning can seem unsettling to the individual user.

In "The Small Personal Voice," Lessing expresses a sense of frustration at this relativism, ascribing it to a loss of communally shared values:

> If there is one thing which distinguishes our literature, it is a confusion of standards and the uncertainty of values. . . . Words, it seems, can no longer be used simply and naturally. All the great words like love, hate; life, death; loyalty, treachery; contain their opposite meanings and half a dozen shades of dubious implication. Words have become so inadequate to express the richness of our experience that the simplest sentence overheard on a bus reverberates like words shouted against a cliff. One certainty we all accept is the condition of being uncertain and insecure.[22]

Despite Lessing's statement that we "accept" the need of "being uncertain and insecure," much of her work contradicts this assertion that she is resigned to contemporary _angst_. Even in this essay, with its demand for a restoration of communal values, Lessing clearly longs nostalgically for a language that stands in a necessary relation to a real referent. She treats reality as static and language as (imperfectly) descriptive, refusing to admit that language confers meaning on, even constitutes, reality and that responsibility for meaning rests with the individual.

Lessing seems to confer value on the collective and to withhold it from the personal, whether the transpersonal Other is political or psychological. What she has called her "failure"[23] to describe this collective reality is inevitable as long as she conceives of language as secondary, a form imposed on meaningful experience. Why does Lessing regard her descriptive attempts as a failure? Why is language inadequate to the task of describing reality? Why is the individual self or persona, and other social constructs for that matter, felt to be false and flawed? It is not that the self fails in its attempts to establish a relationship with reality, and that consequently Lessing condemns it. Rather, because the self is rejected from the outset, it must be foredoomed to "fail."

Martha's (and Lessing's) judgment of failure is not, as they think, freely and independently reached. Instead, Martha's subliminal feeling that her particular self is "bad," leads her to project self-hatred outward: disapproving of her self, she disapproves of selfhood in general. By analyzing Martha's pursuit of self-knowledge and her ultimate rejection of the quest, I hope to show that she has internalized others' criticism of her and consequently feels she lacks the right of selfhood. First I will investigate the nature of her quest, considering how and why Martha seeks dissolution in a collective reality, variously defined. Then it will be important to analyze Lessing's description of the subconscious. In Lessing's fiction, the unconscious mind contains values stemming from Martha's personal history, externally determined effects (like self-hatred) that are attributed to innate psychological causes. As a result, Martha does not so much reject her own ego as continue to be trapped by what others think/ have thought of her. Because of the moral, psychological, and aesthetic attributes of Lessing's conception of the subconscious, Martha's exploration of selfhood is impeded and its outcome foreordained.

* * * * *

In <u>Children of Violence</u>, Martha Quest seeks alternatives to the egocentricity and ethnocentricity of bourgeois family life and white capitalist society in Africa. She seeks literal correlatives for the adolescent "daydream" of a utopian four-gated city where "citizens moved, grave and beautiful, black and white and brown together," their children playing harmoniously. "Yes, they smiled and approved these many-fathered children, running and playing among the flowers and the terraces, through the white pillars and tall trees of this fabulous and ancient city . . ." (<u>MQ</u>, p. 17). This vision of an ideal city is the realization in human terms of that "dissolution of dancing atoms" she first intuited mystically. Its attainment is sought by Martha in a variety of experiences. Communism, personal relationships, and finally psychic communication. At the same time, while seeking dissolution of personality in something greater than herself, Martha is also seeking

to define herself. She needs a vision of wholeness, a Gestalt on which
she can model her own autonomy. That is, identification with some collective Other will enable Martha to see herself from the outside as a
separate whole. These two antithetical impulses--toward dissolution
and toward identification of self--are manifest in Martha's most important experiences, beginning with her political activities.

As a young woman, Martha seeks but cannot find an adequate
explanation for her subjective experience. She studies Victorian
novels and Havelock Ellis fruitlessly: "Books. Words. There must
surely be some pattern of words which would neatly and safely cage what
she felt--isolate her emotions so that she could look at them from outside" (A Proper Marriage, p. 73). She finds no appropriate description
of her experience in traditional literary, sociological, or historical
sources.

Unable to find a conventional image that will embody her
feelings, Martha concludes that "all the terrific, restless force
embodied in her," her "driving individualism," must be submerged in
that mystical dissolution of dancing atoms (MQ, p. 183). Instead of
seeking a self-image, then, Martha remains faithful to that cosmic
unity. She finds its analogue, she thinks, in the Communist vision of
a socialist utopia--"millions of people who were creating a new world"
(PM, p. 315). This vision corresponds to "those parts of her childhood
she still owned, the moments of experience which seemed to her enduring
and true; the moments of illumination and belief" (A Ripple From the
Storm, p. 54). Marxism offers an attractively rational version of this
mystical perception of the individual's relation to the collective:

> "Comrades, the infinite complexity of events, each acting and
> interacting, so that there is no phenomenon in the world which is
> not linked with and affects every other--in nature nothing happens
> alone . . ." and she was returned to a knowledge of the thrust and
> push of knitting natural forces which had grappled with the sub-
> stance of her own flesh, to become part of it, in the moments of
> illumination in her past. (RS, p. 54)

This ideal picture of the human brotherhood does not survive Martha's political initiation. In practice, the Communist Party of Southern Zambesia is as full of contradictions and compulsive repetitiveness as the bourgeois family life Martha has escaped. The tiny Party, operating in a vacuum (no natives are allowed to join), is succeeded by other identically enthusiastic radical cadres, having fallen victim to the petty personal antagonisms and selfish motives of all people, Communist or not. Martha is disappointed not only because the political program brings utopia no nearer realization, but also because Communism fails to offer her an identity. At the end of A Ripple From the Storm, Martha thinks, ". . . I'm not a person at all, I'm nothing yet--perhaps I never will be" (p. 260).

Because relationships between political activists fail to avoid the weaknesses of ordinary human relationships, Martha next experiments with social reformation and brotherhood on the personal level. Through sexual relationships Martha seeks simultaneously dissolution and discovery of self. Selfhood can come, she feels, through identification with a loved partner. She expects "the faceless man who waited in the wings of the future, waiting to free the Martha who was in cold storage. . ." (RS, p. 230). Such a woman requires a man to bring "her 'self' to life. She lives with the empty space at her side, peopled with the images of her own potentialities until the next man walks into the space, absorbs the shadow into himself, creating her, allowing her to be her 'self'--but a new self, since it is his conception which forms her" (RS, p. 38).

In the fourth volume of Children of Violence, Landlocked (1965), Martha finds the lover who "would unify her elements" (LL, p. 30) by presenting her with an authentic image of herself. But this selfhood --a feeling of exalted being paradoxically achieved when she is "dissolved" (LL, p. 99) in love-making with Thomas Stern--is as transitory as her political ardor. The relationship between Martha and Thomas breaks down when she refuses to accept the self-image she sees mirrored in him. Martha is shocked when Thomas goes to Israel to fight for the Zionist cause. She has been denying in Thomas what she will not admit about herself: that both have the capacity, even the inclination, to behave destructively. She "was the essence of violence, she had been conceived, bred, fed and reared on violence" (LL, p. 195). "She, Martha, was as much a child of the 1914-1918 war as she was of Alfred Quest, May Quest" (LL, p. 196). Products of twentieth-century violence, Martha and Thomas cannot break that cycle by willing or dreaming its end; their very selves are "part of a twist and a damage" (LL, p. 196).

Rejecting the image of herself as an aggressive, misanthropic child of violence, Martha seeks fulfillment elsewhere. Politics and love having failed to bring her selfhood, Martha thinks only of escaping Zambesia. The sea about which she fantasizes is both the vehicle of her escape to England and a symbol of the dissolution of personality she longs for. "Somewhere was water, was rescue, was the sea. In this nightmare she was caught in . . . they must remember that outside, somewhere else, was light, was the sound of water breaking on rocks" (LL, p. 238).

Before Martha can cross the sea to England in The Four-Gated City, she is "landlocked" for an entire volume. This sterile period in Africa, "this high dry plateau where Martha was imprisoned, forever, it seemed" (LL, p. 199), symbolizes the drying up of Martha's inner resources. The dissolution of individual life and the sense of identity thus acquired have proved illusory when sought in political commitment and personal relationships. Hereafter, Martha and Doris Lessing lose interest in the quest for identity. Instead of selfhood through merger with an Other, merger alone is sought. In The Golden Notebook (1962), published between A Ripple From the Storm (1958) and Landlocked (1965), Lessing recapitulates Martha's quest in that of Anna Wulf, another autobiographical heroine, one who is primarily a novelist. Like Martha, Anna tries and eventually rejects political and sexual communion with others, yet Anna discovers that language alienates and isolates her. Instead of enabling her to reach them, language impedes unity and wholeness. Finally the disjunction between experience and the expression or description of it seems complete. In The Golden Notebook the problem is first articulated. In The Four-Gated City its implications for Martha's quest for selfhood become prominent. To explain why, it is first necessary to consider how Anna's experience has bearing on that of Martha.

Anna is torn by conflicting impulses that resemble Martha's: toward selfhood through unification of disparate elements of her personality, and toward self-abnegation through merger with some larger Other. Anna, like Martha, turns to Communism out of "a need for wholeness, for an end to the split, divided, unsatisfactory way we all live."[24] She finds it, however, a totally unsatisfying program for living in the world, not merely because of the contradictions between Marxist theory and Stalinist practice. More fundamentally, its rationalistic and idealistic explanations do not accurately account for human behavior, collective or individual, as Anna has experienced it.

Anna's failure to find an identity has left her "incapable of writing the only kind of novel which interests me: a book powered with an intellectual or moral passion strong enough to create order, to create a new way of looking at life. It is because I am too diffused" (GNB, p. 59). Instead of writing this ordered novel, she keeps four notebooks in which she records, separately, thoughts on her African experience during World War II, her Communist activities, her personal life, and, in the fourth, attempts an autobiographical novel. The notebooks are further framed by a conventional novel called "Free Women" which is supposedly the word written by Anna at the end of the experiences recorded in the four notebooks. Her work, obviously, mirrors the fragmentation she feels: It was "as if Anna had, almost automatically, divided herself into four, and then . . . named these divisions" (GNB, p. 55). Before she can unite these fictional parts by synthesizing her stories and meditations, she must unify herself.

In having sex, she is momentarily able to experience the dissolution of personality she craves: "A vaginal orgasm is emotion and nothing else, felt as emotion and expressed in sensations that are indistinguishable from emotion. The vaginal orgasm is a dissolving in a vague, dark generalised sensation like being swirled in a warm whirlpool" (GNB, p. 186). Unfortunately, achieving the "only one real female orgasm" depends upon the male partner: "that is when a man, from the whole of his need and desire takes a woman and wants all her response. Everything else is a substitute and a fake . . . ." (GNB, p. 186). Like Martha Quest, Anna depends on "a real man" who will engulf her and transport her beyond her imperfect, unfulfilled self to wholeness through dissolution. Anna's autobiographical heroine Ella describes this longing: "That when she loved a man again, she would return to normal: a woman, that is, whose sexuality would ebb and flow in response to his. A woman's sexuality is, so to speak, contained by a man, if he is a real man; she is, in a sense, put to sleep by him, she does not think about sex" (GNB, p. 390). Real contentment entails being encompassed by an Other, one's active, conscious identity "put to sleep" and superseded by undivided being.

In The Golden Notebook, however, there is no Thomas Stern; Anna cannot find this transporting experience in a sexual relationship. She does find, on the other hand, a kind of self-image mirrored in her alter ego, Saul. But his near-madness, like Thomas's, is threatening. Like Martha, Anna is reluctant to accept an identity that is so apparently disturbed and marginal, but Anna is more willing to explore irrational alternatives to conventionally sane life.

Through visual projections--dreams and imaginary "films" that repeat, re-organize, and symbolically recreate her waking experience-- Anna heals her self-split. Not the process of psychoanalysis per se, but the dreaming which Anna does deliberately, helps her unite fragments of herself and even relate them to the whole of human history which has seemed chaotic. Through dreams she retrieves a lost sense of the plentitude and unity of being that exists in and through oneness with an Other.

Only in her unconscious dream-life can Anna experience wholeness. Her dream of the unity of the civilized world is an allegory of the disintegration she feels in waking life. It counteracts the disjunction between political idealism and practice, the divisiveness threatening the unity of mankind:

> I dreamed there was an enormous web of beautiful fabric stretched out. It was incredibly beautiful, covered all over with embroidered pictures. The pictures were illustrations of the myths of mankind but they were not just pictures, they were the myths themselves, so that the soft glittering web was alive. . . . Then I look and it is like a vision--time has gone and the whole history of man, the whole long story of mankind, is present in what I see now, and it is like a great soaring hymn of joy and triumph in which pain is a small lively counterpoint. . . . (GNB, p. 256)

After the world becomes whole, one beautiful color mass, there is "a moment of almost unbearable unhappiness" before everything explodes in silence and a chaos of fragments (GNB, p. 256). This dream is reminiscent of the childhood game Anna played, "creating" the world by "naming" everything in it:

> ". . . I would create the world, continent by continent, ocean by ocean (but the point of 'the game' was to create this vastness while holding the bedroom, the house, the street in their littleness in my mind at the same time) until the point was reached where I moved out into space, and watched the world, a sunlit ball in the sky, turning and rolling beneath me. Then, having reached that point . . . I'd try to imagine at the same time, a drop of water, swarming with life, or a green leaf. Sometimes I could reach what I wanted, a simultaneous knowledge of vastness and of smallness." (GNB, p. 469)

Anna's ideal is embodied here: to have simultaneously a sense of individual, atomistic life and a synthesis of the atoms or parts into a vast whole. The act of imagination necessary to achieve this in waking life is beyond Anna's ability at this point. Significantly, she cannot any longer create through "naming." Her discourse does not satisfactorily unite herself and the "world" of her experience.

Anna's linguistic crisis, crystallizing Lessing's own, seems to be this: Do we merely talk to ourselves in our discourse, or do we communicate and even create experience that can be shared by others? In writing a novel, is the author finally only writing about herself, creating a self through the alienated medium of her discourse, but not going beyond that self? Anna's dilemma is exacerbated by an inner conflict between a drive toward individuation and a dread of solipsism. On the one hand she feels "that the human personality, that unique flame, is so sacred to me that everything else becomes unimportant" (GNB, p. 68) and "that the flashes of geniune art are all out of deep, suddenly stark, undisguisable private emotion" (GNB, p. 298). She violently disagrees with the tenets of modernist art: ". . . this antihumanist bullying about the evaporation of the personality becomes meaningless for me at that point when I manufacture enough emotional energy inside myself to create in memory some human being I've known" (GNB, p. 99). Like other modern writers, however, Anna is forced to ask if language can capture that emotional truth and communicate it: "Am I saying then that the certainty I'm clinging to belongs to the visual arts, and not to the novel, not to the novel at all, which has been claimed by the disintegration and the collapse?" (GNB, p. 99). The implicit answer given in The Golden Notebook is, yes.

There is a gulf between reality and the words used to describe it; so Anna comes to feel. Her autobiographical heroine, Ellen, explains: ". . . every time in life I go through a dry time, a period of deadness, I always do this: hold on to a set of words, the phrases of a kind of knowledge, even while they are dead and meaningless, but knowing that life will come back and make them live too" (GNB, p. 390).

This rupture between essence and expression brings about Anna's writing block. In her Communist Party editing job, she ponders this "gap between what they [words] are supposed to mean, and what in fact they say . . ." (<u>GNB</u>, p. 258). For a writer, the implications are twofold. First, discourse cannot communicate a single, necessary meaning. (A sincere but mawkish novel by a "comrade living somewhere near Leeds" dismays Anna because "it could be read as parody, irony or seriously. It seemed to me this fact is another expression of the fragmentation of everything, the painful disintegration of something that is linked with what I feel to be true about language, the thinning of language against the density of our experience" [<u>GNB</u>, p. 259].) The writer cannot be sure his words will refer to the same objects, experiences, and ideas for his audience because language has no stable referent. As Lessing lamented in "A Small Personal Voice," "Words . . . can no longer be used simply and naturally." That meaning is relative leads to the second major difficulty Anna faces.

Discourse--thought, writing, speech--seems to Anna to exclude the part of reality which is Other rather than private. She decries, not solely out of Party loyalty, "'the driving painful individuality of the art of the bourgeois era . . . . the driving egotism of individual art'" (<u>GNB</u>, p. 299). Instead, she wants to write fiction that "'will express not man's self-divisions and separateness from his fellows but his responsibility for his fellows and his brotherhood'" (<u>GNB</u>, p. 299).[25] What alarms Anna most is her intuition that the reality she cannot express in words is <u>within</u> her; Anna comes to realize that the Other occupies the space within her own being.

In *The Golden Notebook*, the Other is the unconscious. Anna learns to accept the fact that this inner landscape includes destructive as well as creative energies. She has a recurring nightmare about a deformed dwarf which "represented something anarchistic and uncontrollable, something destructive," all the more terrifying because it appears in human form. Its power is "an inner vitality . . . caused by a purposeless, undirected, causeless spite" (GNB, p. 408). Anna is reluctant to envision this "joy-in-spite" as human; she has always projected destructive and aggressive impulses onto institutions, other people, and abstractions blamed for distorting human life. Now she must admit that "the malicious male-female dwarf figure, the principle of joy-in-destruction," is within her (GNB, p. 508). The dwarf, representing anarchy, purposelessness, incoherence, is the antithesis of what Anna has always considered the human drive toward creating order. Anna has dreaded disorder and incoherence because they threaten her sense of identity.

Now, however, Anna sees that if chaos resides within her, any unified identity she achieves must falsify the whole of human experience. For, if "words are form," and she defines herself through discourse, this form must be inadequate (GNB, p. 407). "Words mean nothing. They have become, when I think, not the form into which experience is shaped, but a series of meaningless sounds, like nursery talk, and away to one side of experience. Or like the sound tract of a film that has slipped its connection with the film" (GNB, p. 407). The problem is, subconscious experience must necessarily resist articulation because it includes in its essence chaos and incoherence.

> The fact is, the real experience can't be described. I think, bitterly, that a row of asterisks, like an old-fashioned novel, might be better. Or a symbol of some kind, a circle perhaps, or a square. Anything at all, but not words. The people who have been there, in the place in themselves where words, patterns, order, dissolve, will know what I mean and the others won't. (<u>GNB</u>, p. 542)

As an artist, Anna will never be able to write in a way that conveys this knowledge of chaos because language by definition is a kind of order. Another way to put this is that while felt experience may be meaningless and incoherent, discourse cannot be. Therefore, she decides that her art must necessarily fail. Only in visual projections --dreams, films, and so on--can one fuse both orders of experience, rational and irrational.

Anna has an inner "projectionist" who shows films recreating the whole of her past life as her fiction cannot begin to do. The films link her experience with that of others in a collective vision unattainable in language.

> The film was beyond my experience, beyond Ella's, beyond the notebooks, because there was a fusion, and instead of seeing separate scenes, people, faces, movements, glances, they were all together, the film became immensely slow again, it became a series of moments where a peasant's hand bent to drop seed into earth, or a rock stood glistening while water slowly wore it down, or a man stood on a dry hillside in the moonlight, stood eternally, his rifle ready on his arm. Or a woman lay awake in darkness, saying No, I won't kill myself, I won't, I won't. (<u>GNB</u>, p. 543)

In fiction, such anonymity and communality cannot be captured.

What Anna and Doris Lessing strive for instead is a novel that attempts to render more of the communality and multiplicity of experience than has been possible in the traditional realistic novel. Instead of being a <u>Bildungsroman</u> (like the first <u>Children of Violence</u> novels) with its linear narrative, <u>The Golden Notebook</u> is a spatial structure--its notebook extracts woven together in a difficult pattern.

Lessing has said she was trying to exemplify "formlessness with the end of fragmentation," unity through dissolution of difference.[26] The attempt is, as she realizes, self-defeating: "'Well, I do like *The Golden Notebook* because at any rate, though I do believe it to be a failure, at any rate it at least hints of complexity.'"[27] That is, real formlessness and randomness cannot be approximated in purposive discourse. For Lessing, the truth about reality is now "that we must not divide things off, must not compartmentalize."[28] If true, this necessarily dooms to failure any fiction that purports to be about reality, whether that fiction is an articulated personality--a self-- or a novel.

In *The Golden Notebook*, Lessing comes to define Other as self, in a paradoxical sense. Other is the unconscious mind, while personality or ego--the "I"--is merely an imperfect, incomplete form imposed upon this. In *The Golden Notebook*, Lessing rejects the false self (ego) for the true self (the unconscious--primal subjectivity). Since the Other is within, the subject need only dig below the false to the true self to achieve wholeness. It is no longer a question of defining through dialectical process one's relationship to the Other and, in the process, creating a self. Now, as in Virginia Woolf's fiction, the self-as-personality becomes an impediment to true selfhood, really the internalized sense of the Other.

For all its purported "failure" to render the ineffable realm of the Other, the experimental complexity of *The Golden Notebook* does suggest what lies beyond expression. Anna's fitful attempts to order her self and her art convey her liminal experience of the silence (incoherence, irrationality) beyond the forms. *The Four-Gated City* attempts to surpass The Golden Notebook in approaching chaos. Yet instead of experimenting with the limits of fiction, the later novel reaffirms them. Instead of offering a more telling approach to the silence, the novel is a flood of thousands of pages of repetitious utterance. Martha's increasing anonymity is meant to suggest the transcendence of egotism as well as of narrative point of view, since neither self nor literary form can adequately embody the truth, which resists formulation. Yet the novel is problematic, not because it lacks form but because it has too much. That is, in The Four-Gated City the problem is that reality is describable--or rather, it is described. By having Martha's psychic explorations go deeper than those of Anna Wulf, who feared to acknowledge the chaos in her own mind, Lessing implies that Martha discovers the fundamentally collective nature of the unconscious mind. What is collective--transpersonal or interpsychic--becomes intelligible. If rational speech does not establish satisfactory communication between individuals, at least this unconscious discourse--the "sea of sound"--does. Individual, rational discourse becomes useless, unnecessary, even undesirable. In the appendix at the book's end, the mutant "new children" manifest forms of extrasensory perception and other new means of communication that offer the only hope for mankind (4GC, p. 647).

The transcendence (or subversion) of ordinary life leaves behind the realm of fictions--purposive behavior as well as meaningful thought, speech, and writing. It is this subversion of fictionality that is fundamentally, implicitly alarming, I believe. The Golden Notebook suggested that Lessing may have had a change of heart resulting in a sort of political apathy--the renouncing of political change for personal reform on a small scale. Nevertheless, such a loss of interest in overtly political action is not necessarily disquieting. Anna's personal efforts to improve life are unheroic (she becomes a marriage counselor and teacher of delinquent children), but they are the same in kind though not degree as political efforts to reform institutional structures in society. What *is* disquieting, I would suggest, is Lessing's undercutting of even personal, small-scale actions and other "fictive" attempts to imbue experience with meaning. The individual self and language, identity and discourse, are products of the dialectical tension between self and Other. Rejecting them means arresting the process, substituting a stasis (psychic empathy) for the admittedly exhausting process of uniting self and Other. Lessing does not so much resolve the conflict between the two as nullify one pole of the tension--the self.

If silence is reality and discourse only distorts or ineffectually describes it, then why does Lessing write so long a novel if the attempt is by definition doomed to fail? If self is a mirage and a distortion, why is the novel, so lengthy, autobiographical? The answer to both questions is that there remains in her work a subliminal drive toward self-assertion and self-identification through discourse. The definition of self, in separation from Other (defined as political brotherhood, sex, ecstasy, madness, or silence), is implicitly rather than openly desired. The avatar of self in The Four-Gated City is, paradoxically, the collective unconscious.

The psychic underground explored by Martha in the novel embodies elements of conscious, egoic life attributed to the unconscious source. Martha interprets learned feelings and values as innate, universal and necessary. For example, the initial rejection she felt as a tiny child is embodied as the "self-hater." She feels a self-loathing that she interprets as loathing of selfhood--of egocentric identity in any form. Finally, the novel is not problematic because it favors mystical, psychic evolution over political or personal reform. The inherent contradiction is this: it dramatizes the deleterious effects of purposive, malevolent actions even as it apparently denies that purposive action in the sense of reform, mental or physical, is possible. Martha can think of no remedial action to take except to escape from the personal realm entirely. Yet, ironically, she carries within her--in the apparently collective, impersonal unconscious--the rigid, determining values of the realm she seeks to deny. Because she carries the problem with her, escape is impossible.

The Four-Gated City and other recent works convey Lessing's feeling that nothing can be done to alter the underlying structure of consciousness, therefore, such change can only be longingly, passively awaited. In The Four-Gated City, nuclear holocaust liberates people from private and public oppression by causing a genetic mutation that alters the structure of the human mind for the better. The passive receptivity of The Four-Gated City is repeated in The Memoirs of a Survivor (1975). There, the anonymous narrator desires but cannot bring about the transcendence of personal history. Eventually without any volitional act on her part, the barriers between quotidian life and reality break down, permitting a fusion between human beings and the mystical "One," the incarnation of Otherness in this book. What might seem disturbing about this plot is not Lessing's omission of a program of action or blueprint for the mutation or transcendence of human nature. Only if we confuse mental and physical acts can we expect allegorical and utopian fantasies to be prescriptive. What is disturbing, I think, is the painful contradiction between the power of some characters to inflict psychological harm and the powerlessness attributed to the victims. A close look at the unconscious landscape in The Four-Gated City will enable us to map out particular hazards.

* * * * *

In The Four-Gated City, Martha is drawn increasingly toward dissolution of her surface personality, toward exploration of her unconscious mind which, she discovers, is essentially collective. When the novel opens, Martha has recently arrived in London and relishes her anonymity. Looking at her reflection in the Thames which, like the sea, symbolizes the dissolution she longs for, Martha is pleased to see herself as merely "a tiny entity among swarms" (4GC, p. 17). Knowing almost no one in London, Martha is not forced to assume a persona or identity: ". . . one felt like an empty space without boundaries and it did not matter what name one gave a stranger who asked: What is your name? Who are you?" (4GC, p. 18). This anonymous solitude is more authentic than the adoption of a social self: ". . . since she had been in London, she had been alone, and had learned that she had never been anything else in her life. Far from being an enemy, it was her friend. This was the best thing she had known . . ." (4GC, p. 37). For many years (roughly between 1950-1958) Martha will be forced to resume her persona and to play social roles, under the pressure of other people's demands and the images they have of her. She always retains, however, this knowledge of an interior life that is more true and valuable than her conscious life in society.

Martha explores this inner space as she walks unconsciously through London in her early days, discovering that it contains happy and painful memories, feelings, and impulses. In addition to her personal memories, the subterranean mind includes an archetypal demonic figure, like the old dwarf in Anna Wulf's dreams. He is an "enemy, a jiggling fool or idiot," "a maniac ready to dance inwards with idiotic words and phrases" (4GC, p. 38). Like the dwarf, the maniac incarnates chaos, incoherence, random noise. Martha describes this stream of unconscious discourse as "a wavelength, a band where music jigged and niggled, with or without words"(4GC, p. 39). When Martha learns that the "great chaos of sound" is "the human mind," she seems to accept the collectivity of this energy as the true Other she has always sought (4GC, p. 498): "if she did not find a way of getting back there, it would be a self-betrayal" (4GC, p. 495). Betrayal not of her surface identity, but of the pure being she feels when exploring this uncharted "new territory" (4GC, p. 498). The being she feels part of is an impersonal force resembling the cosmic flux, the "dissolution of dancing atoms" in Martha's epiphany on the veld. "Great forces as impersonal as thunder or lightning or sunlight or the movement of the oceans . . . swept through bodies" (4GC, p. 496), impelling people to channel this energy anyhow. Some, like Jack or Mark Coldridge, use sex to experience this dissolution of self. But "The impersonal sea could become the thousand volts of hate as easily as it could become love . . ." (4GC, p. 497), and "the self-hater" is an "aspect" of an individual that can channel this primal energy into destruction.

The capacity for hatred, aggression, prejudice, and so on is innate, in fact, is universal. "Every attitude, emotion, thought, has its opposite held in balance out of sight but there all the time" (4GC, p. 550). Every human being, that is, has the unconscious potential for committing evil as well as good, destructive as well as creative, actions. Martha's political ardor, her humanistic enthusiasm, is merely one of many conflicting impulses: ". . . Hating is . . . the underside of all this lovely liberalism" (4GC, p. 539), she discovers. Self-hatred is the source of political oppression, masochism of sadism, self-destruction of aggression toward others. "If a dictator wishes to control a party, or a country; if a hierarchy of priests wish to control their flock; if any power-seeker anywhere wants to create a manipulated group--he, she, has to embody the self-hater. It is as easy as that. And it is very easy to do" (4GC, pp. 552-553). By embodying the self-destructive impulse in a human form, tyrannical authority wins the identification of the mass.

Yet this negative photographic image of her usual personality--Martha the nurturer, the humanist--is no more real or authentic than her social self. Martha thinks, "'I've seen the underneath of myself. Which isn't me--any more than my surface is me. I am the watcher, the listener . . .'" (4GC, p. 553). That is, the collective unconscious wavelength of energies is something Martha can "plug into" at will, by assuming different guises or personae, both good and bad: "These things are there. Always. I can choose to be them or not" (4GC, p. 551).

The problem is, how does one choose which aspect of self will dominate? How can a person decide whether or not to "plug into" the "self-hater," or any other self? Martha discovers that she can make the power of the "self-hater" diminish merely by accepting him as one impulse of her true self: ". . . because she was very busy, very worried over Lynda, her own Devil retreated. . . . she became careless of him. Soon, the Devil, once histrionic, flamboyant, accusing, violent, had become a silly little nagging voice, which became swallowed in the sea of sound--was just one voice among many" (4GC, p. 556). But this defeat of the "Devil" seems fortuitous, since Martha's choice is not exercised. Indeed, many people with special awareness of the "sea of sound" are unable to control their lives and are victimized by their exceptionalness. Lynda Coldridge, a psychic who heard the inner voices long before Martha's explorations began, is one who suffers for what she knows. Martha and Doris Lessing ascribe Lynda's victimization not to her own powerlessness but to society's refusal to acknowledge the extraordinary perceptiveness that she possesses.

As Mary Shelley and Virginia Woolf knew, society reacts hostilely to any unconventional psychological powers, especially in women and others who violate established norms. It clamps down controls, in the form of rules and conventional responses, to deny the existence of suprarational:

> The mechanisms were always exactly the same, whether political, religious, psychological, philosophic. Dragons guarded the entrances and exits of each layer in the spectrum of belief, or opinion; and the dragons were always the same dragon, no matter what names they went under. The dragon was fear; fear of what other people might think; fear of being different; fear of being isolated; fear of the herd we belong to; fear of that section of the herd we belong to. (4GC, p. 516)

Such repressive mechanisms are society's attempt to prevent psychic explorations that might uncover new ways of being in the world. The established order, psychological and political, must suppress the collective "gleams of life, the authentic note or throb of vitality, the unmistakable pulse" which cannot (by definition) be regimented and reduced to order (4GC, p. 516).

Most people with extraordinary capacities, tuned in to the "sea of sound," are defined by society as mad. Jailed or hospitalized, treated by psychoanalysts who "explode" their energies in catharsis to defuse them (4GC, pp. 243-245), these visionaries become "psychological cripples" (4GC, p. 524): "Like hundreds of thousands of others; probably millions . . . these crippled, destroyed people will become another of our statistics . . ." (4GC, p. 524). Lessing recognizes that extraordinary beings--like Septimus in Mrs. Dalloway--must be certified mad or criminal by society because they threaten its order through their essential anti-rational abilities.

The realization that social personae, rules and conventions are fictions that disguise and distort the true self leads Lessing to take a more extreme position than Virginia Woolf, who did not--could not--elevate her private trauma into a political stand. Lessing simply inverts conventional values. Madness becomes celebrated as positive, for the creative, if anarchistic and incoherent, growth potential it represents:

> Perhaps . . . if society is so organised, or rather has so grown, that it will not admit what one knows to be true, will not admit it, that is, except as it comes out perverted, through madness, then it is through madness and its variants that it must be sought after. (4GC, p. 375)

Lessing's inversion of the usual categories--madness and sanity--to suggest that madness is life-sustaining and creative where sanity entails spiritual death shows the influence of R. D. Laing. In The Politics of Experience, Laing announced, "The texture of the fabric of these socially shared hallucinations is what we call reality, and our collusive madness what we call sanity."[29] "What we call 'normal' is a product of repression, denial, splitting, projection, introjection and other forms of destructive action on experience. . . . It is radically estranged from the structure of being."[30] Schizophrenia is not a disease but "the label is a social fact and the social fact a political event."[31] In The Divided Self, Laing argues that though all people are necessarily divided in having an inner self and a social self, the latter enabling them to interact with others, most of us are dominated by the social self. In schizophrenia, the real, authentic, inner self overpowers the "false" self; in our social being, however, the "false self" has the upper hand.[32]

The problem, in Laing's theory as well as in The Four-Gated City, is how to reform the false self and social institutions that oppress the true self. By what means is the superior, inner self to be accommodated more fully? There are no means, at least not in The Four-Gated City. Ironically, it is not because the unconscious mind is amoral and chaotic that it cannot be brought into contact with conscious life. Rather, it is only too moralistic and orderly. Lessing's view of the unconscious is a space where love and hate, creativity and destruction, order and anarchy clash as primal instincts. She never doubts for a moment, however, that hatred, aggression and destruction are bad.[33] Clearly, these unconscious impulses carry their own labels, representing implicit value judgments on Lessing's part. And if moral and aesthetic values are incorporated into the unconscious itself, then (Lessing implies) there exists no valid, necessary mediating agency between unconscious and conscious life. There can be no mechanism to create and regulate external values and order, no means of translating individual needs and drives into purposive actions. Therefore, no means can be found to bring about social personae or institutions that will be better (i.e., truer to the authentic inner self) than existing ones.

Because she questions the very validity of conscious mechanisms, the "dragons," Lessing cannot recommend any means of reforming individual and social life. She falls back on the "act of imagination" as the means of revolution, psychological and political. Altering the human personality is only possible through mutation of moral, emotional and intellectual faculties. The mutation that produces the "new children" at the end of The Four-Gated City perhaps involves the extinction of some primitive destructive drive in the collective unconscious. Perhaps some creative faculty is augmented, shifting the balance of power between subconscious drives. The means by which this alteration takes place must remain unarticulated.

Similarly, in the public sphere, it is impossible to explain how true community can replace oppressive social institutions. In The Four-Gated City, only in underground culture, subversive of repression itself, is improvement in social life possible. Forming and identifying a group would merely set in motion the intellectual impulses to divide and compartmentalize, which (as Martha has learned) would defeat all reformation attempts. One of the youthful non-leaders (Francis Coldridge) offers a non-definition of their relative success: ". . . our chief characteristic was that we had no ideology, plan, constitution or philosophy. We had grown together as a community" (4GC, p. 600). This communal life, unlike the Communist fraternity or experimental relationships Martha has participated in, fosters the "lively yeast" or vitality by denying rationalism. These nameless, undirected aggregations of people who feel rather than profess the same desire for unity are the nearest realization in Martha's experience of the four-gated city of her childhood vision.

The peaceable kingdom is the outward and visible sign of inner transformation, of wholeness of self making possible social harmony and unity. Significantly, Martha's final recorded thoughts in The Four-Gated City (excluding the appendix) are of a place where life can be unified and made whole, individually and socially:

> She thought, with the dove's voices of her solitude: Where? But where. How? Who? No, but where, where . . . . Then silence and the birth of a repetition: Where? Here. Here?
> Here, where else, you fool, you poor fool, where else has it been, ever . . . . (4GC, p. 591)

The emphasis is on where--in what space this reconciliation of inner and outer, conscious and unconscious life will take place--at the expense of how--by what means it will be effected. Therefore, it is appropriate that the four-gated city, Martha's original annunciated vision, is the key to Lessing's ideas about inner and outer revolution. The four-gated city is perhaps also the key to the problems arising from this vision.

The city has been interpreted as mythic and utopian, symbolizing both psychological and political ideals.[34] It may also stand for very personal needs and wishes, referring not to a future state of collective perfection but instead to the private history of the woman who dreamed it. The four-gated city in a sense symbolizes the perfection of the family Martha has sorely missed all her life. The family appears to be the recurrent motif in the Children of Violence novels, offering an ideal, both structurally and emotionally, for Martha's quest. Structurally, the community of many-fathered, multi-racial children living harmoniously with adults symbolizes the Golden Age of individual autonomy within a collective identity. Emotionally, the original four-gated city embodies at once Martha's longing for an idyllic milieu in which to live and grow, and her bitterness at being denied this.[35]

In Martha Quest, the city offers an alternative to the constriction and pain of family life:

> Outside one of the gates stood her parents, the Van Rensbergs, in fact most of the people of the district, forever excluded from the golden city because of their pettiness of vision and small understanding; they stood grieving, longing to enter, but barred by a stern and remorseless Martha--for unfortunately one gets nothing, not even in a dream, without paying heavily for it, and in Martha's version of the golden age there must always be at least one person standing at the gate to exclude the unworthy. (MQ, pp. 17-18)

Lessing's irony makes clear that Martha's vision is a projection of her own emotional needs: ". . . the pity she refused herself flooded out and surrounded the black child like a protective blanket" (MQ, p. 17). In a way, the vision of the family of man is a direct embodiment of Martha's unmet need for familial love. Even in the collective unconscious and the non-ideological utopias of Lessing's recent work, this primary motivation can be found.

In The Grass is Singing (1950), Lessing's emotional approval was given to the "personal" code of the African natives over the "impersonal," conventional, authoritarian code of the white settlers.[36] In The Memoirs of a Survivor (1975), the mind is divided into two realms, the "personal" and the "impersonal," and the personal space must be transcended:

> The impersonal scenes might bring discouragement or problems that had to be solved--like the rehabilitation of walls or furniture,

> cleaning, putting order into chaos--but in that realm there was a lightness, a freedom, a feeling of possibility. Yes, that was it, the space and the knowledge of the possibility of alternative action. . . . But to enter the "personal" was to enter a prison, where nothing could happen but what one saw happening, where the air was tight and limited, and above all where time was a strict unalterable law and long--oh, my God, it went on, and on and on, minute by decreed minute, with no escape but the slow wearing away of one after another.[37]

This personal realm is one of individual memory--of a claustrophobic infancy, purportedly that of the orphan Emily but at least symbolically that of the anonymous narrator as well. Even the perpetual disorder of the "impersonal" space, its rooms overrun by natural upheaval or human anarchy, is preferable to the suffocating atmosphere of the personal:

> Necessity. The strict laws of this small personal world. Heat. Hunger. A fighting of emotion. . . . And smallness, extreme smallness, weakness, a helplessness reaching out and crying for the little crumbs of food, freedom, variation of choice which were all that could reach this little hot place where the puppets jerk to their invisible strings. (MofS, pp. 152-153)

To escape this dependency and determinism--the repetition of bourgeois family life--the individual will is useless: ". . . I fell into despair at the precariousness of every human attempt and effort. . . . It was that afternoon I tried deliberately to reach behind the wall. . . . trying everything to make the heavy solidity of the thing go down under the pressure of my will" (MofS, p. 150). The wall between "reality" and this impersonal mental space finally dissolves, enabling the narrator (and Emily, her lover Gerald, and their motley group) to cross over "out of this collapsed little world into another order of world altogether" (MofS, p. 217). Not by effort on their part but by the intervention of a female figure ("One," appropriately) is this dissolution of boundaries achieved. In effect, the narrator longs for an idealized version of the primal subjectivity--complete oneness with the mother--that may be the goal of all utopian quests.

The experience of the narrator in The Memoirs of a Survivor clearly parallels that of Martha Quest. In a sense, the whole of The Four-Gated City is about Martha's effort to liberate herself from the emotional oppression she feels, the result of her mother's rejection. One of the voices in the "sea of sound" epitomizes this:

> The tune said: Mother, must I go on dancing? Infuriating, ridiculous, banal, this had recently entered her listening mind as soon as she reached the boundary in it. Always. Mother, must I go on dancing? Yes, she knew only too well she had to go on dancing. She knew it, both now, when she was inside the empty space, away from ordinary living; and inside ordinary living, when the space seemed a very far country. (4GC, p. 40)

The "dance" is the torturous cycle of parent-child relationships in which Martha is trapped ("it was hard to tell whether she was Martha, or her mother who had given birth to her, or Caroline, who would give birth" 4GC, p. 57). When Martha recovers her past in memory, it is in order to comprehend, perhaps forgive, and ideally to leave behind this inheritance of emotional damage.

During psychoanalysis (despite her hostility toward her doctor), Martha has an important realization about her relationship with her mother, attaining "the furthest point she had reached in her life" (4GC, p. 241):

> "My mother was a woman who hated her own sexuality and she hated mine too. She wanted me to be a boy always--before I was born. She knew I was going to be a boy. She had a boy's name for me. My way of fighting her was--to be a clown. . . . She was always making fun of me because I wasn't good at the boy's things. My brother was always beating me. But I never once said, which is what I should have said: I'm a girl, why should I be good at boy's things? No, I did them, but I did them badly and laughed at myself. . . . When at last I became a girl, and spent years and years longing for the moment when I would have breasts and be a woman, I was able to defy her at last. I made myself beautiful clothes, and every man I had, for a long time, was a weapon against her. Do you suppose I don't know that?" (4GC, p. 241)[38]

Adopting, then rebelling against, the images Mrs. Quest has of her, Martha is trapped in an effort to get recognition and approbation of her own identity from her mother.

Martha's need for approval stems from her initial rejection by her mother. In _Martha Quest_ we learn that "Since her earliest years Martha had been offered the information that she was unwanted in the first place, and that she had a double nervous breakdown for godparents . . ." (MQ, p. 262). Her parents, themselves in the throes of personal crises and devastated by the social cataclysm of World War I, were unable to love her as she needed to be loved. Reliving her childhood in memory, "Martha heard herself crying. She wept, while a small girl wept with her, Mama, Mama, why are you so cold, so unkind, why did you never love me?" (4GC, p. 232).

In _The Memoirs of a Survivor_, the baby Emily is depicted in a state of neediness that may, at least symbolically, resemble Martha's original deprivation:

> . . . she was tiny, a baby, and alone. The mother was elsewhere; it was not time to feed. The baby was desperate with hunger. Need clawed in her belly; she was being eaten alive by the need for food. She yelled inside the thick smothering warmth; sweat scattered off her scarlet little face; she twisted her head to find a breast, a bottle, anything; she wanted liquid, warmth, food, comfort. (MofS, p. 153)

The infant's unconscious sense of plentitude comes from such needs being met. Being rejected from birth by their parents means that Lessing's heroines are not even granted that initial identification with the Other that is a prerequisite for selfhood.

May Quest, Martha's mother, has suffered in the same way as her daughter—being rejected by her own mother as a child. Resentment of her beautiful, vivacious mother's early death becomes resentment of

Martha's own desire for independent selfhood:

> That brutal woman, her beautiful mother, remained invisible in her dangerous Heaven. The painful girl, Martha, was locked in her bedroom, under orders. . . . Mrs. Quest had become her own comforter, her own solace. Having given birth to herself, she cradled Mrs. Quest, a small frightened girl, who lay in tender arms against a breast covered in the comfort of bright salmon-pink, home-knitted wool. (LL, pp. 77-78)

The experience of giving birth to oneself becomes a motif in the Children of Violence novels, a symbol of the individual's need to create her own birthright--her self.

Lessing's fiction enacts the rebirth of Martha into a world, not of private pain and suffering, but of wholeness and satisfaction. Lessing has confirmed that Martha's birth struggle was based on her own traumatic experience.[39] Both had forceps deliveries after long, painful labor. Both had parents who were physically and emotionally devastated by the First World War (in which Lessing's father lost a leg) and unprepared to meet the needs of their children. Then, like Martha and Mrs. Quest, Lessing experienced a "rebirth" (after taking mescaline) where she "'was both giving birth and being given birth to. Who was the mother, who was the baby? I was both but neither.'"[40] Lessing interprets this experience as signifying the renunciation of the ego: "'But that creature being born wasn't a "writer." It was immensely ancient, for a start, and it was neither male nor female, and it had no race or nationality.'"[41] This anti-individualism, however, conceals an implicit desire for absolute subjectivity. Lessing wants to give herself "'a good birth--because the whole of this labor was a progress from misery, pain, unhappiness, toward happiness, acceptance, and the birth 'I' invented for myself was not painful.'"[42] In short, the reborn self seeks to replace the world of deprivation of its first, real birth with a world of sensory and emotional surfeit. The state of absolute subjectivity with which the infant begins may become the goal of its personal (and political) questing throughout life.

The question remains, what means will gratify such wants, what panacea alleviate the pain of initial rejection? In The Four-Gated City, Lessing offers no means beyond the alteration of consciousness (comparable to that achieved through drugs) in the "new children" at the book's end. Martha can see the parent-child relationship objectively--"'What is the fight? Who's fighting what? Why is it that we all of us have to get out from under awful parents who damage us?'" (4GC, p. 283)--but this does not remove the emotional pain she still feels when her mother criticizes and abuses her (even on her last, dreadful visit to London).

Political reform cannot affect this private conflict any more than psychoanalysis can. Communism tried to legislate the end of the bourgeois family, and it failed. "'And so we abolished the family. In our minds. And when the war was over and there was Communism everywhere, the family would be abolished. . . . And then there would be the golden age, no family, no neurosis. Because the family was the source of neurosis'" (4GC, p. 70). With the failure of reason to resolve the suffering and confusion inflicted by the family, what remains? For Martha, the end of her torment comes when her mother dies after her visit in London ("'But if I kick her out I sign her death warrant. I know that,'" says Martha, refusing to command her mother to leave [4GC, p. 283].) As when the "self-hater" recedes into the sea of subconscious voices, Mrs. Quest's power over Martha dies with the old woman herself. It seems there is nothing Martha can do to rid herself of her mother's influence, of Mrs. Quest's denial of Martha's right to an identity.

Martha and Doris Lessing want the individual to take control of his or her life: "'Or are we just children, and not responsible at all, ever, for what we live in?'" (4GC, p. 283). To interrupt the cycle of familial pain, it is necessary to declare oneself no longer the child of any parent and to accept responsibility for the good and bad in one's inner and social life. The Four-Gated City moves from Martha's last crisis with her mother (in Part II) to her psychic explorations (Part IV), implying that Martha does cease to be a child. But to shed her private pain, Martha must also shed her surface self-- her personality.

In The Four-Gated City, Martha comes to realize that she can adopt any of a number of false selves or personae--the ironical "Matty" or the archetypal nurturing figure keeping house, among others. To the young women in the Coldridge house, Martha becomes "a hierarchic figure whose function one temporarily had to fulfill, or . . . a character in a play. The rejuvenation a young girl gives her mouther or an older woman is a setting-free into impersonality, a setting-free, also, from her personal past" (4GC, p. 387). Such a role is patently false. In reality, Martha feels "herself (or rather, the surface of herself) to be a mass of fragments, or facets, or bits of mirror reflecting qualities embodied in other people . . ." (4GC, p. 352). Since she doesn't believe in the image of herself as archetypal mother (a figure she has always loathed), Martha cannot unify the complex tensions in the household.

In the end, the nurturing adults can do nothing to help the children--to constitute a whole family--despite their benevolent intentions. In fact, it is the children who take responsibility for saving the world. The mutant "new children" after the holocaust have the capacity lacking in ordinary adults:

> For one thing, they are grown up--no, not physically of course, but mentally, emotionally. One talks to them as if they were adult-- no, not that; one talks to them as if they are superior to us . . . which they are. They all carry with them a gentle strong authority. They don't have to be shielded from the knowledge of what the human race is in this century. . . . It is as if--can I put it like this?--they . . . include that history in themselves and . . . have transcended it. They include us in a comprehension we can't begin to imagine. These seven children are our--but we have no word for it. The nearest to it is that they are our guardians. They guard us. (4GC, p. 647)

In this idyllic island community, Martha's wish--that children take responsibility for the future--comes true. Having superior psychological capacities, the "new children" fulfill the ideal of human maturity ("gentle strong authority," "grown up . . . mentally, emotionally"). Actually, they fulfill Martha's personal need--for nurturing by an emotionally stable authority that comprehends and forgives without criticizing or punishing her neediness.

The sustaining atmosphere of the island, made possible by the extraordinary powers of the children, resembles an idealization of the absolute subjectivity a child first knows before his loss of unity with the Other: "It was as if the far-off sweetness experienced in a dream, that unearthly impossible sweetness, less the thing itself than the need or hunger for it, a question and answer sounding together on the same fine high note--as if the sweetness known all one's life, tantalisingly intangible, had come close . . ." (4GC, p. 374). At the end of The Four-Gated City, Martha's question is answered, her need fulfilled, her "belief in a future for our race" realized (4GC, p. 643).

The "new children" break the inexorable repetition of violence done to children like Martha--private as well as public. (Being the daughter of Alfred and May Quest makes her a "child of violence" as much as being the offspring, historically, of World War I. Perhaps more so.) If the "new children" survive and reproduce, there may be an end to the violence committed by human beings against their fellow men in the guise of political injustice, war, or familial oppression. There will be no more "psychological cripples" like the man in a mental hospital whose destructiveness stems from his own early deprivation:

> What did he want to kill? His father? His mother? His sister? It doesn't matter. Long ago he became filled with an enormous sorrow, he knows that somewhere he lost a birthright, he diverged from himself, he will forever be shut out from some sweet truth that once he sucked in like air through his pores. (4GC, p. 614)

Parenting themselves, the new children will never feel her loss, Martha's anguish at being rejected by the longed-for Other. They have no need of selfhood. In essence, the end of The Four-Gated City is a vision of transcendence, not only of selfhood (private identity), but of the very need for it.

As the "new children" transcend history, public and private, the novel is transmuted from Bildungsroman to science fiction. Doris Lessing seems to be rejecting the role of the author of narrator along with her belief in the ego. She told one interviewer, "'I don't believe anymore that I have a thought. There is a thought around.'"[43] In fact, Lessing's newly experimental fictions (Briefing for a Descent into Hell, The Memoirs of a Survivor) are not simply symbolic of her rejection of the conscious self. Her post-realistic work reflects the difficulty of describing the pre-verbal reality, the "sweet" truth of being, that she is now concerned with. As Martha said of the "new children," "we have no word for" this experience.[44]

Finally, human nature seen from the outside is repellent, Martha learns in her subterranean explorations:

> What an extraordinary race, or near-race of half, uncompleted creatures. . . . these people walked in their fouled and disgusting streets full of ordure and bits of refuse and paper as if they were not conscious of their existence here, were somewhere else. . . . They were essentially isolated, shut in, enclosed inside their hideously defective bodies, behind their dreaming drugged eyes, above all, inside a net of wants and needs that made it impossible for them to think of anything else. (4GC, pp. 506-507)

The repetition of "in" implies that the real self is imprisoned within a false, partial, repressive persona, "a net of wants and needs." Like all human beings, Lessing's heroines reluctantly admit the need for a social self but long for the primal, undifferentiated subjectivity in which all needs are met and no sense of separation or alienation--of Otherness--exists. Lessing seems to reject the essential separateness of a self; consequently she rejects by implication the superstructure of human thought, conventions, institutions--in short, all of man's fictions.

Yet perhaps Lessing is not merely endorsing this attempt to escape but showing Martha's unconscious need for a self. Martha's rejection by her parents, especially by her mother, denied her a stable and positive identity in their eyes, making it impossible for her to see herself as an autonomous being. The image of herself as a broken mirror, a mass of fragments reflecting others' images of herself, implies that she was deprived of the essential early identification with the Other that would have enabled her to see herself as sound and whole. Martha's long quest for a self, which apparently ends in her discovering that she doesn't need one, really dramatizes the urgency of that need.

The Four-Gated City seems a torrent of discourse uttered to fill up a void or lack which is felt but not consciously admitted. It is incongruous but not surprising, then, that Lessing's attempt to escape from the egocentric need for self-assertion is documented in a five-volume autobiographical novel comprising thousands of pages. In the end, Martha fails to achieve self-knowledge, in part because "knowing" (in the sense of identifying and articulating) the unconscious life is impossible. More urgently, she fails to realize that selfhood means acceptance of the essential incompleteness and alienation she has so arduously come to recognize in herself. Though Martha is never reconciled to this fundamental frustration, her story makes us feel vividly how imperative is her need.

As Elaine Showalter says in A Literature of Their Own,

> The change in Lessing's fiction from the individual to the collective, from the personal to the communal, from the female to the global, consciousness seems at first like an abrupt transformation. It has, however, been a systematic, willed process of escape from a very painful encounter with the self, with the anguish of feminine fragmentation.[45]

The seemingly contradictory idea of "willed escape . . . from the self" reminds us of George Eliot's will to power. What Doris Lessing repudiates is not egotism but the ego. The Four-Gated City marks Lessing's evolution from a belief in the "individual conscience" expressed in "A Small Personal Voice" (in 1957). There she insisted,

> The point of rest should be the writer's recognition of man, the responsible individual, voluntarily submitting his will to the collective, but never finally; and insisting on making his own personal and private judgments before every act of submission. . . .

What is dangerous is the inner loyalty to something felt as something much greater than one's self.[46]

In The Four-Gated City, Martha seems to have rejected fierce loyalty to the individual in favor of self-abnegation before a subconscious Other. Yet, paradoxically, the outpouring of her desire for dissolution in The Four-Gated City testifies implicitly to the vastness of her need for assertion, definition, and knowledge of the self.

Epilogue

Doris Lessing sympathizes with women's campaigns for political power but gives her primary allegiance to political movements for racial and economic equality. Reacting against reviews which interpreted The Golden Notebook as a feminist treatise, Lessing wrote a preface to the novel in 1971. She stressed that the ideas it dramatized were not narrowly feminist but tempered her disclaimer by saying ". . . the last thing I have wanted to do was to refuse to support women."[47] In her interview with Jonah Raskin, however, she more carelessly claimed, "I'm impatient with people who emphasize sexual revolution. I say we should all go to bed, shut up about sexual liberation, and go on with the important matters."[48] Despite her insistence that economic, racial and psychological tyranny do more harm than sexual oppression, Lessing's fiction portrays women who are "crippled" by causes linked to their inferior status as women.

Martha Quest's chief struggle for autonomy and self-esteem is fought with her mother rather than with any masculine authority. Martha's obsession with winning her mother's love and approval apparently distinguishes her from the narrators and heroines of Mary Shelley, George Eliot and Virginia Woolf who (unconsciously) conciliate or at least heed a patriarchal authority. Martha finds herself forced to choose between her mother's love and her own free self-assertion--between the approval of another and self-approbation--because Mrs. Quest herself is trapped. She simultaneously envies her daughter's freedom and fearfully obeys repressive ideas of women's duty. Martha and her mother inherit the problem first confronted on a wide scale by

Virginia Woolf's generation: the redefinition of the feminine social role after the dethroning of the Victorian Angel. In a sense, Mrs. Quest is the spokeswoman for patriarchal authority in <u>Children of Violence</u>. Her fear of sexuality, a legacy of Victorian repression, inspires Martha's rebellion. Yet in reality both women are trapped by a shared confusion about their identities. They know what they reject but are less sure what they want to do and to be. Their right to assert themselves is externally, politically sanctioned; however, the prohibitions faced by Lessing's predecessors survive as inhibitions.

Lessing's heroines explore a subterranean unconscious life in an unsuccessful effort to overcome the disabling causes of their insecurity and dissatisfaction. Like Mary Shelley and Virginia Woolf, Lessing describes metaphorically a retreat to an unconscious place ("sea of sound," "wedge-shaped core of darkness," "cave") that, like the Platonic descent into the cave, means an encounter with some reality that is more authentic than quotidian life. Unlike Plato's king, however, the protagonists and narrators who make the exploration in women's novels are unable to apply what they learn underground to their life in society. The dragons of conscience that guard the threshold between conscious and unconscious life successfully intimidate the questers. The woman's need to be loved perhaps proves greater than her will to power. In any case, the political novels of Mary Shelley, George Eliot, Virginia Woolf and Doris Lessing picture women submitting (regretfully, angrily, unconsciously) to a collective will that they both resent and woo.

The political fiction of Doris Lessing culminates with a visionary alternative to an intolerable social world, a world that undermines Virginia Woolf's vision in The Years. Both Lessing and Woolf prefer to entertain the idea that history can be imaginatively transcended, since it apparently resists women's desire to change it. In contrast, George Eliot and Mary Shelley make their peace with history and with society's law for women. Mary Shelley's dysutopian novel is a political statement that explains her need to belong to society-- on society's terms. Of the women represented in this study, George Eliot has the strongest will to power. Not surprisingly, her submission to society's will is also the most absolute. Eliot's characters cannot exist beyond the social "web," a network of human relations that is both reassuring and ominous. In every case, whether the woman writer accepts or evades it, the patriarchal order dominates her political vision.

To the nineteenth-century woman writer, society is the ultimate reality with which the individual must come to terms in order to survive. The twentieth-century writer conceives of the possibility of abolishing society because it is a damaging and deteriorating invention of man's, one that is past reform. For Mary Shelley and George Eliot, egotism is the chief moral obstacle to a woman's acceptance by society. To Virginia Woolf and Doris Lessing, egotism in a woman is not morally unacceptable. Rather, it is the unaccommodating ego that is troublesome because it cannot at once satisfy the woman's needs both to please herself and to please society. The political novels of Shelley and Eliot offer the comfort of society as recompense for the individual woman's renunciation of power. Those of Woolf and Lessing depict an unbearable social world and nostalgically long for escape from it. Yet to stress the element of evasion and escapism in the political fiction of Shelley, Eliot, Woolf and Lessing is to overlook the passion and the clear sight with which they write about the oppression of women—-oppression which is fundamentally political but whose effects have not ceased with women's political emancipation. The Angel in the House and other insidiously innocuous "dragons" have largely vanished from the political landscape but (in fiction as recent as Doris Lessing's) only to retreat within the self. Once exiled from political power over her destiny and society's, the woman writer may still contend with self-exile: lasting ambivalence about the extent and legitimacy of her own power.

NOTES

[1] Sigmund Freud, The Future of an Illusion (London: The Hogarth Press, 1949), p. 32.

[2] Ibid., pp. 85-86.

[3] Doris Lessing, In Pursuit of the English (New York: Popular Library, 1960), p. 5. Subsequently cited parenthetically in the text.

[4] Doris Lessing, "My Father," in A Small Personal Voice: Essays, Reviews, Interviews, ed. Paul Schlueter (New York: Vintage Books, 1975), p. 86. Subsequently cited parenthetically in the text.

[5] Roy Newquist, "Interview with Doris Lessing," in A Small Personal Voice, p. 51.

[6] Doris Lessing, A Ripple from the Storm (New York: New American Library, 1970), p. 38. Other volumes of Children of Violence that will be cited parenthetically in the text include: Martha Quest (London: Panther Books Ltd., 1966); A Proper Marriage (London: Panther Books Ltd., 1966); and Landlocked (New York: New American Library, 1970). The four were originally published in England in, respectively, 1952 (MQ); 1954 (PM); 1958 (RS); 1965 (LL).

[7] In 1969, when interviewed by Jonah Raskin, Lessing said: "I've had Children of Violence set up for twenty years." See "Doris Lessing at Stony Brook: An Interview," in A Small Personal Voice, p. 65. In 1963 Lessing told Roy Newquist, "I planned this out twelve years ago." See "Interview with Doris Lessing," p. 57.

[8] Doris Lessing left the Communist Party after the Hungarian Revolt in 1956 and after being censored by the Stalinist press. This information is available in The Novels of Doris Lessing by Paul Schlueter (Carbondale: Southern Illinois University Press, 1973), p. 4. Chapter 1, "Doris Lessing in Perspective," contains a brief biographical sketch.

[9] Jonah Raskin, "Doris Lessing at Stony Brook: An Interview," p. 73.

[10] Doris Lessing, "Preface to The Golden Notebook," in A Small Personal Voice, p. 32.

[11] Georg Lukács, Realism in Our Time: Literature and the Class Struggle, trans. John and Necke Mander (New York: Harper and Row, 1962), p. 111. In the "Author's Notes" published at the end of The

Four-Gated City (New York: Bantam Books, 1970), pp. 655-656, Doris Lessing writes: "This book is what the Germans call a Bildungsroman. We don't have a word for it. This kind of novel has been out of fashion for some time. This does not mean that there is anything wrong with this kind of novel" (p. 655).

[12] Ibid., p. 28.

[13] Ibid., pp. 93-94.

[14] Doris Lessing, "Preface to The Golden Notebook," p. 23.

[15] Lucien Goldmann, Towards a Sociology of the Novel (London: Tavistock Publications Ltd., 1975), trans. Allan Sheriden, p. 4.

[16] Joyce Carol Oates, "A Visit with Doris Lessing," Southern Review, 9 (1973), says that Lessing's term for her recent fiction is "inner space fiction" (p. 875). Doris Lessing told Florence Howe in another interview that this fiction would more appropriately be called "historical fantasy." See Florence Howe, "A Conversation with Doris Lessing (1966)," in Doris Lessing: Critical Studies, ed. Annis Pratt and L. S. Dembo (Madison: The University of Wisconsin Press, 1974), p. 19.

[17] Doris Lessing, The Four-Gated City (New York: Bantam Books, 1970), pp. 647, 643. Hereafter cited parenthetically as 4GC.

[18] Marion Vlastos, "Doris Lessing and R. D. Laing: Psychopolitics and Prophecy," PMLA, 91 (1976), 245. This assessment of Lessing's shifting allegiances is shared by Karen Ann Kildahl in "The Political and Apocalyptical Novels of Doris Lessing: A Critical Study of Children of Violence, The Golden Notebook, Briefing for a Descent Into Hell," DAI, 35 (1975), 4528A (Univ. of Washington), and by Roberta Rubenstein, "Outer Space, Inner Space: Doris Lessing's Metaphor of Science Fiction," World Literature Written in English, 14 (1975), 187-197.

[19] Lois Marchino, in "The Search for Self in the Novels of Doris Lessing," Studies in the Novel (N. Texas State), 4 (1972), 252-261, believes that the goal of all Lessing's ideological experiments is the finding of the self. On the other hand, Robert Ryf, in "Beyond Ideology: Doris Lessing's Mature Vision," Modern Fiction Studies, 21 (1975), 193-201, argues that Martha's merger with the world around her constitutes a kind of rebellion against social evils though it involves "selflessness." He thinks she "becomes, in effect, a secular saint" (p. 200). Similarly, Marion Vlastos thinks Lessing remains concerned with the ego and has Martha return to society after her psychic explorations to affirm their connection to social life (p. 257). Both attempts to reconcile Martha's selflessness with her need to be in the world seem somewhat strained; however, they may reflect Lessing's own ambivalence toward selfhood.

[20] Lukács is quoted in Goldmann, Towards a Sociology of the Novel, p. 6.

[21] Michel Foucault, The Order of Things: An Archaeology of the Human Sciences (New York: Pantheon Books, 1970), p. 44.

[22] Doris Lessing, "The Small Personal Voice," in A Small Personal Voice, p. 5.

[23] In "A Conversation with Doris Lessing," by Florence Howe, Lessing said of The Golden Notebook "I do believe it to be a failure" (p. 12), meaning that it did not (perhaps could not) capture the complexity of experience as she wished. At the same time she said of Children of Violence, specifically The Four-Gated City, "that when I've finished it I shall think, Christ, what a lie. Because you can't get life into it--that's all there is to it--no matter how hard you try."

[24] Doris Lessing, The Golden Notebook (New York: McGraw-Hill, 1963), p. 142. Subsequently cited parenthetically in the text.

[25] In a way, Anna's problem is a contemporary one as Lessing acknowledges in "Preface to The Golden Notebook": "Once a pressure or a current has started, there is no way of avoiding it: there was no way of not being intensely subjective--it was, if you like, the writer's task for that time" (p. 31). Yet Anna's painful realization that in the very act of writing she affirms her "subjective" isolation from her community is not merely symptomatic of a phase of literary style.

[26] Doris Lessing, "Preface to The Golden Notebook," p. 24.

[27] Florence Howe, "A Conversation with Doris Lessing," p. 12.

[28] Doris Lessing, "Preface to The Golden Notebook," p. 28.

[29] R. D. Laing, The Politics of Experience (New York: Pantheon Books, 1967), p. 47.

[30] Ibid., p. 11.

[31] Ibid., p. 83. Laing is not alone in seeing madness as a political category devised by society to segregate and oppress unconventional behavior. In Women and Madness (New York: Avon Books, 1972), Phyllis Chesler calls insanity in women "an expression of female powerlessness and an unsuccessful attempt to reject and overcome this state." "What we consider 'madness' . . . is either the acting out of the devalued female role or the total or partial rejection of one's sex-role stereotype" (pp. 16, 56). Lessing is closer to Laing's analysis than Chesler's, since she resists feminist ideology as reductive.

[32] R. D. Laing, The Divided Self: A Study of Sanity and Madness (London: Tavistock Publications, 1960), pp. 100-101, 45-48.

[33] In "Doris Lessing at Stony Brook: An Interview," Lessing maintains that "the unconscious can be what you make of it, good or bad, helpful or unhelpful. Our culture has made an enemy of the unconscious" (p. 67). Despite Lessing's criticism of "the Freudian landscape," her own subterranean geography seems far from amoral and value-free.

[34] Mary Ann Singleton, in The City and the Veld: The Fiction of Doris Lessing (Lewisburg: Bucknell University Press, 1977), synthesizes several interpretations of the city. It is "a re-creation of the lost Golden Age; and its destruction by the warlike outer city suggests wholeness lost through the divisions of modern thought and the development of the alienated ego. The City can also be seen as a Utopia, a model for a time when the divisions of contemporary society may be overcome" (p. 199).

[35] As Singleton points out, "In Martha's childhood dream, people are excluded from the City because they are not worthy; and she herself guards the door. Here [in The Four-Gated City], also, people are excluded, but because of their own inability" (p. 199). Perhaps the later exclusion is related to the childish animosity of the earlier one.

[36] Doris Lessing, The Grass Is Singing (New York: New American Library, 1976), pp. 32, 40, 178-182.

[37] Doris Lessing, The Memoirs of a Survivor (New York: Bantam Books, 1976), p. 42. Subsequently cited parenthetically in the text.

[38] Sigmund Freud, A General Introduction to Psychoanalysis (New York: Washington Square Press, Inc., 1952), p. 216, suggests a view of mother-daughter rivalry that (in part) is relevant to Martha and Mrs. Quest's relationship: "The daughter sees in her mother the authority which imposes limits to her will, whose task it is to bring her to that renunciation of sexual freedom which society demands; in certain cases, too, the mother is still a rival, who objects to being set aside."

[39] Roy Newquist, "Interview with Doris Lessing," pp. 58-60.

[40] Ibid., p. 58.

[41] Ibid., p. 60.

[42] Ibid., p. 59.

[43] Jonah Raskin, "Doris Lessing at Stony Brook," p. 173.

[44] Sydney J. Kaplan suggests, "It may well be that the very medium of fiction is not the right one for the kind of vision Doris Lessing is now trying to communicate." See "The Limits of Consciousness in the Novels of Doris Lessing," Contemporary Literature, 14 (1973), 123.

[45] Elaine Showalter, *A Literature of Their Own: British Women Novelists from Brontë to Lessing* (Princeton: Princeton Univ. Press, 1977), p. 309. See also Frederick R. Karl, "Doris Lessing in the Sixties: The New Anatomy of Melancholy," *Contemporary Literature*, 13, No. 1 (1972), 15-33. Karl says that Martha "finds such lack of will attractive as an alternative to setting herself constantly against her destiny" (p. 31).

[46] Doris Lessing, "A Small Personal Voice," p. 12.

[47] Doris Lessing, "Preface to The Golden Notebook," p. 25.

[48] Jonah Raskin, "Doris Lessing at Stony Brook: An Interview," p. 71.

SELECTED BIBLIOGRAPHY

GENERAL BACKGROUND

Abrams, Meyer H. *Natural Supernaturalism: Tradition and Revolution in Romantic Literature*. New York, 1973.

Adam, Ian W. "Society as Novelist." *Journal of Aesthetics and Art Criticism*, 25 (1967), 375-386.

Allen, Walter. *The English Novel: A Short Critical History*. New York: E. P. Dutton, 1954.

Alter, Robert. "History and Imagination in the Nineteenth-Century Novel." *Georgia Review*, 29 (1975), 42-60.

_____. *Partial Magic: The Novel as a Self-Conscious Genre*. Berkeley: University of California Press, 1975.

Altick, Richard D. *The English Common Reader: A Social History of the Mass Reading Public, 1800-1900*. Chicago: University of Chicago Press, 1957.

_____. *Victorian People and Ideas*. New York: W. W. Norton and Co., 1973.

The Art of Victorian Prose. Eds. George Levine and William Madden. New York: Oxford University Press, 1968.

Auerbach, Erich. *Mimesis*. Trans. Willard R. Trask. 1953; rpt. Princeton: Princeton University Press, 1973.

Bald, Marjorie A. *Women Writers of the Nineteenth Century*. New York: Russell and Russell, 1963.

Ball, Patricia M. *The Central Self: A Study in Romantic and Victorian Imagination*. London: Athlone Press, 1968.

Bantock, G. H. "Literature and the Social Sciences." *Critical Quarterly*, 17 (1975), 99-127.

Barker, Sir Ernest. *Political Thought in England. 1848 to 1914*. 2nd ed. 1915; rpt. London: Oxford University Press, 1951.

Barthes, Roland. *Writing Degree Zero*. Trans. Annette Lavers and Colin Smith. New York: Hill and Wang, 1968.

Beer, Patricia. Reader, I Married Him: A Study of the Women Characters of Jane Austen, Charlotte Brontë, Elizabeth Gaskell, and George Eliot. London: Macmillan, 1974.

Blotner, Joseph L. The Political Novel. Garden City, New York: Doubleday and Co., Inc., 1955.

Booth, Wayne C. The Rhetoric of Fiction. Chicago: University of Chicago Press, 1961.

Bradbury, Malcolm. The Social Context of Modern English Literature. New York: Schocken, 1971.

Bragg, Melvyn. "Class and the Novel." Times Literary Supplement, 15 Oct. 1971, 1261-1263.

Branca, Patricia. Silent Sisterhood: Middle Class Women in the Victorian Home. Pittsburgh: Carnegie Mellon University Press, 1976.

Brantlinger, Patrick. "Bluebooks, the Social Organism, and the Victorian Novel." Criticism, 14 (1972), 328-344.

Briggs, Asa. The Making of Modern England 1783-1867: The Age of Improvement. New York: Harper Torchbooks, 1965.

Buckler, William. "A Dual Quest: The Victorian Search for Identity and Authority." Arts and Sciences, I, No. 1 (1963), 27-33.

Buckley, Jerome H. The Triumph of Time. Cambridge: Belknap Press, 1966.

_____. The Victorian Temper. New York: Vintage Books, 1951.

Calder, Jenni. The Victorian Home. London: B. T. Batsford Ltd., 1977.

Cazamian, Louis. The Social Novel in England, 1830-1850: Dickens, Disraeli, Mrs. Gaskell, Kingsley. Trans. Martin Fido. 1903; rpt. London: Routledge and Kegan Paul, 1973.

Chesler, Phyllis. Women and Madness. New York: Avon Books, 1972.

Chesterton, G. K. The Victorian Age in Literature. 1913; rpt. NY: Oxford University Press, 1971.

Clio's Consciousness Raised. Eds. Mary S. Hartman and Lois Banner. New York: Harper Torchbooks, 1974.

Cockshut, A. O. J. The Unbelievers: English Agnostic Thought, 1840-1890. New York: New York University Press, 1966.

Colby, Robert. Fiction with a Purpose: Major and Minor Nineteenth-Century Novels. Bloomington: University of Indiana Press, 1967.

Colby, Vineta. *The Singular Anomaly: Women Novelists of the Nineteenth Century*. London: University of London Press, 1971.

_____. *Yesterday's Woman: Domestic Realism in the English Novel*. Princeton: Princeton University Press, 1974.

Conway, Jill. "Stereotypes of Femininity in a Theory of Sexual Evolution." *Victorian Studies*, 14 (1970), 47-62.

Coveney, Peter. *The Image of Childhood; The Individual and Society: A Study of the Theme in English Literature*. Harmondsworth, England: Penguin Books, 1967.

Craig, David. "Fiction and the Rising Industrial Class." *Essays in Criticism*, 17 (1967), 64-74.

_____. *The Real Foundations: Literature and Social Change*. London: Chatto and Windus, 1973.

Crane, R. S. "Literature, Philosophy, and the History of Ideas." *Modern Philology*, 52 (1964), 73-83.

Crow, Duncan. *The Victorian Woman*. London: George Allen and Unwin, Ltd., 1971.

Culler, A. Dwight. "The Darwinian Revolution and Literary Form." In *The Art of Victorian Prose*. Eds. George Levine and William Madden. New York: Oxford University Press, 1968.

Currell, Melville E. *Political Woman*. Totowa, NJ: Rowman and Littlefield, 1974.

Daiches, David. *The Novel and the Modern World*. Chicago: University of Chicago Press, 1960.

De Beauvoir, Simone. *The Second Sex*. Trans. H. M. Parshley. New York: Vintage Books, 1974.

de Riencourt, Amaury. *Sex and Power in History*. New York: David McKay Co., Inc., 1974.

Dinwiddy, J. R. "Elections in Victorian Fiction." *Victorian Newsletter*, 45 (1974), 8-13.

Douglas, Ann. *The Feminization of American Culture*. New York: Alfred A. Knopf, 1977.

Eagleton, Terry. *Criticism and Ideology: A Study in Marxist Literary Theory*. Atlantic Highlands, NJ: Humanities Press, 1976.

1859: Entering an Age of Crisis. Eds. Philip Appleman, William A. Madden, and Michael Wolff. Bloomington: Indiana University Press, 1959.

Ellis, Mrs. *The Wives of England: Their Relative Duties, Domestic Influence, and Social Obligations*. London: Fisher, Son and Co., 1843.

Erlich, Bruce. "Social Action and Literary Fable." *Minnesota Review*, 5 (1975), 40-52.

Faber, Richard. *Proper Stations: Class in Victorian Fiction*. London: Faber, 1971.

_____. *The Vision and the Need: Late Victorian Imperialist Aims*. London: Faber, 1966.

The Family in History. Ed. Charles E. Rosenberg. Philadelphia: The University of Pennsylvania Press, 1975.

Feminist Literary Criticism: Explorations in Theory. Ed. Josephine Donovan. Lexington: University Press of Kentucky, 1975.

Fernando, Lloyd. *"New Women" in the Late Victorian Novel*. University Park, Pennsylvania: The Pennsylvania State University Press, 1977.

Fiedler, Leslie A. "Class War in British Literature." *Esquire*, 49 (April 1958), 79-81.

Firestone, Shulamith. *The Dialectic of Sex: The Case for Feminist Revolution*. New York: Bantam Books, 1971.

Fleishman, Avrom. *The English Historical Novel: Walter Scott to Virginia Woolf*. Baltimore: The Johns Hopkins University Press, 1971.

Foucault, Michel. *The Order of Things: An Archaeology of the Human Sciences*. New York: Pantheon Books, 1970.

Freud, Sigmund. *Civilization and Its Discontents*. Trans. and ed. James Strachey. New York: W. W. Norton and Co., 1962.

Friedman, Alan. *The Turn of the Novel*. New York: Oxford University Press, 1966.

Fries, Maureen and Anne Daunis. *A Bibliography of Writings By and About British Women Authors, 1957-1969*. Charleston, Illinois: Women's Caucus for the Modern Languages, 1971.

Goldfarb, Russell M. *Sexual Repression and Victorian Literature*. Lewisburg, PA: Bucknell University Press, 1970.

Goldknopf, David. *The Life of the Novel*. Chicago: University of Chicago Press, 1972.

Goldmann, Lucien. *Towards a Sociology of the Novel*. Trans. Allan Sheriden. London: Tavistock Publications, 1975.

Gornick, Vivian. "Woman as Outsider." In Woman in Sexist Society. Eds. Gornick and Moran. New York: Basic Books, 1971.

Greacen, Robert. "Social Class in Post-War English Fiction." Southern Review, 4, No. 1 (1968), 142-151.

Green, Peter. "Aspects of the Historical Novel." Essays by Divers Hands, 31 (1962), 35-60.

Greenberg, Alvin. "The Novel of Disintegration: Paradoxical Impossibility in Contemporary Fiction." Wisconsin Studies in Contemporary Literature, 7 (1966), 103-124.

Greer, Germaine. "Women and Literature--II: Flying Pigs and Double Standards." Times Literary Supplement, 26 July 1974, 784-785.

Guérard, Albert. Literature and Society. Boston: Lothrop, Lee and Shepard Company, 1935.

Halperin, John. Egoism and Self-Discovery in the Victorian Novel: Studies in the Ordeal of Knowledge in the Nineteenth Century. New York: B. Franklin, 1974.

Harrison, John R. The Reactionaries: A Study of the Anti-Democratic Intelligentsia. New York: Schocken, 1967.

Harvey, W. J. Character and the Novel. New York: Cornell University Press, 1965.

Henkin, Leo J. Darwinism in the English Novel. 1860-1910. New York, 1940.

Hinkley, Laura L. Ladies of Literature. New York, 1946.

Holcombe, Lee. Victorian Ladies at Work: Middle-Class Working Women in England and Wales 1850-1914. Hamden, Connecticut: Archon Books, 1973.

Holloway, John. The Victorian Sage: Studies in Argument. New York: W. W. Norton and Co., 1965.

Hough, Graham. The Last Romantics. London: G. Duckworth, 1949.

Houghton, Walter E. The Victorian Frame of Mind: 1830-1870. New Haven: Yale University Press, 1957.

Howe, Irving. Politics and the Novel. New York: Horizon Press, 1957.

Hyman, Lawrence W. "Literature and Political Action." Dissent, 14 (1967), 453-460.

Hynes, Samuel. *The Auden Generation: Literature and Politics in England in the 1930's.* New York: The Viking Press, 1977.

Images of Women in Fiction: Feminist Perspectives. Ed. Susan K. Cornillon. Bowling Green, Ohio: Bowling Green University Popular Press, 1972.

Jameson, Fredric. "Imaginary and Symbolic in Lacan: Marxism, Psychoanalytic Criticism, and the Problem of the Subject." *Yale French Studies,* No. 55/56 (1977), 338-395.

_____. *Marxism and Form: Twentieth-Century Dialectical Theories of Literature.* Princeton: Princeton University Press, 1971.

Jay, Martin. *The Dialectical Imagination: A History of the Frankfurt School and the Institute of Social Research 1923-1950.* Boston: Little, Brown and Co., 1973.

Kaminsky, Alice R. "On Literary Realism." In *The Theory of the Novel: New Essays.* Ed. John Halperin. New York: Oxford University Press, 1974.

Kenny, Anthony. *Will, Freedom and Power.* New York: Barnes and Noble Books, 1976.

Kermode, Frank. *The Sense of an Ending.* New York: Oxford University Press, 1967.

Kettle, Arnold. *An Introduction to the English Novel.* 2 vols. New York: Harper Torchbook, 1951.

Kroeber, Karl. "Fictional Theory and Social History: The Need for a Synthetic Criticism." *Victorian Studies,* 19 (1975), 99-106.

Lacan, Jacques. *The Language of the Self: The Function of Language in Psychoanalysis.* Trans. Anthony Wilden. Baltimore: The Johns Hopkins University Press, 1968.

Leavis, F. R. *The Great Tradition.* Garden City, New York: Doubleday and Co., Inc., 1954.

Levin, Harry. "Toward a Sociology of the Novel." *Journal of the History of Ideas,* 26 (1965), 148-154.

Liberations: New Essays on the Humanities in Revolution. Ed. Ihab Hassan. Middletown, CT: Wesleyan University Press, 1971.

Literature and Politics in the Nineteenth Century: Essays. Ed. John Lucas. London: Methuen and Co., Ltd., 1971.

Literature and Politics in the Twentieth Century. Eds. Walter Laqueur and George L. Mosse. New York: Harper and Row, 1967.

Literature and Revolution. Ed. Jacques Ehrmann. Boston: Beacon Press, 1967.

Lodge, David. The Language of Fiction: Essays in Criticism and Verbal Analyses of the English Novel. London: Kegan Paul, 1966.

Lucas, John. The Literature of Change: Studies in the Nineteenth-Century Provincial Novel. New York: Barnes and Noble, 1977.

Lukács, Georg. The Historical Novel. Trans. Hannah and Stanley Mitchell. London, 1962.

_____. Realism in Our Time: Literature and the Class Struggle. Trans. John and Necke Mander. New York: Harper and Row, 1962.

_____. The Theory of the Novel. Trans. Anna Bostock. 1920; rpt. Cambridge, MA: The MIT Press, 1971.

Meakin, David. Men and Work: Literature and Culture in Industrial Society. New York: Holmes and Meier, 1976.

Mews, Hazel. Frail Vessels: Women's Role in Women's Novels from Fanny Burney to George Eliot. London: Athlone Press, 1969.

Miles, Rosalind. The Fiction of Sex: Themes and Functions of Sex Difference in the Modern Novel. London: Vision Press, 1969.

Miller, Joseph Hillis. The Disappearance of God. Cambridge, MA: Harvard University Press, 1963.

_____. The Form of Victorian Fiction. Notre Dame: Notre Dame University Press, 1968.

_____. "Narrative and History." Journal of English Literary History, 41, No. 3 (1974), 455-473.

Millett, Kate. Sexual Politics. Garden City, NY: Doubleday and Co., 1970.

The Mind and Art of Victorian England. Ed. Josef L. Altholz. Minneapolis: The University of Minnesota Press, 1976.

Mitchell, Juliet. Psychoanalysis and Feminism. New York: Pantheon Books, 1974.

Moers, Ellen. Literary Women: The Great Writers. Garden City, New York: Doubleday and Co., 1976.

Moore, Katherine. Victorian Wives. New York: St. Martin's Press, 1974.

Morgan, David. Suffragists and Liberals: The Politics of Woman Suffrage in England. Totowa: NJ: Rowman and Littlefield, 1975.

Neff, Emery. "Social Background and Social Thought." In The Reinterpretation of Victorian Literature. Ed. Joseph E. Baker. Princeton: Princeton University Press, 1950.

O'Brien, Conor Cruise. Writers and Politics. New York: Pantheon Books, 1965.

Parrinder, Patrick. "Historical Imagination and Political Reality: A Study in Edwardian Attitudes." Clio: An Interdisciplinary Journal of Literature, History, and the Philosophy of History, 4 (1974), 5-25.

Peckham, Morse. Beyond the Tragic Vision: The Quest for Identity in the Nineteenth Century. New York: G. Braziller, 1962.

──────. Victorian Revolutionaries: Speculations on Some Heroes of a Cultural Crisis. New York: G. Braziller, 1970.

Poirier, Richard. "The Aesthetics of Radicalism." Partisan Review, 41, No. 2 (1974), 176-196.

The Politics of Twentieth-Century Novelists. Ed. George A. Panichas. New York: Thomas Y. Crowell Co., 1974.

Power and Consciousness. Eds. Conor Cruise O'Brien and William Dean Vanoch. New York: New York University Press, 1969.

Praz, Mario. The Hero in Eclipse in Victorian Literature. Trans. Angus Davidson. London: Oxford University Press, 1956.

Rance, Nicholas. The Historical Novel and Popular Politics in Nineteenth-Century England. New York: Barnes and Noble, 1974.

Reed, John. Victorian Conventions. Athens, Ohio: Ohio University Press, 1975.

Rowbotham, Sheila. Hidden from History: Rediscovering Women in History from the Seventeenth Century to the Present. New York: Vintage Books, 1976.

Roudiez, Leon S. "In Dubious Battle: Literature vs. Ideology." Semiotexte, 1, No. 1 (1974), 87-95.

Russell, Frances Theresa. Satire in the Victorian Novel. New York: The Macmillan Co., 1920.

Ryals, Clyde. "The Nineteenth Century Cult of Inaction." Tennessee Studies in Literature, 4 (1959), 51-60.

Sacks, Sheldon. Fiction and the Shape of Belief. Berkeley: University of California Press, 1967.

Sage, Lorna. "Women and Literature--III: The Case of the Active Victim." Times Literary Supplement, 26 July 1974, 803-804.

Said, Edward. Beginnings: Intention and Method: New York: Basic Books, 1975.

Schochet. Gordon. Patriarchalism in Political Thought. Oxford: Basil Blackwell, 1975.

Searle, John. Speech Acts: An Essay in the Philosophy of Language. Cambridge: Cambridge University Press, 1969.

Showalter, Elaine. A Literature of Their Own: British Women Novelists from Brontë to Lessing. Princeton: Princeton University Press, 1977.

──────. Women's Liberation and Literature. New York: Harcourt Brace, 1971.

Smith, Sheila M. "Blue Books and Victorian Novelists." Review of English Studies, 21 (1970), 23-40.

──────. "Truth and Propaganda in the Victorial Social Problem Novel." Renaissance and Modern Studies, 8 (1964), 75-91.

Society and Self in the Novel: English Institute Essays, 1955. New York: Columbia University Press, 1956.

Spacks, Patricia Meyer. The Female Imagination. New York: Alfred A. Knopf, 1972.

──────. Imagining a Self: Autobiography and Novel in Eighteenth-Century England. Cambridge: Harvard University Press, 1976.

Speare, Morris Edmund. The Political Novel: Its Development in England and in America. New York: Oxford University Press, 1924.

Stevenson, Lionel. "Darwin and the Novel." Nineteenth-Century Fiction, 15 (1960), 29-38.

──────. "The Intellectual Novel in the Nineteenth Century." Personalist, 31 (1950), 42-56, 157-166.

Stone, Donald D. "Victorian Feminism and the Nineteenth-Century Novel." Women's Studies, 1 (1972), 65-92.

Style in Prose Fiction: English Institute Essays. 1958. Ed. Harold C. Martin. New York: Columbia University Press, 1959.

Suffer and Be Still: Women in the Victorian Age. Ed. Martha Vicinus. Bloomington, Indiana: Indiana University Press, 1972.

Sussman, Herbert L. *Victorians and the Machine: The Literary Response to Technology.* Cambridge, MA: Harvard University Press, 1968.

Swingewood, Alan. *The Novel and Revolution.* New York: Barnes and Noble/Harper, 1976.

Sypher, Wylie. *Literature and Technology: The Alien Vision.* New York: Random House, 1968.

Thale, Jerome. "History, Consciousness, Imaginative Vision: A Proposal and a Method." *Southern Humanities Review*, 9 (1975), 125-139.

Thompson, E. P. *The Making of the English Working Class.* New York: Vintage Books, 1963.

Thomson, Patricia. *The Victorian Heroine: A Changing Ideal, 1837-1873.* London: Oxford University Press, 1956.

Tillotson, Geoffrey and Kathleen. *Mid-Victorian Studies.* London: Athlone Press, 1965.

Tillotson, Kathleen. *Novels of the Eighteen-Forties.* Oxford: Oxford University Press, 1955.

Tomlinson, T. B. *The English Middle-Class Novel.* New York: Barnes and Noble/Harper, 1976.

_____. "Literature and History--The Novel." *Melbourne Critical Review*, 4 (1961), 93-101.

_____. "Love and Politics in the Early-Victorian Novel." *The Critical Review* (Melbourne), 17 (1974), 127-139.

Tradition and Tolerance in Nineteenth-Century Fiction. Eds. John Goode, David Howard, and John Lucas. London: Routledge and Kegan Paul, 1966.

Trilling, Lionel. *The Liberal Imagination.* New York: Viking Press, 1950.

Trudgill, Eric. *Madonnas and Magdalens: The Origins and Development of Victorian Sexual Attitudes.* New York: Holmes and Meier, 1976.

Turkle, Sherry. *Psychoanalytic Politics: Freud's French Revolution.* New York: Basic Books, Inc., 1978.

Utter, Robert P. and Gwendolyn B. Needham. *Pamela's Daughters*, 1936.

Van Ghent, Dorothy. *The English Novel: Form and Function.* New York: Holt, Rinehart and Winston, 1953.

The Victorians and Social Protest: A Symposium. Eds. J. Butt and I. F. Clarke. Hamden, CT: Archon Books, 1973.

Von Wright, Georg Henrik. Explanation and Understanding. Ithaca, New York: Cornell University Press, 1971.

Watson, George. The English Ideology. Studies in the Language of Victorian Politics. London: Allen Lane, 1973.

———. Politics and Literature in Modern Britain. London: The Macmillan Press, 1977.

Watt, Ian. The Rise of the Novel. Berkeley: University of California Press, 1957.

White, Hayden. "The Historical Text as Literary Artifact." Clio, 3 (June 1974), 277-303.

———. Metahistory: The Historical Imagination in Nineteenth-Century Europe. Baltimore: The Johns Hopkins University Press, 1973.

A Widening Sphere: Changing Roles of Victorian Women. Ed. Martha Vicinus. Bloomington: Indiana University Press, 1977.

Willey, Basil. Nineteenth Century Studies. London: Chatto and Windus, 1955.

———. More Nineteenth Century Studies. London: Chatto and Windus, 1956.

Williams, Raymond. The Country and the City. London: Chatto and Windus, 1973.

———. Culture and Society: 1780-1950. New York: Columbia University Press, 1958.

———. Keywords: A Vocabulary of Culture and Society. New York: Oxford University Press, 1976.

Wollstonecraft, Mary. Thoughts on the Education of Daughters: With Reflections on Female Conduct, in the More Important Duties of Life. London: J. Johnson, 1787.

———. A Vindication of the Rights of Women. In A Wollstonecraft Anthology. Ed. Janet M. Todd. Bloomington: Indiana University Press, 1977.

Woman, Culture and Society. Eds. Michelle Z. Rosaldo and Louise Lamphere. Stanford: Stanford University Press, 1974.

Wood, Neal. Communism and British Intellectuals. New York: Columbia University Press, 1959.

Young, G. M. *Victorian England: Portrait of an Age*. 2nd ed. 1936; rpt. New York: Oxford University Press, 1971.

MARY SHELLEY

Shelley, Mary. *Falkner*. London: Saunders and Otley, 1837.

———. *The Fortunes of Perkin Warbeck, a Romance by the Author of "Frankenstein."* London: Henry Colburn & Richard Bentley, 1830.

———. *Frankenstein: Or, The Modern Prometheus*. New York: The New American Library, 1965.

———. *The Last Man*. Ed. Hugh J. Luke, Jr. Lincoln: University of Nebraska Press, 1965.

The Letters of Mary W. Shelley. 2 vols. Ed. Frederick L. Jones. Norman: University of Oklahoma Press, 1954.

———. *Lodore*. London: Richard Bentley, 1835.

Mary Shelley's Journal. Ed. Frederick L. Jones. Norman: University of Oklahoma Press, 1947.

———. *Mathilda*. Ed. Elizabeth Nitchie. Chapel Hill: The University of North Carolina Press, 1959.

My Best Mary: The Selected Letters of Mary Wollstonecraft Shelley. Eds. Muriel Spark and Derek Stanford. London: Allan Wingate, 1953.

———. *Tales and Stories*. Ed. Joanna Russ. Boston: Gregg, 1975.

———. *Valperga, Or, the Life and Adventures of Castruccio, Prince of Lucca*. London: G. & W. B. Whittaker, 1823.

* * * * *

Bigland, Eileen. *Mary Shelley*. London: Cassell, 1959.

Brownstein, Rachel. "Portrait of the Artist as a Young Woman: Mary Shelley." *Book Forum*, 2 (1976), 600-608.

Cameron, Kenneth N. "Shelley and the Reformers." *ELH*, 12 (1945), 62-85.

Church, Richard. *Mary Shelley*. London: Gerald Howe, Ltd., 1928.

Clements, Frances M. "The Rights of Women in the Eighteenth-Century Novel." *Enlightenment Essays* (Chicago), 4, No. 3-4 (1973), 63-70.

Clifford, Gay. "Caleb Williams and Frankenstein: First-Person Narrative and 'Things as They Are.'" Genre, 10 (1977), 601-617.

Detre, Jean. A Most Extraordinary Pair: Mary Wollstonecraft and William Godwin. Garden City, NY: Doubleday and Co., 1975.

Dussinger, John A. "Kinship and Guilt in Mary Shelley's Frankenstein." Studies in the Novel (North Texas State University), 8 (1976), 38-55.

The Endurance of Frankenstein: Essays on Mary Shelley's Novel. Eds. George Levine and U. C. Knoepflmacher. Berkeley: University of California Press, 1979.

Evans, Frank B. "Shelley, Godwin, Hume, and the Doctrine of Necessity." Studies in Philology, 37 (1940), 632-640.

Gardner, Joseph H. "Mary Shelley's Divine Tragedy." Essays in Literature (Western Illinois University), 4, No. 2 (1977), 182-197.

George, Margaret. One Woman's "Situation": A Study of Mary Wollstonecraft. Urbana: University of Illinois Press, 1970.

Gerson, Noel B. Daughter of Earth and Water: A Biography of Mary Wollstonecraft Shelley. New York: Morrow, 1973.

Godwin, William. The Adventures of Caleb Williams, Or, Things As They Are. New York: Holt, Rinehart and Winston, 1967.

──────. An Enquiry Concerning Political Justice and Its Influence on General Virtue and Happiness. Ed. Raymond A. Preston. New York: Alfred A. Knopf, 1926.

Goldberg, M. A. "Moral and Myth in Mrs. Shelley's Frankenstein." Keats-Shelley Journal, 8, Part I (1959), 27-38.

Grylls, Rosalie Glynn. Mary Shelley: A Biography. London: Oxford University Press, 1938.

Hildebrand, William H. "On Three Prometheuses: Shelley's Two and Mary's One." Serif, 11, No. 2 (1974), 3-11.

Le Gates, Marlene. "The Cult of Womanhood in Eighteenth-Century Thought." Eighteenth-Century Studies, 10 (1976), 21-39.

Leighton, Margaret. Shelley's Mary: A Life of Mary Godwin Shelley. New York: Farrar, Straus and Giroux, 1973.

Levine, George. "Frankenstein and the Tradition of Realism." Novel, 7 (1973), 14-30.

Lovell, Ernest J., Jr. "Byron and Mary Shelley." Keats-Shelley Journal, 2 (1953), 35-49.

Luke, Hugh J., Jr. "*The Last Man*: Mary Shelley's Myth of the Solitary." *Prairie Schooner*, 39 (1966), 316-327.

Lund, Mary Graham. "Mary Godwin Shelley and the Monster." *University of Kansas City Review*, 28 (1962), 253-258.

Lyles, W. H. *Mary Shelley: An Annotated Bibliography*. New York: Garland Publishing, 1975.

Miller, Arthur McA. "*The Last Man*: A Study of the Eschatological Theme in English Poetry and Fiction from 1806 through 1839." *Dissertation Abstracts International*, 28 (1967), 687A.

Miyoshi, Masao. *The Divided Self: A Perspective on the Literature of the Victorians*. New York: New York University Press, 1969.

Neumann, Bonnie R. "Mary Shelley." *Dissertation Abstracts International*, 33 (1973), 5689A.

Nitchie, Elizabeth. *Mary Shelley: Author of "Frankenstein."* New Brunswick, NJ: Rutgers University Press, 1953.

Norman, Sylva. *The Flight of the Skylark: The Development of Shelley's Reputation*. Norman: University of Oklahoma Press, 1954.

Palacio, J. de. "Mary Shelley and *The Last Man*." *Révue de Littérature Comparée*, 42 (1968), 37-49.

Peck, W. E. "The Biographical Element in the Novels of Mary Wollstonecraft Shelley." *PMLA*, 38 (1923), 196-219.

Pollin, Burton R. "Philosophical and Literary Sources of *Frankenstein*." *Comparative Literature*, 17, No. 2 (1965), 97-108.

Powers, Katherine R. "The Influence of William Godwin on the Novels of Mary Shelley." *Dissertation Abstracts International*, 33 (1973), 4359A.

Rubenstein, Marc A. "'My Accursed Origin': The Search for the Mother in *Frankenstein*." *Studies in Romanticism*, 15 (1976), 165-194.

Sencourt, Robert. "Mary Wollstonecraft Shelley." *Contemporary Review*, No. 1102 (1957), 215-218.

Shelley and His Circle. Ed. Kenneth Neill Cameron. 4 vols. Cambridge: Harvard University Press, 1961.

Small, Christopher. *Ariel Like a Harpy: Shelley, Mary and Frankenstein*. London: Gollancz, 1972.

Smith, Susan Harris. "*Frankenstein*: Mary Shelley's Psychic Divisiveness." *Women and Literature*, 5, No. 2 (1977), 42-53.

Spark, Muriel. _Child of Light: A Reassessment of Mary Wollstonecraft Shelley_. Hadleigh, Essex: Tower Bridge Publications Ltd., 1951.

_____. "Mary Shelley: A Prophetic Novelist." _The Listener_, 45 (Feb. 22, 1951), 305-306.

Spatt, Hartley S. "Mary Shelley's Last Men: The Truth of Dreams." _Studies in the Novel_ (North Texas State University), 7 (1975), 526-537.

Sterrenberg, Lee. "_The Last Man_: Anatomy of Failed Revolutions." _Nineteenth-Century Fiction_ (1978), 324-347.

Todd, Janet M. "Frankenstein's Daughter: Mary Shelley and Mary Wollstonecraft." _Women and Literature: A Journal of Women Writers_, 4, No. 2 (1976), 18-27.

Tropp, Martin. _Mary Shelley's Monster: The Story of Frankenstein_. Boston: Houghton Mifflin Co., 1976.

Uphaus, Robert W. "_Caleb Williams_: Godwin's Epoch of Mind." _Studies in the Novel_, 9, No. 3 (1977), 279-296.

Walling, William. _Mary Shelley_. New York: Twayne Publishers, Inc., 1972.

Wardle, Ralph M. "Mary Wollstonecraft, Analytical Reviewer," _PMLA_, 62 (1947), 1000-1009.

Weissman, Judith. "A Reading of _Frankenstein_ as the Complaint of a Political Wife." _Colby Library Quarterly_, 12 (1976), 171-180.

White, Newman I. "Shelley and the Active Radicals of the Early Nineteenth Century." _South Atlantic Quarterly_, 29 (1930), 248-261.

A Wollstonecraft Anthology. Ed. Janet M. Todd. Bloomington: Indiana University Press, 1977.

GEORGE ELIOT

Eliot, George. *The Works of George Eliot*. 24 vols. The Cabinet Edition. Edinburgh and London: William Blackwood [n.d.].

Essays of George Eliot. Ed. Thomas Pinney. London: Routledge and Kegan Paul, 1963.

The George Eliot Letters. Ed. Gordon S. Haight. 7 vols. New Haven: Yale University Press, 1954-1955.

* * * * *

Austen, Zelda. "Why Feminist Critics Are Angry with George Eliot." *College English*, 37 (1976), 549-561.

Baker, William. "George Eliot's Readings in Nineteenth-Century Jewish Historians: A Note on the Background of *Daniel Deronda*." *Victorian Studies*, 15, No. 4 (1972), 463-473.

Bamber, Linda. "Self-Defeating Politics in George Eliot's *Felix Holt*." *Victorian Studies* (June 1975), 419-435.

Basch, Francoise. *Relative Creatures: Victorian Women in Society and the Novel 1837-67*. Trans. Anthony Rudolf. London: Allen Lane, 1974.

Beaty, Jerome. "*Daniel Deronda* and the Question of Unity in Fiction." *Victorian Newsletter*, 15 (1959), 16-20.

———. "History by Indirection: The Era of Reform in *Middlemarch*." *Victorian Studies*, 1 (1957), 173-179.

———. *Middlemarch from Notebook to Novel: A Study of George Eliot's Creative Method*. (ISLL, Vol. 47) Urbana: University of Illinois Press, 1960.

Bedient, Calvin. *Architects of the Self: George Eliot, D. H. Lawrence, and E. M. Forster*. Berkeley: University of California Press, 1972.

Beebe, Maurice. "'Visions are Creators': The Unity of *Daniel Deronda*." *Boston University Studies in English*, 1, No. 3 (1955), 166-177.

Beer, Patricia. *Reader, I Married Him: A Study of the Women Characters of Jane Austen, Charlotte Brontë, Elizabeth Gaskell, and George Eliot*. London: The Macmillan Press Ltd., 1974.

Bennett, Joan. *George Eliot: Her Mind and Her Art*. Cambridge: The University Press, 1948.

Bissell, Claude T. "Social Analysis in the Novels of George Eliot." *Journal of English Literary History*, 18 (1951), 221-239.

Blake, Kathleen. "Middlemarch and the Woman Question." *Nineteenth-Century Fiction*, 31 (1976), 285-312.

Bonaparte, Felicia. *Will and Destiny: Morality and Tragedy in George Eliot's Novels*. New York: New York University Press, 1975.

Burke, Edmund. *Reflections on the Revolution in France*. Garden City, NY: Doubleday and Co., 1961.

Carroll, David R. "*Felix Holt* Society as Protagonist." *Nineteenth-Century Fiction*, 17, No. 3 (1962), 237-252.

_____. "The Unity of *Daniel Deronda*." *Essays in Criticism* (Oxford), 9 (1959), 369-380.

A Century of George Eliot Criticism. Ed. Gordon S. Haight. London: Methuen and Co., Ltd., 1965.

Christ, Carlo. "Aggression and Providential Death in George Eliot's Fiction." *Novel*, 9 (1976), 130-140.

Cirillo, Albert R. "Salvation in *Daniel Deronda*: The Fortunate Overthrow of Gwendolen Harleth." In *Literary Monographs*, I. Eds. Eric Rothstein and Thomas K. Dunseath. Madison: University of Wisconsin Press, 1967.

Cox, C. B. *The Free Spirit: A Study of Liberal Humanism in the Novels of George Eliot, Henry James, E. M. Forster, Virginia Woolf, and Angus Wilson*. London: Oxford University Press, 1963.

Craig, David. "Fiction and the Rising Industrial Classes." *Essays in Criticism* (Oxford), 17 (1967), 64-71.

Critical Essays on George Eliot. Ed. Barbara Hardy. London: Routledge and Kegan Paul, 1970.

Deegan, Thomas. "George Eliot's Novels of the Historical Imagination." *Clio*, 1, No. 3 (1972), 21-33.

Doheny, John. "George Eliot and Gwendolen Harleth." *Recovering Literature*, 5, No. 2 (1976), 19-37.

Emery, Laura Comer. *George Eliot's Creative Conflict: The Other Side of Silence*. Berkeley: University of California Press, 1976.

Fernando, Lloyd. "George Eliot, Feminism and Dorothea Brooke." *Review of English Literature* (Leeds), 4 (1963), 76-90.

Fisch, Harold. "Daniel Deronda or Gwendolen Harleth?" *Nineteenth-Century Fiction*, 19, No. 4 (1965), 345-356.

Gaeddert, Lou Ann Bigge. *All-in-All: A Biography of George Eliot*. New York: Dutton, 1976.

George Eliot: A Collection of Critical Essays. Ed. George Creeger. Englewood Cliffs, NJ: Prentice-Hall, Inc., 1970.

George Eliot: The Critical Heritage. Ed. David Carroll. London: Routledge and Kegan Paul, 1971.

George Eliot and Her Readers: A Selection of Contemporary Reviews. Eds. John Holstrom and Laurence Lerner. London: The Bodley Head, 1966.

George Eliot's Life as Related in Her Letters and Journals. Ed. John W. Cross. Edinburgh and London: W. Blackwood and Sons, 1885.

Haight, Gordon S. *George Eliot: A Biography*. Oxford: The Clarendon Press, 1968.

Hardy, Barbara. *The Appropriate Form: An Essay on the Novel*. London: The Athlone Press, 1964.

_____. "Middlemarch: Public and Private Worlds." *English*, 25, No. 121 (1976), 5-26.

_____. "Mrs. Gaskell and George Eliot." In *The Victorians*. Ed. Arthur Pollard. London: Cresset, 1969.

_____. *The Novels of George Eliot: A Study in Form*. University of London: The Athlone Press, 1959.

Harvey, W. J. *The Art of George Eliot*. London: Chatto and Windus, 1961.

Hester, Erwin. "George Eliot's Use of Historical Events in *Daniel Deronda*." *English Language Notes*, 4 (1966), 115-118.

Horowitz, Lenore W. "George Eliot's Vision of Society in *Felix Holt, the Radical*." *Texas Studies in Literature and Language*, 17 (1975), 175-191.

Jackson, R. L. P. "George Eliot, J. S. Mill and Women's Liberation." *Quadrant*, 94 (1975), 11-33.

Jones, Peter. *Philosophy and the Novel. Philosophical Aspects of Middlemarch, Anna Karenina, The Brothers Karamazov, A la Recherche de Temps Perdu, and of the Methods of Criticism.* Oxford: Clarendon Press, 1975.

Jones, R. T. *George Eliot.* Cambridge: The University Press, 1970.

Ker, I. T. "George Eliot's Rhetoric of Enthusiasm." *Essays in Criticism* (Oxford), 26 (1976), 134-155.

Kettle, Arnold. "*Felix Holt the Radical.*" In *Critical Essays on George Eliot.* Ed. Barbara Hardy. London: Routledge and Kegan Paul, 1970.

Kitchel, Anna Theresa. *George Lewes and George Eliot: A Review of Records.* New York, 1933.

Knoepflmacher, Ulrich C. *George Eliot's Early Novels: The Limits of Realism.* Berkeley: University of California Press, 1968.

_____. *Laughter and Despair: Readings in Ten Novels of the Victorian Era.* Berkeley: University of California Press, 1971.

_____. *Religious Humanism and the Victorian Novel.* Princeton, NJ: Princeton University Press, 1965.

Kroeber, Karl. *Styles in Fictional Structure: The Art of Jane Austen, Charlotte Brontë, George Eliot.* Princeton: Princeton University Press, 1971.

Laski, Marghanita. *George Eliot and Her World.* London: Thames and Hudson, 1973.

Leavis, F. R. *The Great Tradition: George Eliot, Henry James, Joseph Conrad.* New York: New York University Press, 1963.

Lerner, Lawrence. *The Truthtellers: Jane Austen, George Eliot, D. H. Lawrence.* London: Chatto and Windus, 1967.

Levine, George. "Determinism and Responsibility in the Works of George Eliot." *PMLA*, 77 (1962), 268-279.

Marcus, Steven. "Human Nature, Social Orders, and Nineteenth-Century Systems of Explanation: Starting in with George Eliot." *Salmagundi*, 28 (1975), 20-42.

Milner, Ian. *The Structure of Values in George Eliot.* Praha: Universita Karlova. Universitatis Carolinae Philologica Monographia, 23, 1968.

Mintz, Alan. *George Eliot and the Novel of Vocation.* Cambridge: Harvard University Press, 1978.

Myers, W. F. T. "Politics and Personality in *Felix Holt*." *Renaissance and Modern Studies*, 10 (1966), 5-33.

Paris, Bernard J. *Experiments in Life: George Eliot's Quest for Values*. Detroit: Wayne State University Press, 1965.

_____. "George Eliot's Religion of Humanity." *Journal of English Literary History*, 29 (1962), 418-443.

_____. *A Psychological Approach to Fiction: Studies in Thackeray, Stendhal, George Eliot, Dostoevsky, and Conrad*. Bloomington: Indiana University Press, 1974.

Pearce, T. S. *George Eliot*. London: Evans Brothers Ltd., 1973.

Pinney, Thomas. "The Authority of the Past in George Eliot's Novels." *Nineteenth-Century Fiction*, 21, No. 2 (1966), 131-147.

Preyer, Robert. "Beyond the Liberal Imagination: Vision and Unreality in *Daniel Deronda*." *Victorian Studies*, 4 (1960), 33-54.

Redinger, Ruby V. *George Eliot: The Emergent Self*. New York: Alfred A. Knopf, 1975.

Roberts, Neil. *George Eliot: Her Beliefs and Her Art*. London: Paul Elek, 1975.

Robinson, Carole. "*Romola*: A Reading of the Novel." *Victorian Studies*, 6, No. 1 (1962), 29-42.

Scott, James F. "George Eliot, Positivism, and the Social Vision of *Middlemarch*." *Victorian Studies*, 16 (1972), 59-76.

Sedgely, Anne. "*Daniel Deronda*." *The Critical Review* (Melbourne), 13 (1970), 3-19.

Speaight, Robert. *George Eliot*. New York: Roy Publishers, 1955.

Stump, Reva. *Movement and Vision in George Eliot's Novels*. Seattle: University of Washington Press, 1959.

Sudrann, Jean. "*Daniel Deronda* and the Landscape of Exile." *Journal of English Literary History*, 37, No. 3 (1970), 433-455.

Svaglic, Martin J. "Religion in the Novels of George Eliot." *Journal of English and Germanic Philology*, 53 (1954), 145-159.

Swann, Brian. "George Eliot's Ecumenical Jew, or, The Novel as Outdoor Temple." *Novel*, 8, No. 1 (1974), 39-50.

_____. "George Eliot and the Play: Symbol and Metaphor of the Drama in *Daniel Deronda*." *Dalhousie Review*, 52 (1972), 191-202.

This Particular Web: Essays on "Middlemarch." Ed. Ian Adam. Toronto: University of Toronto Press, 1975.

Thale, Jerome. The Novels of George Eliot. New York: Columbia University Press, 1959.

_____. "Daniel Deronda: The Darkened World." Modern Fiction Studies, 3, No. 2 (1957), 119-126.

Thomson, Fred C. "Felix Holt as Classic Tragedy." Nineteenth-Century Fiction, 16 (1961), 47-58.

_____. "The Genesis of Felix Holt." PMLA, 74, No. 5 (1959), 576-584.

_____. "Politics and Society in Felix Holt." In The Classic British Novel. Eds. Howard M. Harper, Jr. and Charles Edge. Athens, Georgia: University of Georgia Press, 1972.

Woolf, Gabriel. "In the Vanguard of Women's Liberation: George Eliot." George Eliot Fellowship Review, 4 (1973), 11-13.

Woolf, Virginia. "George Eliot." In The Common Reader. New York: Harcourt Brace and World, Inc., 1953.

Wright, Walter F. "George Eliot as Industrial Reformer." PMLA, 56, No. 4 (1941), 1107-1115.

VIRGINIA WOOLF

The Diary of Virginia Woolf. 2 vols. Ed. Anne Oliver Bell. New York: Harcourt Brace Jovanovich, 1977-1978.

The Letters of Virginia Woolf. 4 vols. Eds. Nigel Nicolson and Joanne Trautmann. London: The Hogarth Press, 1975-1978.

Woolf, Virginia. Between the Acts. New York: Harcourt Brace Jovanovich, Inc., 1941.

_____. Collected Essays. 4 vols. New York: Harcourt Brace Jovanovich, 1967.

_____. Moments of Being: Unpublished Autobiographical Writings. Ed. Jeanne Schulkind. New York: Harcourt Brace Jovanovich, 1976.

_____. Mrs. Dalloway. New York: Harcourt, Brace and World, 1925.

_____. A Room of One's Own. 1925; rpt. London: Penguin Books, 1970.

_____. Three Guineas. 1938; rpt. New York: Harcourt, Brace and World, 1963.

_____. To the Lighthouse. New York: Harcourt, Brace and World, 1972.

_____. The Waves. New York: Harcourt, Brace and World., Inc., 1931.

_____. A Writer's Diary. Ed. Leonard Woolf. New York: Harcourt Brace Jovanovich, 1954.

_____. The Years. New York: Harcourt Brace Jovanovich, 1937.

* * * * *

Alexander, Jean. The Venture of Form in the Novels of Virginia Woolf. Port Washington, NY: Kennikat Press, 1973.

Batchelor, J. B. "Feminism in Virginia Woolf." English, 17 (1968), 1-7.

Bazin, Nancy Topping. Virginia Woolf and the Androgynous Vision. New Brunswick, NJ: Rutgers University Press, 1973.

Bell, Barbara C. and Carol Ohmann. "Virginia Woolf's Criticism: A Polemical Preface." Critical Inquiry, 1 (1974), 361-371.

Bell, Millicent. "Portrait of the Artist as a Young Woman." Virginia Quarterly Review, 52 (1976), 670-686.

Bell, Quentin. Bloomsbury. London, 1968.

_____. Virginia Woolf: A Biography. New York: Harcourt Brace Jovanovich, 1972.

Bennett, Joan. Virginia Woolf: Her Art as a Novelist. Cambridge: Cambridge University Press, 1964.

Blackstone, Bernard. Virginia Woolf: A Commentary. New York: Harcourt Brace and World, 1949.

Blanchard, Margaret. "Socialization in Mrs. Dalloway." College English, 34 (1972), 287-305.

Brewster, Dorothy. Virginia Woolf. London: George Allen, 1962.

Chapman, Robert T. "The 'Enemy' vs. Bloomsbury." Adam: International Review, 364-366 (1972), 81-84.

Comstock, Margaret. "The Loudspeaker and the Human Voice: Politics and the Form of The Years." Bulletin of the New York Public Library, 80, No. 2 (1977), 252-275.

Daiches, David. Virginia Woolf. Norfolk: New Directions, 1942.

de Selincourt, Basil. "Infinity in Experience: Virginia Woolf's New Novel." The Observer, 14 March 1937, p. 5, cols. 3-5.

Deiman, Werner J. "History, Pattern, and Continuity in Virginia Woolf." Contemporary Literature, 15 (1974), 49-66.

Edwards, Lee R. "War and Roses: The Politics of Mrs. Dalloway." In The Authority of Experience: Essays in Feminist Criticism. Eds. Arlyn Diamond and Lee R. Edwards. Amherst: University of Massachusetts Press, 1976.

Farwell, Marilyn, R. "Virginia Woolf and Androgyny." Contemporary Literature, 16 (1975), 433-451.

Fleishman, Avrom. Virginia Woolf: A Critical Reading. Baltimore: The Johns Hopkins University Press, 1975.

Forster, E. M. "Virginia Woolf." The Rede Lecture. New York: Harcourt Brace and Co., Inc., 1942.

Freedman, Ralph. The Lyrical Novel: Studies in Hesse, Gide and Woolf. Princeton: Princeton University Press, 1963.

Gillespie, Diane F. "Virginia Woolf's Miss La Trobe: The Artist's Last Struggle Against Masculine Values." Women and Literature, 5, No. 1 (1976), 38-46.

Graham, John. "Time in the Novels of Virginia Woolf." University of Toronto Quarterly, 18 (1948), 186-201.

Guiget, Jean. Virginia Woolf and Her Works. New York: Harcourt Brace Jovanovich, 1962.

Hafley, James. The Glass Room: Virginia Woolf as Novelist. Berkeley: University of California Press, 1954.

Hawthorn, Jeremy. Virginia Woolf's Mrs. Dalloway: A Study in Alienation. London: Sussex University Press, 1975.

Hoffman, Charles G. "Virginia Woolf's Manuscript Revisions of The Years." PMLA, 84 (1969), 79-89.

Holtby, Winifred. Virginia Woolf. London: Wishart, 1932.

Humphry, Robert. Stream of Consciousness in the Modern Novel. Berkeley: University of California Press, 1954.

Hynes, Samuel. "Stephen into Woolf." Sewanee Review, 84 (1976), 510-517.

Johnson, Manly. Virginia Woolf. New York: Ungar, 1973.

Johnstone, J. K. The Bloomsbury Group: A Study of E. M. Forster, Lytton Strachey, and Virginia Woolf and Their Circle. New York: 1963.

Kelly, Alice Van Buren. The Novels of Virginia Woolf: Fact and Vision. Chicago: University of Chicago Press, 1973.

Kelsey, Mary E. "Virginia Woolf and the She-Condition." Sewanee Review, 39 (1931), 425-444.

Leaska, Mitchell A. The Novels of Virginia Woolf: From Beginning to End. New York: The John Jay Press, 1977.

_____. "Virginia Woolf, the Pargeter: A Reading of The Years." Bulletin of the N.Y. Public Library, 80, No. 2 (1977), 172-210.

Lee, Hermione. The Novels of Virginia Woolf. London: Methuen and Co., Ltd., 1977.

Lipking, Joanna. "Looking at the Monuments: Woolf's Satiric Eye." Bulletin of the N.Y. Public Library, 80, No. 2 (1977), 141-145.

Lorberg, Aileen D. "Virginia Woolf, Benevolent Satirist." The Personalist, 33 (1952), 148-158.

Love, Jean O. _Worlds in Consciousness: Mythopoetic Thought in the Novels of Virginia Woolf_. Berkeley: University of California Press, 1970.

Lyons, Richard S. "The Intellectual Structure of Virginia Woolf's _Between the Acts_." _Modern Language Quarterly_, 38 (1976), 149-166.

Majumdar, Robin. _Virginia Woolf: An Annotated Bibliography of Criticism, 1915-1974_. New York: Garland, 1976.

Marcus, Jane. "_The Years_ as Greek Drama, Domestic Novel, and Götterdämmerung." _Bulletin of the N.Y. Public Library_, 80, No. 2 (1977), 276-301.

Marder, Herbert. "Beyond _The Lighthouse_: _The Years_." _Bucknell Review_, 15, No. 1 (1967), 61-70.

―――. _Feminism and Art_. Chicago: University of Chicago Press, 1968.

McIntyre, Clara F. "Is Virginia Woolf a Feminist?" _The Personalist_, 61 (1960), 176-184.

McLaurin, Allen. _Virginia Woolf: The Echoes Enslaved_. New York: Cambridge University Press, 1973.

Mellers, W. H. "Mrs. Woolf and Life." Rpt. in _The Importance of Scrutiny_. Ed. Eric Bentley. New York: George W. Stewart, 1948.

―――. "Virginia Woolf: The Last Phase." _Kenyon Review_, 4 (1942), 381-387.

Mendilow, A. A. _Time and the Novel_. London: Peter Nevill Ltd., 1952.

Miller, J. Hillis. "Virginia Woolf's All Souls' Day: The Omniscient Narrator in _Mrs. Dalloway_." In _The Shaken Realist: Essays in Honor of Frederick J. Hoffman_. Eds. Melvin J. Friedman and John B. Vickery. Baton Rouge: Louisiana State University Press, 1970.

Moody, A. D. _Virginia Woolf_. New York: Grove Press, 1963.

Naremore, James. _The World Without a Self: Virginia Woolf and the Novel_. New Haven: Yale University Press, 1973.

Novak, Jane. _The Razor Edge of Balance: A Study of Virginia Woolf_. Coral Gables: University of Miami Press, 1974.

Ozick, Cynthia. "Mrs. Virginia Woolf." _Commentary_, 56, No. 2 (1973), 33-44.

Pippett, Aileen. _The Moth and the Star: A Biography of Virginia Woolf_. Boston: Little, Brown and Co., 1953.

Pratt, Annis. "Sexual Imagery in To the Lighthouse: A New Feminist Approach." Modern Fiction Studies, 18 (1972), 417-431.

Proudfit, Sharon L. "Virginia Woolf: Reluctant Feminist in The Years." Criticism, 17 (Winter 1975), 59-73.

Radin, Grace. "'Two enormous chunks': Episodes Excluded during the Final Revision of The Years." Bulletin of the N.Y. Public Library, 80, No. 2 (1977), 221-251.

Rantavaara, Irma. Virginia Woolf and Bloomsbury. Helsinki: Annales Academiae Fennicae, 1953.

──────. Virginia Woolf's "The Waves." Port Washington, NY: Kennikat Press, 1960.

Richter, Harvena. Virginia Woolf: The Inward Voyage. Princeton: Princeton University Press, 1970.

Roberts, John Hawley. "The End of the English Novel?" Virginia Quarterly Review, 13 (1973).

Rose, Phyllis. Woman of Letters: A Life of Virginia Woolf. New York: Oxford University Press, 1978.

Rosenbaum, S. P. "The Philosophical Realism of Virginia Woolf." In English Literature and British Philosophy: A Collection of Essays. Ed. S. P. Rosenbaum. Chicago: University of Chicago Press, 1971.

Ruddick, Lisa. The Seen and the Unseen: Virginia Woolf's "To the Lighthouse." Cambridge: Harvard University Press, 1977.

Samuelson, Ralph. "Virginia Woolf, Orlando, and the Feminist Spirit." Western Humanities Review, 15 (1961), 51-58.

Schaefer, Josephine O'Brien. The Three-Fold Nature of Reality in the Novels of Virginia Woolf. London: Mouton and Co., 1965.

Schlack, Beverly Ann. "Virginia Woolf's Strategy of Scorn in The Years and Three Guineas." Bulletin of the N.Y. Public Library, 80, No. 2 (1977), 146-150.

Sears, Sallie. "Notes on Sexuality: The Years and Three Guineas." Bulletin of the N.Y. Public Library, 80, No. 2 (1977), 211-220.

Sharma, O. P. "Feminism as Aesthetic Vision: A Study of Virginia Woolf's Mrs. Dalloway." Women's Studies, 3 (1975), 61-73.

Showalter, Elaine. "Killing the Angel in the House: The Autonomy of Women Writers." Antioch Review, 32 (1973), 339-353.

Spater, George and Ian Parsons. *A Marriage of True Minds: An Intimate Portrait of Leonard and Virginia Woolf*. New York: Harcourt Brace and Co., 1976.

Stewart, Jack F. "Historical Impressionism in *Orlando*." *Studies in the Novel* (North Texas State University), 5 (1973), 71-85.

Summerhayes, Don. "Society, Morality, Analogy: Virginia Woolf's World in *Between the Acts*." *Modern Fiction Studies*, 9 (1964), 329-337.

Tobin, Gloria J. "Virginia Woolf's *The Waves* and *The Years* as Novel of Vision and Novel of Fact." *Dissertation Abstracts International*, 35 (1974), 483A.

Virginia Woolf: The Critical Heritage. Eds. Robin Majumdar and Allen McLaurin. London: Routledge and Kegan Paul, 1975.

Zwerdling, Alex. "*Between the Acts* and the Coming of War." *Novel*, 10 (1976), 220-236.

DORIS LESSING

Lessing, Doris. *The Four-Gated City*. New York: Bantam Books, 1970.

_____. *Going Home*. New York: Ballantine Books, 1968.

_____. *The Golden Notebook*. New York: McGraw-Hill, 1963.

_____. *The Grass Is Singing*. New York: New American Library, 1976.

_____. *In Pursuit of the English*. New York: Popular Library, 1960.

_____. *Landlocked*. 1965; rpt. New York: New American Library, 1970.

_____. *Martha Quest*. 1952; rpt. London: Panther Books Ltd., 1966.

_____. *The Memoirs of a Survivor*. New York: Bantam Books, 1976.

_____. *A Proper Marriage*. 1954; rpt. London: Panther Books, Ltd., 1966.

_____. *A Ripple from the Storm*. 1958; rpt. New York: New American Library, 1970.

_____. *A Small Personal Voice: Essays, Reviews, Interviews*. Ed. Paul Schlueter. New York: Vintage Books, 1975.

* * * * *

Aycock, Linnea. "The Mother/Daughter Relationship in the *Children of Violence* Series." *Anonymous*, 1 (1974), 48-55.

Brewer, Joseph E. "The Anti-Hero in Contemporary Literature." *Iowa English Yearbook*, 12 (1967), 55-60.

Brooks, Ellen W. "The Image of Women in Lessing's *The Golden Notebook*." *Critique: Studies in Modern Fiction*, 15, No. 2 (1973), 101-109.

Brown, Lloyd W. "The Shape of Things: Sexual Images and the Sense of Form in Doris Lessing's Fiction." *World Literature Written in English*, 14, No. 1 (1975), 176-186.

Burkom, Selma R. *Doris Lessing: A Checklist of Primary and Secondary Sources*. Troy, New York: Whitston Publishing Co., 1973.

_____. "'Only Connect': Form and Content in the Works of Doris Lessing." *Critique*, 11, No. 1 (1969), 51-68.

Carey, Father Alfred Augustine: "Doris Lessing: The Search for Reality. A Study of the Major Themes in Her Novels." *Dissertation Abstracts International*, 26 (1965), 3297.

Carey, John L. "Art and Reality in *The Golden Notebook*." *Contemporary Literature*, 14 (1973), 437-456.

Carnes, Valerie. "'Chaos, That's the Point': Art as Metaphor in Doris Lessing's *The Golden Notebook*." *World Literature Written in English*, 15 (1976), 17-28.

Doris Lessing: Critical Studies, Eds. Annis Pratt and L. S. Dembo. Madison: University of Wisconsin Press, 1974. [Reprint of special issue on Doris Lessing of *Contemporary Literature*, 14 (1973).]

Freud, Sigmund. *The Future of an Illusion*. London: The Hogarth Press, 1948.

_____. *A General Introduction to Psychoanalysis*. New York: Washington Square Press, Inc., 1952.

Graves, Nora. "Doris Lessing's Two Antheaps." *Notes on Contemporary Literature*, 2, No. 3 (1972), 6-8.

Howe, Irving. "Neither Compromise Nor Happiness." *The New Republic*, 147 (1962), 17-20.

Hynes, Joseph. "The Construction of *The Golden Notebook*." *Iowa Review*, 4, No. 3 (1973), 100-113.

Johnson, Sally Hickerson. "Form and Philosophy in the Novels of Doris Lessing." *Dissertation Abstracts International*, 38, No. 1 (1977), 282A.

Joyner, Nancy. "The Underside of the Butterfly: Lessing's Debt to Woolf." *Journal of Narrative Technique*, 4 (1974), 204-211.

Kaplan, Sydney Janet. *Feminine Consciousness in the Modern British Novel*. Urbana: University of Illinois Press, 1975.

Karl, Frederick R. "Doris Lessing in the Sixties: The New Anatomy of Melancholy." *Contemporary Literature*, 13, No. 1 (1972), 15-33.

Kildahl, Karen Ann. "The Political and Apocalyptical Novels of Doris Lessing: A Critical Study of *Children of Violence*, *The Golden Notebook*, *Briefing for a Descent into Hell*." *Dissertation Abstracts International*, 35 (1975), 4528A.

Krouse, Agate N. "A Doris Lessing Checklist." *Contemporary Literature*, 14 (1973), 590-597.

_____. "The Feminism of Doris Lessing." Dissertation Abstracts International, 34 (1973), 322A.

Laing, R. D. The Divided Self: A Study of Sanity and Madness. London: Tavistock Publications, 1960.

_____. The Politics of Experience. New York: Pantheon Books, 1967.

Lessing, Doris. "On The Golden Notebook." Partisan Review, 40 (1973), 14-30.

Lewis, M. Susan. "Conscious Evolution in The Four-Gated City." Anonymous, 1 (1974), 56-71.

Libby, Marion V. "Sex and the New Woman in The Golden Notebook." Iowa Review, 5 (1974), 56-71.

Marchino, Lois A. "The Search for Self in the Novels of Doris Lessing." Studies in the Novel (North Texas State University), 4 (1972), 252-261.

Markow, Alice B. "The Pathology of Feminine Failure in the Fiction of Doris Lessing." Critique, 16, No. 1 (1974), 88-100.

Mulkeen, Anne M. "Twentieth-Century Realism: The 'Grid' Structure of The Golden Notebook." Studies in the Novel (North Texas State University), 4 (1972), 262-274.

Mutti, Giuliana. "Female Roles and the Function of Art in The Golden Notebook." Massachusetts Studies in English, 3 (1972), 78-83.

Oates, Joyce Carol. "A Visit with Doris Lessing." Southern Review, 9 (1973), 873-882.

O'Fallon, Kathleen. "Quest for a New Vision." World Literature Written in English, 12 (1973), 180-189.

Porter, Dennis. "Realism and Failure in The Golden Notebook." Modern Language Quarterly, 35 (1974), 56-65.

Porter, Nancy. "Silenced History: Children of Violence and The Golden Notebook." World Literature Written in English, 12 (1973), 161-179.

Pratt, Annis. "The Contrary Structure of Doris Lessing's The Golden Notebook." World Literature Written in English, 12 (1973), 150-160.

Rapping, Elayne Antler. "Unfree Women: Feminism in Doris Lessing's Novels." Women's Studies, 3 (1975), 29-44.

Raskin, Jonah. "Doris Lessing at Stony Brook: An Interview." New American Review, 8 (1970), 166-179.

Rose, Ellen C. "Doris Lessing's Children of Violence as a Bildungsroman: An Eriksonian Analysis." Dissertation Abstracts International, 35 (1974), 3006A-3007A.

──────. "The End of the Game: New Directions in Doris Lessing's Fiction." Journal of Narrative Technique, 6 (1976), 66-75.

Rubenstein, Roberta. The Novelistic Vision of Doris Lessing: Breaking the Forms of Consciousness. Urbana: The University of Illinois Press, 1979.

──────. "Outer Space, Inner Space: Doris Lessing's Metaphor of Science Fiction." World Literature Written in English, 14 (1975), 187-197.

Ryf, Robert S. "Beyond Ideology: Doris Lessing's Mature Vision." Modern Fiction Studies, 21 (1975), 193-201.

Schlueter, Paul. The Novels of Doris Lessing. Carbondale and Edwardsville: Southern Illinois University Press, 1973.

Seligman, Claudia Dee. "The Autobiographical Novels of Doris Lessing." Dissertation Abstracts International, 37 (1976), 1544A.

──────. "The Sufi Quest." World Literature Written in English, 12 (1973), 190-206.

Singleton, Mary Ann. The City and the Veld: The Fiction of Doris Lessing. Lewisburg: Bucknell University Press, 1976.

Spacks, Patricia Meyer. "Free Women." Hudson Review, 24 (1971), 559-573.

Spencer, Sharon. "'Femininity' and the Woman Writer: Doris Lessing's The Golden Notebook and the Diary of Anaïs Nin." Women's Studies, 1 (1973), 247-257.

Spilka, Mark. "Lessing and Lawrence." Contemporary Literature, 16 (1975), 218-240.

Thorpe, Michael. Doris Lessing. London: Longman for British Council, 1973.

Vlastos, Marion. "Doris Lessing and R. D. Laing: Psychopolitics and Prophecy." PMLA, 91 (1976), 245-258.

Wells, Dorothy Bergquist. "The Unity of Doris Lessing's Children of Violence." Dissertation Abstracts International, 37 (1976), 1573A-1574A.

M